DATE DUE

SELF-OBSERVATION
in the SOCIAL SCIENCES

SELF-OBSERVATION
in the SOCIAL SCIENCES

Joshua W. Clegg
editor

Transaction Publishers
New Brunswick (U.S.A.) and London (U.K.)

Library of Congress Catalog Number: 2012013891
ISBN: 978-1-4128-4949-4
Printed in the United States of America

Library of Congress Cataloging-in-Publication Data

Self-observation in the social sciences / Joshua W. Clegg, editor.
    p. cm.
  Includes bibliographical references and index.
  ISBN 978-1-4128-4949-4
  1. Introspection. 2. Self-perception. 3. Observation (Psychology)
I. Clegg, Joshua W.
  BF316.S45 2013
  150.72—dc23
                           2012013891

Contents

Foreword

Breaking a Social Taboo: Introspection Restored

There is no doubt—*introspection as a method needs to be restored to its central place among all the methods that are aimed at studying human psychology.* This is a simple necessity to maintain the specific nature of psychology as a science in its own rights—rather than reduce it "downwards" (to physiology or to functional neuroanatomy) or "upwards" (to treating human beings as "texts" in the socio-narrative traditions). This new book that Joshua Clegg has assembled is a constructive continuation of his first treatise in 2009—*The Observation of Human Systems: Lessons from the History of Anti-reductionistic Empirical Psychology* (Clegg 2009). The lessons of 2009 have led to a positive new methodological program by 2012—one of the clear and prominent restoration of introspection as the primus inter pares in human psychology. However, that restoration of the misunderstood, discredited, and feared method is not a return to where that method was in the beginning of the twentieth century. It comes to us a hundred years later with a new twist—the explicit focus on the social context of both the introspecting Observer and the Experimenter. The present volume stands at the intersection of the history of holistic approaches in psychology (Diriwächter and Valsiner 2008) and its emerging new dynamic ways of constructing methods (Abbey and Surgan 2012).

A Science in Trouble: Where Psychology Lost Its Scientific Soul

Psychology has—from its beginning in the eighteenth and nineteenth centuries—been ambivalent as to its primary object of investigation—the *psyche* (Rosa 2007). It has gone through various fashions of denying that object—and replacing it with others— "behavior," "cognition," and even "positive psychology." Different "*-isms*" have dominated the minds of psychologists—from behavior*ism* to cognitiv*ism* to evolution*ism* and sociocultural*ism*. Who knows what fashion—labeled by an *-ism*—comes next, but what is clear is that invention and proliferation of such "schools of thought" distances psychology's research enterprise precisely from what science needs to do—to study its object phenomena. If a psychologist claims "I take a X-ist (or Y-ian, e.g., 'vygotskian') perspective on Z" one can guarantee that Z will be pushed into a framework of an orthodox belief system, rather than kept as the source for innovative understanding. The *-isms* fixate the perspective taken—rather than enable its flexible move. They try to standardize science, while scientific discovery necessarily runs ahead of any effort toward its fixation. Categorization units of thought systems—"schools" in science or "systems" in psychology—may be useful for didactic purposes in teaching beginning undergraduates to navigate through the grand confusion of psychological perspectives. Yet, such systematization fails to capture the essence of science—to always be striving toward the horizons that we do not know yet. Science is not about sure knowledge that we can proudly present to outsiders, but a discovery process (Valsiner 2012b, viii) of something less than knowledge (of the past) and not yet knowledge (in the present—see Polanyi 1962, 135).

Psychological evidence does not come in neatly sealed packages. Knowledge is not a consumer product—with dates of usability institutionally printed on the packages. Thus, any science operates on the outer frontier of knowledge—rather than "collects data" by established procedures—"standardized methods." The latter are in vogue in psychology. In tandem with socially obligatory quantification of psychological phenomena into data—an operation proven to be fallacious (Michell 1999)—psychology has generated a vast flow of empirical artifacts that do not stand the test of time, or reality. Phenomena in psychology have remained lost—as my friend and former colleague Bob Cairns once eloquently pointed out (Cairns 1986). Psychology—striving to show its allegiance with what is supposed to be a science—becomes highly effective in that social game. The result of such success in social recognition is the failure in providing solutions to deep, basic, human problems—that range from the deep privacy of sexuality to the hyperinflated public discourses about genocides, peace, democracy, and those heroic villains of the stock market that are easy to blame for any economic problem.

The Root of the Problem: Forgetting that the Human *Psyche* Creates Forms

Human lives are not reducible to their constituent elements. Human beings create affective and cognitive complexes with the help of which they live. Wherever we look we are surrounded by dynamic structures—in music (Langer 1953), in paintings (Kandinsky 1979) and photographs (Barthes 1982), and in the ornaments that surround us (Valsiner 2008). These structures undergo constant transformation—as human beings actively change them to act *forward*—toward their futures—*into* their worlds. In such coping with uncertainty—while acting toward my future-to-become-my present—I do not precisely know how to act best. Redundancy—acting both by parallel ways to reach the same goal, or creating a hierarchical "command and meaning center" for my action—are ways to cope with such uncertainty. Human beings create, execute, and abandon multilevel action plans that include both tools for acting and reflection upon that process of acting. The human *psyche* creates its own hierarchical order.

Hence it is at least mildly ironic that psychology over the twentieth century has successfully lost from focus the consideration of hierarchical Gestalts that transform *as they are being used* by their constructors. The relevant phenomena of human psyche have been replaced by counting of elementary constituents as if these could be treated separately from the whole within which they function.

It was Lev Vygotsky—a young literary scholar turned into a psychologist—who warned about the need for psychology to find its own unit of analysis, if it were to become an autonomous science. As Vygotsky claimed:

> Psychology, as it desires to study complex wholes . . . needs to change the methods of analysis into elements by the analytic method that reveals the parts of the unit [literally: breaks the whole into linked units—*metod . . . analiza, . . . razchleniayushego na edinitsy*]. It has to find the further undividable, surviving features that are characteristic of the given whole as a unity—<u>units within which in mutually opposing ways these features are represented</u> [Russian: *edinitsy, v kotorykh* **v protivopolozhnom vide** *predstavleny eti svoistva*].[1] (Vygotsky 1999, 13)

Putting in to practice Vygotsky's suggestion would have required psychology in the twentieth century to become dialectical—which could not happen after the discipline was caught between the warring sides of *Naturwissenschaften* and *Geisterwissenschaften* in its nineteenth-century German context (Valsiner 2012a).

Movement in the Reverse Direction: Anxiety of Distrust

The loss of complexity of phenomena in psychology has been on the rise in the twentieth century—psychology's methodology has failed by being developed in a direction of precise tools that do not fit the phenomena any more (Toomela 2007, 2011). Psychological complexity is the rule for every human life—and reflection upon it is accessible—at best—to the person who carries it. Hence the Subject of research (=the agent, the Researcher) is confined to the very same person ("research participant," formerly known as "subject" or "observer"—Bibace et al. 2009). Psychology as science has avoided the treatment of such complexity—using different disguises of "objectivity" and the reliance on methods as separated from methodology (Branco and Valsiner 1997). Observing *others* has been a major pastime for psychologists—but observing *themselves* (*Selbstbeobachtung*) has triggered various kinds of sentiments of distrust.

This is more than curious. Psychology seems to have become a self-suspecting science: no trust in scientists' subjective experience, and preference for the import of methods of other sciences, rather than developing some of its own. Alan Costall in this book puts it succinctly:

> The unthinking distrust of introspection within modern psychology goes hand in hand with the unchallenged prestige of methodological behaviorism. Neither are the result of critical disciplinary reflection, but stem from a dualism of the subjective and the objective that has insinuated itself into psychological thought through a potent historical myth. (Costall 2012, 77).

I would add that it is not only the conceptual dualism but the social–institutional control that is at work here. History of the notion of objectivity has its interesting past (Daston and Gallistel 2007) that includes complete reversal of the Subject–Object relationship. Fixing the tension of trust< >distrust axiomatically by making extrospection trustable (and introspection not) has created a discipline where knowledge obtained from observing others says little or nothing about the complexity of the human *psyche*.

Toward a New Solution: Socially Negotiated Self-Observation

How can psychology in the twenty-first century find its way? This volume provides a good start—instead of methodological pietism (of finding "biases" and punishing researchers for using "wrong methods") one can move to negotiation between all parties in the knowledge construction enterprise. This is a revolutionary solution—researchers leave their control monopoly behind. It is here that the direction for the future is specified most succinctly in the conclusion to this volume:

> . . . some of the principal challenges in formulating a theory of self-observation are generally construed in terms of bias *but can be more fruitfully conceptualized in terms of negotiations between multiple parties, including researcher, participant, and scientific community.* So, instead of trying to correct for fallible memory, a good theory of self-observation needs to account for, and make sense of, the differences in inter and intrasubjective agreement across both experience-near and experience-distant self-observations; instead of assuming a fundamentally inadequate self-knowledge in self-observers, or attempting to mitigate "observer bias," a *good theory will start with the assumption that there is no simplistic isomorphism between the observer's and the interpreter's frames of reference and will attempt to account for, to describe and document, the negotiations that bring these multiple and nonstandard frames of reference into relation.* A theory that accounts for such negotiations must model both the multiplicity—i.e., multiple levels of intention, attention, commitment, etc.—and the fundamentally dynamic nature of those individuals in negotiation, but it cannot start from the privileged and theoretically naïve assumptions that localize "error" in individuals. (Clegg 2012, 14, added emphases)

The new solution offered in this book builds on the history of the discipline. It takes a key idea—guided self-observation—and situates it in a new context (of social situations of knowledge construction). Most of our contemporary psychological science works with self-imposed conceptual blinders that overlook many potentials produced in early psychology (Valsiner 2012a). It is my hope that the readers of this volume will appreciate being silent participants in the widening of the scope of psychology's methodology, and join to make psychology a scientifically human endeavor.

Jaan Valsiner
Worcester, MA, February 2012

Note

1. It is important to note that the intricate link with the dialectical dynamicity of the units—which is present in the Russian original—is lost in English translation, which briefly stated the main point: "Psychology, which aims

at a study of complex holistic systems, must replace the method of analysis into elements with the method of analysis into units" (Vygotsky 1986, 5). Yet it remains unclear in the English translation what kinds of units are to be constructed—while in the Russian original it is made evident.

References

Abbey, E. A. and Surgan, S eds. 2012. *Emerging Methods in Psychology*. New Brunswick, NJ: Transaction Publishers.

Barthes, R. 1982. *Camera Lucida*. New York: Hill and Wang.

Bibace, R., Clegg, J., and Valsiner, J. 2009. "What Is in a Name? Understanding the Implications of Participant Terminology." *IPBS: Integrative Psychological & Behavioral Science* 43, no. 1: 67–77.

Branco, A. U. and Valsiner, J. 1997. "Changing Methodologies: A Co-constructivist Study of Goal Orientations in Social Interactions." *Psychology and Developing Societies* 9, no. 1: 35–64.

Cairns, R. B. 1986. "Phenomena Lost: Issues in the Study of Development." In *The Individual Subject and Scientific Psychology*, edited by J. Valsiner, 97–111. New York: Plenum.

Clegg, J. W. ed. 2009. *The Observation of Human Systems: Lessons from the History of Anti-reductionistic Empirical Psychology*. New Brunswick, NJ: Transaction Publishers.

———. 2012. "The Inferential Context of Self-Observation." In *Self Observation in the Social Sciences*, edited by J. W. Clegg, 277–284. New Brunswick, NJ: Transaction Publishers.

Daston, L. and Gallistel. P. 2007. *Objectivity*. New York: Zone Books.

Diriwächter, R. and Valsiner, J. eds. 2008. *Striving for the Whole: Creating Theoretical Syntheses*. New Brunswick, NJ: Transaction Publishers.

Innis, R. E. 2009. *Susanne Langer in Focus: The Symbolic Mind*. Bloomington, IN: Indiana University Press.

Kandinsky, V. 1979. *Point and Line to Plane*. New York: Dover.

Langer, S. 1953. *Feeling and Form*. New York: Charles Scribner's sons.

Michell, J. 1999. *Measurement in Psychology: Critical History of a Methodological Concept*. Cambridge: Cambridge University Press.

Polanyi, M. 1962. *Personal Knowledge*. Chicago, IL: University of Chicago Press.

Rosa, A. 2007. "Acts of Psyche: Acting and Meaning-Making for the Future. In *Cambridge Handbook of Socio-Cultural Psychology*, edited by J. Valsiner and A. Rosa. New York: Cambridge University Press.

Toomela A. 2007. "Culture of Science: Strange History of the Methodological Thinking in Psychology. *IPBS: Integrative Psychological & Behavioral Science* 41: 6–20.

———. 2011. "Travel into a Fairy Land: A Critique of Modern Quantitative and Mixed Methods Psychologies. *IPBS: Integrative Psychological & Behavioral Science* 45: 21–47.

Valsiner, J. 2008. "Ornamented Worlds and Textures of Feeling: The Power of Abundance." *Outlines: Critical Social Studies* 10, no. 1: 67–78.

———. 2012a. *A Guided Science: History of Psychology in the Mirror of Its Making*. New Brunswick, NJ: Transaction Publishers.

———. 2012b. "Methods, Methodology, and Meaning: Psychology's Struggles in the Game of "Being a Science." In *Emerging Methods in Psychology*, edited by E. A. Abbey and S. Surgan, vii–x. New Brunswick, NJ: Transaction Publishers.

Vygotsky, L. S. 1986. *Thought and Language*, 2nd edn. Cambridge, MA: MIT Press.

———. 1999. *Myshlenie i rech*, 5th edn. Moscow: Labirint.

Part I
Introduction

1

Developing an Adequate Theory of Self-Observation

Joshua W. Clegg

The persistence of something like a "debate" over the status of self-observation is written deeply into the soul of psychology—in every generation, self-observation seems always to find its legions of detractors and yet always remains, in one form or another, at the heart of psychological research. The most basic points of debate have not changed a great deal—for example, the possibility of a divided consciousness (which pitted Comte against Mill), the comparative limitations of introspection and retrospection (as debated by James and the Wurzburgers), etc.—but the "official" history of the discipline often seems to imply that the debate ended in a decided loss for introspection. Most have argued, following Boring (1953), that the disciplinary struggles of the first few decades of the twentieth century exposed the fundamental unreliability of introspection and so led to its demise in the wake of a behaviorist revolution.

The assumption that introspection somehow vanished has issued in periodic calls to revisit some form of self-observation. In the 1920s and 1930s, we see many defenses of introspection against the various objectivist onslaughts (e.g., DeSilva 1930; Washburn 1922; Wheeler 1923) and as early as 1954 we see Bakan citing the "need for a psychology which is more appropriate to its problems" (Bakan 1954, 105) and so a return to introspective research practices. We see similar calls throughout the twentieth century—e.g., Lieberman (1979) advocating for "greater acceptance of introspection and the mind" (332), Grover (1982) defending the value of "introspective verbal reports" (211), and Gould (1995) advocating for introspection as a method in consumer research.

From the hindsight of history, however, we can see that the so-called "death" of introspection was greatly exaggerated. As Costall (2006) and others have shown, the rise and fall of introspection is more of a creation myth than a history—an oversimplification that served particular goals but did little to reflect the actual practices of psychologists. Even Boring, who contributed significantly to this creation myth, asserted in 1953 that "introspection is still with us, doing its business under various aliases, of which verbal report is one" (169). The social sciences have always relied on various forms of self-observation and so the periodic resurfacing of "introspection" in the literature has not been so much a call to resurrect introspection as to acknowledge the ongoing practice of self-observation and to more rigorously define its epistemological status (and, to a lesser degree, to define the proper forms for producing self-observation data).

The current volume, then, belongs to a long tradition of scholarship intended to bring the discipline of psychology back to a theoretical project that we have continually re-abandoned in the name of "objectivity"—namely, the development of robust and empirically adequate theories of self-observation. This volume begins from the assumption that this project cannot be avoided through the obvious self-deception that behavioral observations, fMRI scans, or scaled self-reports do not involve self-observation. The reality is that all of the psychological disciplines share a "reliance on introspection and subjective reports" (den Boer et al. 2008, 381) because, as Overgaard (2006) argues, "no physical phenomenon can be a more reliable indication of a given conscious state than the introspective report" (Overgaard 2006, 630–31). We cannot ignore the centrality of self-observation in the psychological disciplines and so there is a serious need for more adequate self-observation theories and practices. In the remainder of this introduction, I will outline what I consider to be the most basic questions that any theory of self-observation must address and I will then indicate how the subsequent chapters attempt to address those questions.

The Wrong Questions

Most theories of self-observation treat it as an ontologically and epistemologically special case—that is, they assume that the observation of "objects" is a fundamentally different kind of activity than is the observation of "consciousness." This distinction derives from the assumption that self-observation cannot "be 'consensually validated,' as other people cannot observe anyone's consciousness but their own" (Locke 2009, 24). "Objective" knowledge, it is assumed, is based on public, verifiable, external, and transparent entities while self-observation concerns only private, idiosyncratic, and internal experience. Objective analysis provides us with universal categories of meaning like length and not hopelessly idiosyncratic categories of meaning like imagination and, as such, the study of "objects" provides a different, and in fact more reliable, kind of knowledge than does the study of the "subjective."

The necessary consequence of this familiar distinction is a fundamental solipsism—that is, an a priori assumption that the consciousness of another is always a postulate and never a datum; something we infer but never really know:

> This conception of behaviour not only entails the assumption that our understanding of other people's intentions, feelings, and so forth, can only be based on inferences, but also—given the assumed logical disconnection between behaviour, and intentions, etc.—such inferences lack any premises. (Costall 2006, 638)

The inevitable ending for such a beginning is the denial of, or at least the permanent reservation of judgment concerning, the consciousness of another. The assumption that "the minds of others are closed territory" and that "all that I have experiential access to is their behavior" essentially "imprisons me within my own mind" (Zahavi 2008, 519). This sort of solipsism is where the behaviorists arrived and seems the logical destination for the various forms of physicalism.

And yet, nearly every human being experiences some others as conscious and can quite reliably distinguish the conscious from the nonconscious (as though these were "real," i.e., consistent, categories). It is easy, and certainly fashionable, to reduce the experience of another's consciousness to a sort of epiphenomenal fantasy; to face the "hard truth" that we can directly know only physically sensible traces and so must infer, perhaps wrongly, everything else we think we know of one another. If this is our starting place, however, then there is not much meaning to self-observation as a method for producing general knowledge. Indeed, the very idea of genuinely public knowledge becomes suspect. If what I know of others is only what I know of myself, then all knowledge becomes private knowledge and all observation becomes self-observation; the Cartesian anxiety presides over all of our reasoning. One of the most basic challenges in developing a theory of self-observation, then, is to find a better starting place, one where we can account for what is being observed such that meaningful intersubjectively validated inferences are possible. But this problem needs to be defined more precisely if it is to be addressed in any useful way.

First of all, the traditional distinction between external and internal objects of perception is surely a specious one and deserves to be abandoned. It is not, in fact, the case that experiences of length or EEG readings or key presses are the properties of an external world, while experiences of imagination, or anger, or daydreams are properties of the internal world. At the level of experience, in fact, there is no meaningful way to conceptualize an "external" perception. As Burt (1962) argues, "strictly speaking, *every* first-hand observation is necessarily 'private'" (231). When a scientist records a reading from an instrument, she is recording her own experience, her own perception, and no quantity or sophistication of mechanical interface can change that fact. I can no more directly "feel" your perception of length than I can "feel" your experience of anger and, in this sense, both of these experiences can be called "private." But we can both experience anger in response to the same state of affairs in precisely the same way that we can both experience length in response to the same state of affairs and, in this sense, both of these experiences can be called "public."

The essential point here is that all experiences are private in the sense that they are "mine" and all can be made public in essentially the same way—i.e., through various forms of language—and so we cannot coherently maintain the hard distinction between subjective and objective:

> We cannot ignore the epistemological tradition that since Kant demonstrates that we do not have access to the objects "in themselves" apart from the very accessing process. A scientific model is not the exact reproduction of an independent external reality, but a set of technological acts which highlight a set of invariants, acts which have stabilized, and which have obtained an intersubjective agreement. (Petitmengen and Bitbol 2011, 95)

If pushed, I suspect most of us would grant that the scientist possesses no special access to an independent and objective reality. The problem, however, is that though we may all agree that the experiential qualities of both length and anger are roughly equivalent elements of an interpreted human experience, yet we still talk about measuring length "as such"—instead, for example, of talking about the intersubjective variability in particular experiences of extension. We maintain this sloppy mental habit, presumably, because the variability between different visual experiences of extension is so small. It is this stability of interpretation which has allowed the natural sciences to reify and externalize sensory, interpretive qualities as independent of human experience and intrinsic to stable, external objects. But this distinction does not withstand scrutiny. Length and anger are both "private" and "public." Both expressions of length and expressions of anger are intersubjective, both are born out of collisions between embodied conscious beings and their world; neither of them can be fully described as "inside" or "outside," "private," or "public." Both are built and maintained in the intersubjective negotiation of symbolic meaning and to the extent that one can be public or verifiable, so can the other.

The Right Questions

The most basic theoretical problem, then, for any theory of self-observation is not to account for some special kind of nonpublic, purely subjective knowledge; the problem is the same one encountered by all kinds of scientific knowledge—namely, to define the conditions under which we can intersubjectively validate reports of individual experience. The physical sciences have approached this problem essentially by attempting to suppress and transform the languages and subjectivities of observers, stripping away culture, sociality, history, and personality, through discourses that imply an independent, uninterpreted object. This has been possible because of the relative simplicity of "natural" objects, but in the social sciences we cannot profitably labor under such simplistic philosophy of science. We must acknowledge, theorize, and work with the full complexity of the intersubjective negotiation if we are to ever account for how we build shared inferences.

The essential implication of this line of argument is that the most basic unit of analysis in any self-report or self-observation context is not a narrative report, an fMRI scan, a survey score, or any other particular "data set." The basic unit of analysis is always the relationship or context within which those data are produced—"the communication of experience involves an exchange" (Jack and Roepstorff 2002, 335) and so data only make sense in terms of the whole intra and interpersonal interplay that produced them: "scientific results are gained from and refer back to a life-world of shared intersubjectivity" (den Boer et al. 2008, 397). The point here is that when we attempt to interpret any form of self-observation, we are not interpreting the data point, but the data negotiation. Even the most basic forms of research interaction are "embedded in a second-person interaction which involves exchange of frames of reference and of attentional focus" (Roepstorff and Jack 2004, vi).

The minimal analytic case, then, for an inference based on self-observation (and, for that matter, any kind of observation) is what we might call the local inferential relationship—that is, the relationship between an interpreter who is embedded in and embodies the values, norms, and codes of a scientific tradition (as well as more idiosyncratic personal traditions) and a self-observer who expresses his or her experience from a particular sociohistorical location (which may also include a particular scientific tradition). This minimal case embraces "introspective" and "self-report" contexts, and other contemporary self-observation traditions, and dispenses with the untenable distinction between "internal" and "external" forms of observation. Even in this minimal case, the layered forms of interpersonal negotiation involved in "data production" are of daunting complexity—at the very least, a viable theory of self-observation would require an account[1] of how the intrapersonal and interpersonal negotiations involved in a particular reporting process produce "data" and related interpretive conclusions.

Inferential Negotiations

The intrapersonal negotiations of the self-observer—that is, the navigation within oneself of different recollections, interpretations, moral shadings, individual purposes or commitments, etc.—and the resulting ambiguity and indeterminacy of self-reports, are, of course, a notorious aspect of self-observation and one of the chief targets of critique. The source of so-called "error" in self-report has almost always been conceptualized in terms of the simplistic subjective/objective divide and so the various irregularities in the inferential context have been primarily localized "inside" the self-observer. The self-observer is essentially accused of: (1) unreliable memory, (2) limited self-knowledge, and (3) biased self-interpretations (and occasionally of outright deceit, but that is a problem not considered unique to self-observation). In the following discussion, however, it should become clear that all of the possible sources of inferential error involved in self-observation research can be more meaningfully conceptualized in terms of a relational negotiation, rather than in terms of a set of personal or internal "biases."

Unreliable Memory

Error is ascribed to the self-observer, first, in terms of the transformation of memory across time: "one problem with retrospective recall of events as data concerning actual behavior stems from the well-substantiated finding that memory is reconstructive and degrades over time" (Wallendorf and Brucks 1993, 343). Of course, any report of a self-observation will, to some degree, be retrospective and so this critique is not reserved for experience-distant self-observations: "the absolute veracity of our immediate inner apprehension of a conscious state should be considered in the light of the fallibility of our memory a moment later" (den Boer et al. 2008, 385).

There are some obvious theoretical leaps in talking about "memory degradation" and so this assumption should be taken with some caution—the kinds of inferences that we can justifiably make on the basis of memory research all relate to how memory *reporting* is produced and negotiated among researchers and participants, and it is naïve to assume that all of the irregularities in that process are purely a function of fallible participant memory. Speaking within the confines of empirical warrant, then, the sweeping ontological generalization of a fundamentally "fallible memory" can be more prudently expressed in terms of the modest assertion that there is greater inter and intrasubjective agreement about experience-near than about experience-distant self-reports. Stated in this way, adequate memory reporting becomes a meaningful boundary condition for any valid theory of self-observation but not an insurmountable barrier rooted in all of the ancient agonies of dualism.

Limited Self-knowledge

A second source of error commonly attributed to the self-observer is the assumption that he is perfectly willing to report on aspects of his experience about which he has no direct knowledge. Research participants regularly provide information on their motives and yet "lack of awareness of and inability to report on general principles that guide their behavior, or the relevant contextual contingencies that situate and modify these regularities, is a fundamental premise of social science research" (Wallendorf and Brucks 1993, 345). This assumption was most explicitly defended by Nisbett and Wilson (1977), who argued that research participants have "little or no direct introspective access to higher order cognitive processes" (231). Their principal contention was that, in laboratory research, participants provide explanations that do not coincide with what the researchers take to be demonstrable influences on participant behavior. They further argued that participants can be "shown" to respond to stimuli that they themselves do not acknowledge, and in ways that they themselves do not accurately report. Nisbett and Wilson's conclusion was that participants "base their reports on implicit, a priori theories about the causal connection between stimulus and response" and so even when subjective reports about higher mental processes are correct this is "not due to direct introspective awareness" but "to the incidentally correct employment of a priori causal theories" (233).

Of course, a number of critiques of Nisbett and Wilson (1977) have been forwarded. Ericsson and Simon (1980), for example, argued that the unreliable reports of cognitive processes produced in the studies reviewed by Nisbett and Wilson were the result of technical limitations, rather than of the fundamental inaccessibility to consciousness of cognitive processes. Even Wilson, himself, later qualified the scope of the original argument:

> To the extent that people's responses are caused by the adaptive unconscious, they do not have privileged access to the causes and must infer them, just as Nisbett and I argued. But to the extent that people's responses are caused by the conscious self, they have privileged access to the actual causes of these responses; in short, the Nisbett and Wilson argument was wrong about such cases. (Wilson 2002, 106)

These critiques notwithstanding, the basic premise that self-observers do not really know why they do what they do, remains a standard assumption in experimental psychology.

Such an assumption, however, reveals a basic inattention to the full data production context—there is no acknowledgment of the fact that when researchers ask participants to speculate about causal processes, they are projecting onto the self-observer an idiosyncratic and completely implicit set of personal theories about causality, consciousness, and even science itself: "there has been a tendency, unfortunately, to assume that the theorist's models (e.g., of dissonance and attribution processes) define the S's 'psychological reality.' An S's failure to report verbally on such process is often taken as *ipso facto* evidence for the unreliability of introspective reports" (Grover 1982, 211). There is something fundamentally unreflective and egocentric in the assumption that when researcher and participant reach different conclusions, this is the result of the participant's limited self-knowledge. The only thing that such an outcome clearly demonstrates is that researcher and participant do not clearly understand one another, and this is surely as much the responsibility of the researcher as it is of the participant.

Despite their obvious inattention to researcher positionality, there is an important lesson inherent in Nisbett and Wilson's argument (and in the many similar arguments that have both preceded and followed it): we cannot assume simplistic isomorphisms between our conceptualizations of the categories of consciousness, our formulations of questions about that consciousness, the reports these questions generate, and the consciousness of any given self-observer. Every point in that chain of inference involves a sociohistorically situated negotiation and assuming that the researcher's interpretation of the self-observer's self-explanation will somehow directly map onto any given set of empirical predictions is not only discouraged by existing empirical research, as Nisbett and Wilson did in fact demonstrate, but is at best theoretically naïve. As researchers, we should not expect our questions to simply bypass all of the vagaries of interpretation, self-interest, interpersonal politics, etc., and reveal the consciousness of the other in perfectly unambiguous self-talk. Any adequate theory of self-observation will have to describe and document, rather than simply ignore, how such self-talk is produced and interpreted.

Biased Self-Interpretations

The final general way in which the self-observer is considered error-prone is in terms of personal interpretive bias—that is, because a self-observation report will always be an interpretation of one's experience it will always be subject to various forms of cognitive distortion. The most obvious of these presumed distortions is the result of "focused attention on conscious experience" which "arguably alters the very experience attended to" (Weisberg 2011, 11). This is an ancient objection to self-observation, forming in fact, one of Comte's original objections. Comte essentially argued that observing one's own conscious states changes them, an assertion with which J. S. Mill, his principal opponent, agreed and which led both Comte and Mill to conclude that if we are to know our consciousness it must be through retrospection. Early proponents of systematic self-observation in psychology wrestled with similar difficulties, with both William James and the members of the Wurzburg school advocating, on these same grounds, for some form of retrospective self-observation.

Beyond this presumed fundamental distortion, many have also argued that "no interviewee will be without presuppositions" (Froese et al. 2011, 47–48) and so "interpretation and (often implicit) theorizing is ever-present in introspection" (Weisberg 2011, 11). This layering of "interpretation" over "perception" was precisely the problem that the stimulus error was meant to express and remains a primary concern among contemporary practitioners of self-observation. Participants are also generally considered subject to interpersonal biases, such that "interviewees may alter the reports of their experience because they are keen to please the interviewer, or they may be disinclined to fully cooperate, perhaps because of trust issues" or traditional "demand characteristics," where the participant "forms an interpretation of the purpose of the study and unconsciously changes their behaviour accordingly" (Froese et al. 2011, 47–48).

At one level, these kinds of arguments are difficult to interpret, as they seem to imply the ideal of a "pure" consciousness, unmediated by individual interpretation—yet it is hard to imagine an uninterpreted report of consciousness, given that any communication, indeed any reflection at all, is an interpretive act. There is little doubt that we can and do continually transform our self-interpretations according to all sorts of exigencies, implicit and explicit, personal and interpersonal, and there are certainly good reasons for trying to understand consciousness in an experience-near way, but it makes no sense to talk about any sort of self-report as somehow pre-interpretive or to idealize the unmediated report as somehow more truthful or revelatory. All self-reports are interpreted and any self-report, no matter how transformed, will still be illuminating in some way. In self-observation (and, in fact, in science of every kind), self-interpretation is not the problem—it is the point of observation in the first place.

In any case, it is not really the interpretive nature of self-observation that presents a unique challenge. When I am interpreting self-interpretations, I am not doing something on an epistemologically distinct plane from what all scientists do when they build general inferences. All scientific knowledge consists in general inferences made on the basis of self-interpretations (also called "observations"). We might imagine, for example, a particular scientist who records her interpretations of her own experiences of a set of DNA molecules. Other scientists will draw general conclusions about the nature of DNA on the basis of her reported self-interpretations, but what is being intersubjectively validated in this case is not something like "the nature of DNA molecules." What is being validated is the fact that under comparable conditions, comparable interpretations occur—i.e., if another scientist interprets his experiences of DNA molecules under conditions similar to those of the original report, he will draw similar conclusions. In the case of classical introspection (where the scientist is also the self-observer), this is precisely how scientific inference is produced and there is really no meaningful epistemological distinction between the inferential processes involved in physical and in psychological observation. There is, however, a meaningful practical distinction, given that in psychological self-observation there may, indeed, be a fair number of cases for which there are no comparable conditions (e.g., self-observations based on particularly unique personal experiences). This limitation is certainly a challenge for any theory of self-observation and may constitute a hard limit on what psychological self-observation can accomplish.

Of course, classical introspection is less common than it once was and in those cases where the researcher is not the self-observer—e.g., interviews, scaled self-report, brain imaging research, behavioral observations, etc.—the inferential process is, indeed, more complex than in the physical sciences. As in all research, the scientist's self-interpretations are the basis for the inferences of other scientists, but because the researcher bases those interpretations on the self-interpretations of others, an additional link is added to the inferential chain (self-observer → researcher → other scientists). This is primarily a problem of degree, as this new inferential link is of the same kind as the others, except in the sense that it involves nonscientist self-interpreters. In traditional natural science, the chain of inferences involves a negotiation among a community of scientists who all share the same highly technical language and tradition of practice. When we are drawing inferences from self-reports, however, we are introducing an entirely new negotiation, this time with an audience who shares none of our linguistic or technical points of reference.[2] The unique inferential problem in self-observation, then, is not so much that we must draw inferences from potentially "biased" self-interpretations (as this is what all researchers do) but that we must integrate inferences constructed within multiple nonstandard frames of reference.

Conclusions and Introduction to the Volume

In summary, some of the principal challenges in formulating a theory of self-observation are generally construed in terms of bias but can be more fruitfully conceptualized in terms of negotiations between multiple parties, including researcher, participant, and scientific community. So, instead of trying to correct for fallible memory, a good theory of self-observation needs to account for, and make sense of, the differences in inter and intrasubjective agreement across both experience-near and experience-distant self-observations; instead of assuming a fundamentally inadequate self-knowledge in self-observers, or attempting to mitigate "observer bias," a good theory will start with the assumption that there is no simplistic isomorphism between the observer's and the interpreter's frames of reference and will attempt to account for, to describe and document, the negotiations that bring these multiple and nonstandard frames of reference into relation. A theory that accounts for such negotiations must model both the multiplicity—i.e., multiple levels of intention, attention, commitment, etc.—and the fundamentally dynamic nature of those individuals in negotiation, but it cannot start from the privileged and theoretically naïve assumptions that localize "error" in individuals.

Each of these basic issues is taken up from many different perspectives in the chapters that follow. In the first section, self-observation is considered from a primarily historical point of view. In the second chapter of the book, Adrian Brock reviews some of the important waypoints in the history of psychological self-observation, focusing particularly on the many myths surrounding the instrospectionist tradition. Brock argues, along with Danziger, Costall and others, that introspection per se was a specific methodological tradition that was never particularly dominant in either American or European psychology and that the supposed struggle between introspection and behaviorism is largely a fabrication. He suggests that the tensions between behaviorism and experimental self-observation were largely confined to a narrow American context and that these had less to do with any particular disciplinary struggle than with the financial and political advantages of a behavioral focus for psychology.

In the third chapter, Jacy Young outlines the early history of self-report measures in psychology, beginning with a discussion of Galton's early questionnaires and anthropometric tests and their influence on Cattell and Osborn in the United States. She also outlines William James' relatively brief work on self-reports of hallucinatory phenomena and G. Stanley Hall's much more involved self-reports of children's experiences. Young shows that these early self-reports were largely open-ended until Thurstone and his students began their highly influential work with scaled self-reports.

In the fourth chapter, Alan Costall revisits his deconstruction of psychology's three-stage history—from introspection to behaviorism to cognitivism—focusing particularly on the methodological implications. According to Costall, from the methodological point of view, the three-stage myth asserts that (1) introspection was attempted on a large scale but was shown to be unreliable, (2) that behaviorism brought psychology into line with the methodological rigor of science but inappropriately narrowed the theoretical field of the discipline, and (3) that the cognitive revolution maintained the methodological strengths of behaviorism while re-introducing the indispensable breadth of cognitive concepts. Costall's basic argument is that this way of telling the story has locked psychology into a kind of methodological dualism. He argues, in fact, that the terms of the so-called behaviorist revolution created a dualism of objective and subjective methods that never really existed. Costall suggests that introspection was neither unreliable nor really abandoned and that the idealized reductionist and physicalist form of behaviorism was rarely actually carried out in practice, either by behaviorists or their cognitivist descendants. This commitment to a largely fabricated history, he claims, prevents the discipline from moving beyond the false metaphysics of methodological behaviorism.

In the next section of the book, authors from various traditions explore both the theory and practice of contemporary self-observation. In the fifth chapter of the volume, Brady Wagoner argues for a theory of self-observation as a linguistic and social practice. He begins by outlining the ways in which language was used in early self-report traditions, showing, for example, that, despite the attempt to approximate "objective" conditions through the use of external stimuli and immediate reporting, early self-observation reports depended on a complex and usually unacknowledged negotiation of meaning. Wagoner traces language use in other self-observation traditions, including the Wurzburg school, the Gestalt and Ganzheit traditions, and the theoretical work of James and Bergson, and argues that these traditions show the ambiguity and adaptability of research language as well as the creative resources inherent in metaphorical language use. Wagoner then takes up the functionalist/pragmatist arguments that cast self-observation as situated in an inherently social process and not separable as an independent reflective activity. He argues for a conception of self-observation that accounts for the way that the context of reporting, the history of research relationships, institutional constraints, etc., frame how knowledge is reported and what it can mean. Through a qualitative analysis of how participants make decisions about completing scaled self-reports, Wagoner shows that even simple scaled self-reports involve complex negotiations of meaning that are obscured under a simplistic questionnaire format. He argues that, for any kind of self-report to be meaningfully interpreted, our methods need to foreground the negotiational and mediational aspects of self-report.

In the sixth chapter, Christopher Heavey outlines some basic principles for doing self-observation research, focusing on the method of Descriptive Experience Sampling (DES). According to Heavey, the best self-observation reports will be those that are made as close to the naturally occurring context in which they occur. His argument is that transformations in the memories, intentions, and interpretive stances of both the self-observer and the interpreter also transform the qualities of any experience reported and that this process is only exacerbated with time. Following Comte, James, The Wurzburgers and others, Heavey argues that experience-near retrospective reports best minimize these transformations. Heavey then outlines the ways in which DES attempts to realize these ideals, including using nondirective prompting strategies, participatory interpretive strategies, and by attempting to create naturalistic experience sampling using a randomized beeper. Heavey frames this approach to self-observation under the assumption that interpreting self-reports involves a negotiation between self-observer and interpreter about the meanings and functions of words. He also acknowledges that in DES, and presumably in any form of self-observation research, the self-observation task and the associated interpretive languages are not natural, or indigenous, to the self-observer and so require training, or perhaps more accurately, socialization, in the theory and practice framing the research activity.

In the seventh chapter, Stephen Gould describes what he calls Multi-modal Introspection Theory, a set of insights gleaned from his experiences in experimental psychology, poststructural philosophy, and Eastern meditation. Gould divides introspective traditions along a number of dimensions, including narrative and the metacognitive introspections, conceptual and nonconceptual introspections, hypothesis-testing (i.e., deductive) and grounded theory (i.e., inductive) introspections, outward and inward focused introspections, and mind and body focused introspections. Through discussions of various introspective theories and controversies, as well as through introspective exercises, Gould describes how he has tried to turn the traditional critiques of the knowable toward an enriched vision of meditative introspection. He concludes with a series of examples, showing how his theory of an embodied and embedded introspection can help us both explore and develop the self.

In the third section of this volume, three authors discuss the history, theory, and practice of self-observation in the phenomenological traditions. In the eighth chapter, Edwin Gantt and Jeffrey Thayne trace the historical and theoretical origins of phenomenological self-observation through the works of Franz Brentano, Edmund Husserl, and Martin Heidegger. They argue that Husserlian phenomenology took its earliest inspiration from Brentano's act psychology, which emphasized the intentional nature of consciousness and thus the importance of studying psychological acts. Husserl, however, diverged from Brentano's vision in that he abandoned the more natural scientific view of psychology as an enumeration of the contents of consciousness through direct inner perception. Husserl, Gantt and Thayne argue, recast the notion of intentionality to imply the indissolubility of subject and object in the lifeworld. As a result, phenomenology focused not on examining the contents of an independent consciousness, but instead on uncovering the essential features of experience itself. Gantt and Thayne then argue that Heidegger moved phenomenology even further from the basic positivist perspective and toward the study of an experience that is fundamentally embedded in a social and historical world. These transformations in phenomenological approaches, the authors argue, led phenomenology from "an *observation of the self* to the *self's detached observations of experience* (and the observation of the meaning of experience), and finally to the *self's engagement with the meaning of lived experience*" (2012, 27).

In the ninth chapter, Samuel Downs outlines a phenomenological theory of self-observation. He frames his argument against the theoretical difficulties that have long plagued dualistic theories of self-observation and offers as a solution to these difficulties a kind of hermeneutic reduction. Downs argues that the phenomenological perspective redefines self-observation as an intentional act and thus not as purely internal or external. He also argues, following Heidegger, that intentional acts are inseparable from history, culture, and context, and so are constrained by these influences. This approach collapses inner and outer, subjective and objective, and so reframes introspection as intraspection. This kind of hermeneutic "reduction focuses on what my own actions disclose about myself. While disclosure often emphasizes the way the world is revealed to me, self-observation simply emphasizes the self as participatory in the hermeneutic" (Downs 2012, 18). Downs argues that this conception of intraspection avoids the basic philosophical problems that have plagued self-observation, essentially eliminating the difficulty of accounting for how knowledge can move between, and distinguish, subjective and objective, by collapsing that distinction into a single lifeworld.

In the tenth chapter, Svend Brinkmann discusses how the general phenomenological traditions have informed and transformed self-observation research. Brinkmann defines both the subject and the object of self-observation in terms of Harre's distinction between three types of "self"—self 1, which consists in the agentive, personal self (more or less, James' "I"); self 2, which consists in what I can call my own (James' "Me"); and self 3, which consists in the self we are taken to be by others, the self negotiated in conversation with others. Brinkmann argues that which of these kinds of self is taken as the object of self-observation determines to a great degree the kind of observation one does—e.g., self 1 implies a kind of experiential, felt phenomenology, self 2 a narrative approach, and self 3 a discursive approach. Brinkmann also discusses some of the unique challenges involved in different forms of self-observation, and then outlines the strengths and limitations of three traditions, namely, creative analytical practices, experience sampling methods, and systematic self-observation, arguing that different methods are appropriate to different questions.

In the final section of the book, three authors discuss self-observation from within the narrative traditions. In the eleventh chapter, Andrew McCarron offers insights into self-observation provided by the biographical narrative tradition. He outlines theoretical work from this tradition, focusing on the ways that identity is ordered and expressed in life narratives or myths and on the challenges of reflexivity in self-observers and interpreters. McCarron then provides a detailed analysis of the poetry and life story of a well-known New York area poet as a way of demonstrating the narrative approach to self-observation, as well as of arguing for the importance and relevance of both conceptions of self and of artistic media in the excavation of personal meanings. Pursuing his analysis in terms of Harre's three selves, McCarron shows how both the narrative perspective and the aesthetic one provide important insights into how story-telling and language use can reveal important aspects of self.

In the twelfth chapter, Mark Freeman considers the various possibilities for self-understanding and argues for a fundamentally narrative conceptualization of self-discovery—that is, for something less like a direct self-observation and more like a retrospective self-interpretation. Freeman first discusses the inherent challenges to self-observation imposed by history, memory, and narrative—i.e., the fundamentally interpreted, multiple, dynamic, and motivated qualities of self-understanding and self-narrative. But Freeman argues that, despite these well-worn difficulties, narrative self-understanding is still possible. He argues, first, that the present experience is not less interpretive, or interested, than a retrospective account and that, in fact, the distance of retrospection may serve to counteract the prejudices and blindnesses of the present, or experience-near, interpretation. He also points out that the meaning of any given experience is as much defined by the events that follow it as by those that precede it. Ultimately, Freeman argues that, strictly speaking, self-observation may not be possible from the narrative perspective, but hindsight can serve as a means of self-understanding, a way of knowing the self that can actually help us see the interpreted, moral, and historical qualities of our experience—to "unself" our self-understandings in a way that makes them more truthful.

In the thirteenth chapter, Alessandra Fasulo describes the meaning and practice of self-observation within an ethnographic perspective. She first reviews the basic nature of ethnographic research, focusing on the way in which the self of the ethnographer is the fundamental instrument of research. Fasulo then discusses the difficulties inherent in a research instrument that is self-interpreting and so continually producing dynamic, ambiguous, and fundamentally perspectival interpretations, noting that this ambiguous character has contributed to a progressively more reflexive approach to ethnography. Fasulo also argues that as ethnographic research has come to center more on the local cultures of the researchers, the practice of ethnography has "come home" to self-interpretation as a primary locus of research. Fasulo then describes a particularly reflexive form of ethnography—namely, auto-ethnography, which produces an array of creative, dynamic, and adaptive forms of first-person description, production, and self-interpretation. Auto-ethnography deconstructs analytical distance and objectivity and emphasizes the contextual and reflexive aspects of research, thus, Fasulo argues, making self-observation even more central to ethnographic practice.

In the final chapter of this volume, I revisit the arguments made here and consider how they are addressed throughout the volume, providing an outline of the basic implications for future theories of self-observation.

Notes

1. By "account" I do not mean a philosophical justification of the possibility of self-observation, but a form of design and reporting that exposes, documents, and interprets the phases of data production.
2. The incredible complexity and difficulty of such a negotiation sheds light on the original introspectionist contention that only highly trained scientists could act as self-observers.

References

Bakan, D. 1954. "A Reconsideration of the Problem of Introspection." *Psychological Bulletin* 51, no. 2: 105–18.

Boring, E. G. 1953. "A History of Introspection." *Psychological Bulletin* 50, no. 3: 169–86.

Burt, C. 1962. "The Concept of Consciousness." *British Journal of Psychology* 53, no. 3: 229–42.

Costall, A. 2006. "'Introspectionism' and the Mythical Origins of Scientific Psychology." *Consciousness and Cognition: An International Journal* 15, no. 4: 634–54.

den Boer, J. A., Reinders, A., and Glas, G. 2008. "On Looking Inward: Revisiting the Role of Introspection in Neuroscientific and Psychiatric Research." *Theory & Psychology* 18, no. 3: 380–403.

Downs, S. D. 2012. "A Phenomenologically Informed Theory of Self-Observation: Intra-Spection as Hermeneutic Reduction on the Self." In *Self-Observation in the Social Sciences*, edited by J. W. Clegg, 173–194. New Brunswick, NJ: Transaction Publishers.

DeSilva, H. R. 1930. "The Common Sense of Introspection." *Psychological Review* 37, no. 1: 71–87.

Ericsson, K. and Simon, H. A. 1980. "Verbal Reports as Data." *Psychological Review* 87, no. 3: 215–51.

Froese, T. T., Gould, C. C., and Seth, A. K. 2011. "Validating and Calibrating First- and Second-Person Methods in the Science of Consciousness." *Journal of Consciousness Studies* 18, no. 2: 38–64.

Gantt, E. E. and Thayne, J. L. 2012. "A Conceptual History of Self-Observation in the Phenomenological Tradition: Brentano, Husserl, and Heidegger."

In *Self-Observation in the Social Sciences*, edited by J. W. Clegg, 147–171. New Brunswick, NJ: Transaction Publishers.

Gould, S. J. 1995. "Researcher Introspection as a Method in Consumer Research: Applications, Issues, and Implications." *Journal of Consumer Research* 21, no. 4: 719–22.

Grover, S. C. 1982. "A Re-evaluation of the Introspection Controversy: Additional Considerations." *Journal of General Psychology* 106, no. 2: 205–12.

Jack, A. and Roepstorff, A. 2002. "Introspection and Cognitive Brain Mapping: From Stimulus-Response to Script-Report." *Trends in Cognitive Sciences* 6, no. 8: 333–39.

Lieberman, D. A. 1979. "Behaviorism and the Mind: A (Limited) Call for a Return to Introspection." *American Psychologist* 34, no. 4: 319–33.

Locke, E. A. 2009. "It's Time We Brought Introspection Out of the Closet." *Perspectives on Psychological Science* 4, no. 1: 24–25.

Nisbett, R. E. and Wilson, T. D. 1977. "Telling More Than We Can Know: Verbal Reports on Mental Processes." *Psychological Review* 84, no. 3: 231–59.

Overgaard, M. 2006. "Introspection in Science." *Consciousness and Cognition: An International Journal* 15, no. 4: 629–33.

Petitmengin, C. and Bitbol, M. 2011. "Let's Trust the (Skilled) Subject! A Reply to Froese, Gould and Seth." *Journal of Consciousness Studies* 18, no. 2: 90–97.

Roepstorff, A. and Jack, A. I. 2004. "Trust or Interaction? Editorial Introduction." *Journal of Consciousness Studies* 11, no. (7–8): v–xxii.

Wallendorf, M. and Brucks, M. 1993. "Introspection in Consumer Research: Implementation and Implications." *Journal of Consumer Research* 20, no. 3: 339–59.

Washburn, M. F. 1922. "Introspection as an Objective Method (Address of the President, before the American Psychological Association, Princeton Meeting, December, 1921)." *Psychological Review* 29, no. 2: 89–112.

Weisberg, J. 2011. "Introduction." *Journal of Consciousness Studies* 18, no. 1: 7–20.

Wheeler, R. H. 1923. "Introspection and Behavior." *Psychological Review* 30, no. 2: 103–15.

Wilson, T. D. 2002. *Strangers to Ourselves: Discovering the Adaptive Unconscious.* Cambridge, MA: Belknap Press/Harvard University Press.

Zahavi, D. 2008. "Simulation, Projection and Empathy." *Consciousness and Cognition: An International Journal* 17, no. 2: 514–22.

Part II

The History of Scientific Self-Observation

2

The History of Introspection Revisited

Adrian C. Brock

Introspection was less a victim of its intrinsic problems than a casualty of historical forces far bigger than itself.
—Danziger (1980, 259).

My involvement with this topic goes back a long way. The first research I ever did on the history of psychology was a master's thesis on the so-called "imageless thought controversy" that I wrote in 1987. A summary of this research was subsequently published as a book chapter (Brock 1991). It was on the basis of this research that I was recommended to the editor of the present volume. My first reaction on being asked to write another chapter on the history of introspection was to say that the topic had already been thoroughly investigated and I was not sure that I could add much to the research that was new. His response was to say that the target audience for the book was not specialist historians of psychology and so many of its readers would not be familiar with this research. He also suggested that the book would be lacking if it did not contain some historical material. I accepted these points and agreed to write a chapter on this basis. I mention it so that no one will expect the chapter to contain groundbreaking new research. It is more a summary of the research that I and others, mainly Kurt Danziger (1980, 1990, 2001), have already published in the specialist literature on the history of psychology and it is directed to the nonspecialist reader.

The starting point of my account is a view that is widely held among psychologists to the effect that introspection was once the favored method of psychology. The names of the Wilhelm Wundt and Edward B. Titchener are often mentioned in this connection. It is also held that the use of introspection led to unresolvable controversies because introspection is essentially a private affair. According to this view, which tends to be assumed rather than debated, I can tell you what is going on in my mind but I have no idea what is going on in yours. It is also said to be because of this situation that the founder of behaviorism, John B. Watson, argued that psychology should be based on publicly observable behavior and it has done this ever since. For much of the twentieth century, psychologists restricted themselves to accounts of human and animal behavior and did not concern themselves with minds or mental events. From the 1960s onwards, behaviorism was replaced by cognitive psychology, which did not share the same reticence with regard to mental events. On the contrary, it concerned itself with topics like a memory and attention, and even mental imagery, but it did so on the basis of behavioral rather than introspective evidence. Thus, even postbehaviorist psychology has not abandoned this long-standing commitment to methodological behaviorism.

The traditional view of the history of introspection can be found in introductory textbooks on psychology and in textbooks on the history of psychology. It can also be found in the work of eminent scholars in the field (Brock 1991, 1993; Costall 2006). It is sometimes communicated in the classroom. One of the more curious aspects of human knowledge is that anyone who wants to challenge an accepted view will usually be expected to provide copious evidence in support of that challenge but someone who is expressing an accepted view is usually not required to present any supporting evidence at all. It is partly because of this situation that popular myths are able to survive.

For those who do not know it yet, the traditional view of these events is a mythical account. History is a messy affair and does not usually lend itself to being divided up into neat stages. Although it is true that introspection enjoyed a brief period of popularity in the first decade of the twentieth century, it has never been the dominant approach to psychology at any time in its history. It also did not disappear from the discipline in the years that behaviorism prevailed. Our first task is, therefore, to provide a more accurate account of the history of introspection in psychology.

The Philosophical Background

Introspection no doubt has its origins in traditional religious practices, such as the examination of one's conscience, but the term did not appear in the English language until the end of the seventeenth century (Danziger 2001; Lyons 1986). It is, of course, derived from the Latin words for "to look within." The use of the term is closely linked to the rise of empiricism in British philosophy. One of the key figures in this movement, John Locke, famously argued that knowledge is based on experience and he believed that we had two types of experience, experience of an external physical world and experience of an inner mental world. The former was experienced through the traditional senses and the term "inner sense" was frequently used to account for our ability to experience the latter. It should be noted that these views did not extend to Continental Europe where figures like Leibniz and Kant believed that rational enquiry, rather than conscious experience, was the royal road to understanding the mind (Danziger 1980).

Introspection was the main method used by British philosophers of mind prior to the establishment of modern psychology but it was not without its critics. The father of positivism, Auguste Comte, had little time for traditional psychology and believed that phrenology would be the key to understanding the human mind. He famously argued that we cannot split ourselves into two so that one part of the mind can engage in complex tasks while the other part observes it engaging in these tasks. He also suggested in an argument that was later to be widely adopted by psychologists, that the results of introspection were unreliable (Wilson 1991). John Stuart Mill was a follower of Comte in some respects but he was also one of the heirs to the British empiricist tradition and he defended introspection with what subsequently came to be a standard response to the criticism that Comte had made: He argued that there was no need to split the mind into two; we could engage in complex tasks and then recall what we had done while our memories of them were still fresh. This view is frequently described in the literature as "introspection as retrospection."

A common language and culture led to British philosophy being particularly influential in the United States in the nineteenth century and so William James held similar views. In his famous book, *Principles of Psychology*, he vividly described his conscious experience (James 1890). James regarded introspection as the main method of psychology and also defended it against the criticisms of Comte. For example, in response to the claim that the results of introspection were unreliable, he argued that all observation was fallible and introspection was no different in this respect (James 1894). James owes his eminent position in the history of psychology to the fact that he was the first person in the United States to become aware of the developments that were taking place in experimental psychology in Europe and to make them widely known among his contemporaries. In spite of this, he was not a typical psychologist. He once famously said that psychophysics could only have arisen in a country where the natives were incapable of being bored. He also became disillusioned with psychology, describing it as "a nasty little subject," and devoted himself to philosophy in his later years (James 1920).

The Beginnings of Experimental Psychology

Wilhelm Wundt was more representative of the spirit of the new psychology. He established what many people consider to be the first laboratory for experimental psychology, with the date usually being given as 1879. He also wrote its first textbook and published its first journal. Perhaps most important of all, he trained around 150 graduate students from different parts of the world, many of whom went back to their own countries and established laboratories for experimental psychology along similar lines. Even James imported one of Wundt's former students, Hugo Münsterberg, to take charge of the laboratory at Harvard University.

It is somewhat strange that Wundt came to be regarded as the arch-introspectionist in the early history of psychology since he did not share the commitment of James to this method. One point that is often overlooked is that Wundt devoted a great deal of his life to a subject that he called "Völkerpsychologie" (Wundt 1900–1920). The term is usually translated as social or cultural psychology by English-language writers but there is actually no direct equivalent for the term in English. The word, "Volk" can mean "people" or "nation" in German and so the literal translation of Völkerpsychologie is either "the psychology of peoples" or "the psychology of nations." It was concerned with those aspects of mental life that members of linguistic and cultural communities had in common and could not be explained in terms of individual consciousness. Its main method was to examine the cultural products of these communities, in particular language, myth, and custom (Wundt 1888; see also Danziger 1983). Introspection was completely irrelevant in this task since it was centered on the individual mind.

Wundt's experimental psychology was concerned with the individual mind but it relied to a large extent on behavioral measures like reaction times (Danziger 1980, 1990). Wundt was not a behaviorist, however, and his psychology did incorporate the results of subjective reports, though it was a limited form of introspection, if it can be described as introspection at all. He accepted the argument of Comte that we could not divide ourselves into two and compared the introspector to Baron von Münchhausen who claimed to have pulled himself out of a swamp with his pigtail (Wundt 1887). Wundt also did not accept the argument of Mill that introspection can operate by way of retrospection, arguing that we were unlikely to be able to remember something that we were incapable of observing in the first place. In order for subjective reports to be valid, they had to be tied to external events and repeatable. The kind of thing that Wundt had in mind was psychophysics where two physical objects, weights for example, could be presented to a blindfolded subject and the difference between them increased until a just noticeable difference could be found. This is not introspection in the usual sense of the term.

Part of the problem here is that "introspection" was not used in German at the time and it would be naive in the extreme to think that the concepts and categories of every language are exactly the same. The closest term in German was "Selbstbeobachtung," which literally translates as "self-observation." This term also exists in English and it does not have exactly the same meaning as "introspection" since it does not necessarily involve "looking within." It can also be used to describe observations of our own behavior. In a paper titled "Selbstbeobachtung und innere Wahrnehmung" ("Self-observation and inner perception"), Wundt expressed his opposition to traditional introspection or "Selbstbeobachtung" and contrasted it with what he called "inner perception." The latter involved reports of subjective experience that were tied to external stimuli and repeatable. It is unfortunate that influential English-language authors, such as Boring (1953), translated both of these terms as "introspection," with the result that the subtle differences between them were overlooked. One of the problems that anyone writing a history of introspection has to face is the way in which diverse practices have been lumped together under this label. This is all part of the legacy of behaviorism. As Boring (1953) noted: "Introspectionism got its *ism* because protesting new schools needed a clear and stable background against which to exhibit their novel features" (172).

The Next Generation of Experimental Psychologists

How did Wundt come to be mistakenly characterized as an "introspectionist"? The question can be answered on different levels but the origins of the problem lie with his former student, Edward B. Titchener. Titchener was an Englishman who had studied philosophy in Oxford prior to traveling to Leipzig to do his PhD in experimental psychology. It was in Oxford that he was immersed in British empiricist philosophy and this was the basis of his approach to psychology. Like his empiricist predecessors, he believed that introspection was the key to understanding the mind (Titchener 1912a, 1912b). Also, like his empiricist predecessors, he believed that complex thought could be broken down into its sensory components. The main difference between him and his empiricist predecessors was that he used experimental methods to accomplish this task rather than examining the content of his own mind. Titchener spent only two years in Leipzig and had very little contact with Wundt during this time. Wundt was officially a professor of philosophy and he published extensively on traditional philosophical topics like ethics, logic, and metaphysics. He had temporarily put experimental psychology to one side in order to pursue these other interests and had left the day-to-day running of his laboratory to his assistants. On completing his studies in Leipzig, Titchener found that British universities had been slow to take an interest in the new field of experimental psychology and so he looked for employment in the United States. He found it at Cornell University in upstate New York where he spent the rest of his career.

Titchener was very much at odds with the mainstream of American psychology, partly because of his elitist Oxford background. He believed that psychology needed to establish itself as a science before it could develop useful applications. It was possible for him to pursue what he considered to be "pure science" from his tenured position at Cornell but many American psychologists did not have the luxury of pursuing knowledge that would have no practical applications. They relied on funding from advertisers, industrialists, educational administrators and the like, and they would only provide support for psychological research if it resulted in knowledge that they considered to be useful. Titchener's estrangement from the mainstream of American psychology can be seen from the fact that he withdrew from the American Psychological Association, believing it to have been taken over by "mental testers," and founded his own rival Society of Experimental Psychologists, an organization which still exists today.

Titchener liked to portray himself as Wundt's loyal disciple in the United States. This was no doubt due to the fact that he was such a marginal figure. Wundt made himself very unpopular in the United

States during World War I when he passionately argued Germany's case but prior to that his name carried a certain amount of prestige. He had after all trained many of the first generation of American psychologists. Titchener's psychology was still rooted in the British empiricist tradition. It was more a matter of *claiming* to be a loyal disciple of Wundt rather than actually being one. He is far from unique in this regard. I have lost count of the number of psychologists I have encountered over the years who have claimed, and continued to claim, that their views on psychology are the same as those of Wundt. I have also never found a single instance where the claim was true. Politicians who are standing for election will often seek the endorsement of senior figures in their party and psychologists sometimes engage in a similar strategy to gain support from their views. There is, of course, no figure in the history of psychology who is more "senior" than Wundt.

Titchener's attempt to reconstruct Wundt in his own image became a major problem for the history of psychology largely due to the influence of his student, E. G. Boring, whose work has already been mentioned. Boring wrote a textbook on the history of experimental psychology, which was first published in 1929 and which appeared as a second edition in 1950 (Boring 1929, 1950). This textbook was widely used in classes on the history of psychology and came to be regarded as an authoritative source. It was unfortunate from the point of view of gaining accurate knowledge since Boring rarely checked the original sources of his work. His interest in the history of psychology had been sparked off by the lectures of Titchener and much of what he wrote about Wundt was derived from these lectures.

It should be noted in Boring's defense that he was writing at a time before the history of psychology became an area of specialist research. This did not happen until the 1960s in the United States and even later elsewhere (Ash 1983; Brock 1998). Prior to that it was an exclusively pedagogical field and the broad sweep of Boring's textbook made it virtually impossible for him to check the original sources. This has been a problem for textbook writers ever since, a problem that is discussed in more detail below. It should also be noted that Boring pointed to some important differences between Wundt and Titchener but the stories of Titchener's devotion to Wundt became increasingly exaggerated over the years so that their approaches to psychology were thought to be exactly the same (Brock 1993; Danziger 1979a).

Titchener was not the only former student of Wundt who advocated the use of introspection. Another was Oswald Külpe, who served as

Wundt's assistant and right-hand man for several years. It is very likely that Titchener had more contact with Külpe than he had with Wundt during the two years that he spent in Leipzig. One of the tasks that Wundt gave to Külpe during the early 1890s was to write an introductory textbook on psychology. Wundt had written a standard work on experimental psychology in the 1870s, which was constantly updated and served as a kind of handbook for the field. It was, however, directed at people who already had some knowledge of the field. As Wundt's lectures on psychology became increasingly popular in the university, he found that he needed an introductory text. Külpe duly carried out this task and published a book with the title, *Grundriss der Psychologie* (*Outline of Psychology*) in 1893 (Külpe 1893). Wundt was extremely disappointed with this work and published his own textbook with exactly the same title in 1895 (Wundt 1895). The main problem was that Külpe had made public his differences with Wundt in the book. It was mentioned earlier that Wundt devoted a great deal of his life to a subject that he called "Völkerpsychologie" and that this was concerned with the cultural products of human communities. Wundt assigned the study of what he called the "higher" mental functions, such as language and thought, to this field, arguing that they were essentially social and could not be understood by studying isolated individuals in the laboratory. Thus, experimental psychology, according to Wundt, had a very limited role. It was on this point that Külpe departed from Wundt and suggested that there is no part of psychology that could not be studied using experimental methods, a view that Titchener would have endorsed. Both Külpe and Titchener represented a new generation of psychologists who believed that experimentation was the only appropriate method for psychology and it is interesting to note that it was Külpe's textbook that Titchener translated into English rather than that of Wundt (Külpe 1895; see also Danziger 1979a).

Külpe's departure from the views of his mentor must have made life difficult for him in Leipzig and he accepted an offer to set up his own Psychological Institute at the University of Würzburg in 1895. He gathered around him a group of able researchers who set out to conduct experiments on thought and the favored method for doing this was what they called "systematische experimentelle Selbstbeobachtung," which is literally "systematic experimental self-observation," but which has traditionally been translated as "systematic experimental introspection." As mentioned earlier, the word "introspection" did not exist in the German language at the time. The Würzburg researchers also claimed to have discovered a phenomenon which they called "Bewusstseinslagen." The term has no direct equivalent in English. It was translated by Titchener and his students as "conscious attitudes" (e.g., Clarke 1911), though it is perhaps best translated as "states of consciousness" (Ach 1905; see also Brock 1991). It is these "Bewusstseinslagen" that subsequently came to be characterized as "imageless thought." However, if one reads the original works of Würzburg researchers, it was not the lack of sensory images that was their defining characteristic. It was Titchener who believed that thought was accompanied by sensory images and it was he who was offended by the suggestion that there could be such a thing as imageless thought. This is just one example of the way in which psychologists in English-speaking countries have come to see the controversy from Titchener's point of view. It is for this reason that I tend to use scare quotes when referring to the "imageless thought" controversy.

The "Imageless Thought" Controversy

It was Wundt who fired the first salvoes in the controversy. He was concerned not so much with the findings of the Würzburg psychologists but with the methods that they used to obtain them. It was the work of Karl Bühler that particularly offended him (e.g., Bühler 1907). Bühler had given his research participants a complex problem, got them to solve the problem and then asked them how they had arrived at the answer. This was the classic method of "introspection as retrospection" and Wundt's opposition to it was entirely consistent with the views that he had expressed in his paper from 1887 where he had opposed the use of "self-observation" and contrasted it with "inner perception," which was tied to external objects and repeatable. Wundt (1907) referred to Bühler's use of what he called the "interview method" (*Ausfragemethode*) and dismissed the work as "pseudo-experiments" (*Scheinexperimente*).

It was some time later when Titchener entered the fray. Being an advocate of introspection, he did not share Wundt's views on this subject and openly stated that he did not agree with them. Titchener subscribed to the classic empiricist view that complex thought could be broken down into its sensory components and much of his experimental work, as well as that of his students, was carried out with this aim in mind. He was not willing to accept the existence of imageless thought and tried to explain away the Würzburg results by suggesting that they had committed what he called the "stimulus error."

This involved confusing the object of thought with the thoughts themselves. He also suggested that the "Bewusstseinslagen" were accompanied by weak kinesthetic images which had been merely overlooked (Titchener 1909).

A few observations need to be made about the controversy here. According to the traditional view, it was the essentially private nature of introspection which had led to this impasse. This was definitely not the case as far as Wundt was concerned. His involvement in the controversy was the result of his opposition to introspection in the way that the term is usually understood. Also, if we look at the work of the advocates of introspection around this time, we will find little evidence that introspection is essentially a private affair. As I pointed out in my master's dissertation many years ago, the disagreement did not center on different reports from isolated individuals. It was a clash of two different *schools.* The two schools of psychology differed in important respects but the members of each school were in agreement (Brock 1987, 1991). In this respect, it was no different from many of the other controversies that have occurred in the history of science.

The traditional view of these events also gives the impression that scientific controversy is a kind of aberration. It encourages the view that scientists are mere collectors of "facts" and that there will be no disagreement between them if they deal with publicly observable facts. I probably do not need to point out that there is little evidence from the history of psychology to support such a view. The results of intelligence tests are publicly observable and yet this has not prevented the existence of controversy surrounding them over the years. In fact, as a Boring (1929) wryly noted, the adoption of behaviorism did not lead to psychologists being in agreement with each other. On the contrary, different schools of behaviorism began to emerge. The inescapable conclusion is that the total abandonment of introspection in response to the controversy was neither justified nor inevitable.

The Rise of Behaviorism

In fact, behaviorism was not a response to the controversy. It is certainly true that John B. Watson's "behaviorist manifesto," as it has come to be known, appeared in 1913 when memories of the controversy were still fresh. There is little evidence in his article to suggest that he had adopted behaviorism as a result of the failure of introspectors to agree. He briefly mentions the "imageless thought" controversy in a footnote but this seems to be little more than an attempt to exploit the perceived weakness of his opponents (163). Watson (1936) traced his own views on the subject back to 1904 before the controversy had even begun. There is also plenty of evidence to suggest that Watson's ideas were not as revolutionary as is generally thought. Walter Pillsbury (1911) had published a textbook in 1911 in which he had defined psychology as "the science of human behavior" (1) and added: "man may be treated as objectively as any physical phenomena" (4). As early as 1904, James McKeen Cattell (1904) had written: "the rather widespread notion that there is no psychology apart from introspection is refuted by the brute argument of accomplished fact" (176). Articles that were critical of introspection had also appeared (e.g., Dodge 1912; Dunlap 1912). Indeed, the only important contemporary of Watson in the United States who was still advocating the use of introspection was Titchener and he is the only psychologist who is mentioned in this connection by name. Watson was merely giving voice to a trend that had already occurred in American psychology, not outlining changes that still needed to be made.

It is important to remember that behaviorism was popular only in the United States. This point is often overlooked because of an unfortunate but widespread tendency to confuse the history of psychology in the United States with the history of psychology in general (Brock 2006). George Miller (2003) has written:

> Behaviorism flourished primarily in the US and the cognitive revolution in psychology re-opened communication with some distinguished psychologists abroad. In Cambridge, UK, Sir Frederic Bartlett's work on memory and thinking had remained unaffected by behaviorism. In Geneva, Piaget's insights into the minds of children had inspired a small army of followers. And in Moscow, A. R. Luria was one of the first to see the brain and mind as a whole. None of these three spent time at the Center but we knew their work well. Whenever we doubted ourselves we thought of such people and took courage from their accomplishments. (142)

There has been a great deal of discussion over whether the transition from behaviorism to cognitivism in American psychology is best portrayed as "revolution" or "evolution" (e.g., Leahey 1992) but it was a non-event from a European perspective because psychology there had never gone behaviorist in the first place. One only need look at the kind of psychology that European refugees brought to the United States with them in the 1930s. Gestalt psychology, for example, did not reject the study of conscious experience and placed great emphasis on it. It is because of this difference that the work of figures like Piaget and Vygotsky from the 1920s and -30s was belatedly discovered by American psychologists in the 1960s.

If we are going to find an adequate explanation for the rise of behaviorism in the United States, we need to look at social factors that were operating in the United States. It was primarily in the United States that the so-called "applied" fields of psychology—clinical psychology, educational psychology, industrial psychology, consumer psychology, forensic psychology, etc.—began to emerge. The main reason for this is that American psychologists were more reliant than their European counterparts on private sources of support. Educational administrators, industrialists, advertisers, law enforcement agencies, the military, etc., were unlikely to provide funds for psychological research unless it resulted in knowledge that was relevant to their interests. It is this more than anything else that explains the rise of behaviorism in the United States. There is an important passage in Watson's behaviorist manifesto that is often overlooked. He writes:

> If psychology would follow the plan I suggest, the educator, the physician, the jurist and the businessman could utilise our data in a practical way, as soon as we are able, experimentally, to obtain them. Those who have occasion to apply psychological principles practically would find no need to complain as they do at the present time. Ask any physician or jurist today whether scientific psychology plays a practical part in his daily routine and you will hear him deny that the psychology of the laboratories finds a place in the scheme of work. I think the criticism is extremely just. One of the earliest conditions which made me dissatisfied with psychology was the feeling that there was no realm of application of the principles which were being worked out in content terms. (168–69)

He continues:

> What gives me hope that the behaviorist position is a defensible one is the fact that those branches of psychology which have already partially withdrawn from the parent, experimental psychology, and which are consequently less dependent upon introspection are to-day in a most flourishing presentation. Experimental pedagogy, the psychology of drugs, the psychology of advertising, legal psychology, the psychology of tests, and psychopathology are all vigorous growths. (169)

The amount of space that Watson devotes to this issue stands in sharp contrast to his brief mention of the imageless thought controversy in a footnote.

It must be acknowledged here that Watson was onto something important. The social agencies that fund psychological research are not particularly interested in the content of people's minds. Some years ago, the former US President, Jimmy Carter was asked if he had ever committed adultery. He replied that he had committed adultery "in his heart." The statement resulted in amusement because our views on morality are generally concerned with behavior rather than thoughts. I can covet my neighbor's Mercedes Benz but I am not committing a crime unless I damage or steal it. It is only then that the law enforcement agencies will get involved. The same is true of other agencies in society that are concerned with the management of people. For example, children become a problem in schools when they misbehave, not when they have deviant thoughts. A similar situation pertains to advertisers. They might want people to remember the names of their products but the advertising will not be considered successful unless it leads people to buy their products. What all these agencies have in common is an interest in human behavior and Watson was correct in asserting that psychology would flourish if this was to become its main concern.

This is not to say that introspection is not without its practical uses. Kroker (2003) writes about a former student of Titchener who used introspection as a relaxation technique. The point remains, however, that the social agencies that are likely to fund psychological research are interested primarily in behavior and so this is the side of psychology's bread on which the butter is likely to be found. It also does not help that many of these social agencies are concerned with groups such as children and the mentally ill where introspection is impossible or unreliable. It was possible for someone like Titchener to pursue this kind of psychology from his tenured position at Cornell but many of his contemporaries did not have the luxury of investigating topics that were unlikely to lead to practical results. This situation did not apply in Europe or it applied to a lesser extent. For example, in Germany, psychology continued to be a branch of philosophy until World War II (Danziger 1979b).

The Persistence of Introspection

The ban on introspection is better seen as a social taboo rather than a rational response to a crisis. This may explain why introspection as a practice never died out. It is often written that introspection survived under the guise of "verbal report" but there is an important difference between the two. The latter is akin to witness testimony; that is, something we are unlikely to accept without corroborating evidence of another kind. It did continue, however, in psychophysics, Gestalt psychology, psychoanalysis, and other forms of clinical practice. One has to be careful in using the term "introspection" because of the sloppy way in which it has been traditionally applied. I am using it here in the sense of examining subjective experience.

It would also explain why there have always been dissenting voices. Titchener was not convinced by Watson's arguments and there was a series of polemics between the two. According to Titchener (1914), behaviorism was not science but technology. Other dissenting voices have appeared in the literature over the years. For example, David Bakan (1954) published an article with the title "A reconsideration of the problem of introspection" in 1954. Arguments in favor of introspection were made by Cyril Burt and by R. B. Joynson in British journals (Burt 1962; Joynson 1974). There were also articles in favor of introspection in the *American Psychologist*, such as "Reflections on introspection" by John Radford (1974) and "Behaviorism and the mind: A (limited) call for a return to introspection" by David Lieberman (1979). It is interesting to note that, although both these articles appeared in the *American Psychologist*, their authors were British. It seems that introspection has continued to be a British obsession. Further evidence of this can be seen from the fact that the British Psychological Society has a section devoted to "Consciousness and Experiential Psychology," something that the American Psychological Association does not have.

This situation may change in the future. It seems that consciousness has started to make a comeback in psychology. There are now journals such as *Consciousness and Cognition*, which devoted a special issue to the topic of introspection in 2006 (Overgaard 2006), as well as the *Journal of Consciousness Studies*. The rise of consciousness as an object of investigation in psychology will inevitably lead to the mythical account of the history of introspection being increasingly challenged. For the moment, it continues to survive.

Why the Mythical Account Survives

Psychologists with little experience of the history of psychology might think that once a mythical account has been exposed by scholarly research, it is unlikely to survive. Nothing could be further from the truth. Part of the problem here is the unusual status of history of psychology with regard to the discipline as a whole. We can broadly classify the various specialities in psychology into two types; fields like social or developmental psychology that are considered to be central to the discipline and fields that are relatively peripheral, such as community or cross-cultural psychology. History of psychology does not fall neatly into either of these categories. Courses on the history of psychology are regularly offered in departments of psychology but it is relatively peripheral as an area of research (Brock 1998).

A consequence of this situation is that the courses are rarely taught by psychologists whose main area of specialization is the history of psychology and this is even true of the authors of some of the popular textbooks in the field. While they may pay lip-service to original sources and to the professional literature in their reference lists, their knowledge of the subject is largely derived from other textbooks. "Textbook history," which is generally the only kind of history to which psychologists are exposed, is often a culture unto itself. This is why textbooks continue to appear in which Wundt is described as an "introspectionist," in spite of the fact that some of the scholarly work on this subject is now over thirty years old (e.g., Danziger 1980; see also Brock 1993).

In some respects, history of psychology has suffered the same fate as introspection in that it has been neglected because it does not produce the kind of knowledge that is likely to appeal to psychology's paymasters. There is, however, a certain logic to this situation as well. In a well-known article titled, "Should the history of science be rated 'X'," Brush (1974) suggests that the main purpose of offering courses on the history of science to science students is to socialize them into the ways of their discipline. He also suggests that scholarly historical accounts are not particularly useful in this regard and that myths can perform the task much better. Further evidence for this view can be found in the anthropological literature on myth. While writing my master's thesis on the "imageless thought" controversy many years ago, I came across the work of Malinowski (1926) on this subject. He noted that myths were always connected to particular social rules. They generally provided an account of the origins of a rule and the rationale for it. In this respect, it is misleading to understand the term, "myth" in the pejorative sense of something false. It is certainly that but it has a sociological dimension to it as well. In the case of the mythical account of the history of introspection, it explains the origins of the rule that "psychologists study behavior" and warns of dire consequences if the rule is not observed. It is the persistence of the rule that explains the persistence of the myth. Should the day come when psychologists abandon this rule, the mythical account will have outlived its usefulness and can be given a well-earned retirement.

Conclusions

Brush's juxtaposition of "history" and "myth" points to the more subversive aspects of history. If myth helps to reinforce a social rule, then exposing it as myth can help to undermine the rule. No doubt the advocates of a return to introspection will welcome the news that the traditional view of these events is a mythical account, if they were not aware of it already. It should be noted, however, that the rise of behaviorism in the United States did not occur for no reason. Watson's claim that introspection will lead to unresolvable controversies may be without substance but the same thing cannot be said of his claim that the social agencies that provide support for psychology are primarily interested in the behavior of people, not the content of their minds. This problem will not be easily overcome.

It was not my intention in this chapter to provide support for the view that consciousness is a proper object of psychological investigation or that introspection is a useful method in this task. One of the points that was instilled into me during my initial training as a historian of science was: "It is not the job of a historian to tell scientists how they should do their work." This seemed like a reasonable piece of advice and it is one that I have tried to follow ever since. History that is written with the aim of advocating a particular approach to psychology is usually considered to be bad history. At the very least, it ceases to be "history" in the usual sense of the term and becomes something else. A wise historian of economics once wrote in a different context:

> I conclude that both critics and defenders . . . could improve upon their arguments through knowledge of the episode in intellectual history that has been recounted here. This is probably all one can ask of history, and of the history of ideas in particular: not to resolve issues, but to raise the level of the debate. (Hirschmann 1977, 135)

In recounting this particular episode in intellectual history, I have tried to do the same.

References

Ach, N. 1905. *Über die Willenstätigkeit und das Denken*. Göttingen: Vandenhoeck und Ruprecht.

Ash, M. G. 1983. "The Self-Presentation of a Discipline: History of Psychology in the United States between Pedagogy and Scholarship." In *Functions and Uses of Disciplinary Histories*, edited by L. Graham, W. Lepenies, and P. Weingart, 143–89. Dordrecht: Reidel.

Bakan, D. 1954. "A Reconsideration of the Problem of Introspection." *Psychological Bulletin* 51: 105–18.

Boring, E. G. 1929. *A History of Experimental Psychology*. New York: Appleton Century.

_____. 1950. *A History of Experimental Psychology*, 2nd edn. New York: Appleton Century Crofts.

_____. 1953. "A History of Introspection." *Psychological Bulletin* 50: 169–89.

Brock, A. 1987. "The Imageless Thought Controversy: An Examination of the Myths." Unpublished M.Phil. Dissertation, University of Cambridge.

_____. 1991. "Imageless Thought or Stimulus Error? The Social Construction of Private Experience." In *World Views and Scientific Discipline Formation*, edited by W. R. Woodward and R. S. Cohen, 97–106. Dordrecht: Kluwer.

_____. 1993. "Something Old, Something New: The 'Reappraisal' of Wilhelm Wundt in Textbooks." *Theory & Psychology* 3: 235–42.

Brock, A. C. 1998. "Pedagogy and Research." *The Psychologist* 11: 169–71.

_____. 2006. "Introduction." In *Internationalizing the History of Psychology*, edited by A. C. Brock, 1–15. New York: New York University Press.

Brush, S. G. 1974. "Should the History of Science Be Rated 'X'?" *Science* 183: 1164–72.

Bühler, K. 1907. "Tatsachen und probleme zu einer Psychologie der Denkvorgänge." *Archiv für die gesamte Psychologie* 9: 297–369.

Burt, C. 1962. "The Concept of Consciousness." *British Journal of Psychology* 53: 229–42.

Cattell, J. M. 1904. "The Conceptions and Methods of Psychology." *Popular Science Monthly* 60: 176–86.

Clarke, H. M. 1911. "Conscious Attitudes." *American Journal of Psychology* 22: 214–49.

Costall, A. 2006. "'Introspectionism' and the Mythical Origins of Scientific Psychology." *Consciousness and Cognition* 15: 634–54.

Danziger, K. 1979a. "The Positivist Repudiation of Wundt." *Journal of the History of the Behavioral Sciences* 15: 205–30.

_____. 1979b. "The Social Origins of Modern Psychology: Positivist Sociology and the Sociology of Knowledge." In *Psychology in Social Context: Towards a Sociology of Psychological Knowledge*, edited by A. R. Buss, 27–45. New York: Irvington.

_____. 1980. "The History of Introspection Reconsidered." *Journal of the History of the Behavioral Sciences* 16: 240–62.

_____. 1983. "Origins and Basic Principles of Wundt's Völkerpsychologie." *British Journal of Social Psychology* 22: 303–13.

_____. 1990. *Constructing the Subject: Historical Origins of Psychological Research*. Cambridge: Cambridge University Press.

_____. 2001. "Introspection: History of the Concept." In *International Encyclopedia of the Social and Behavioral Sciences*, edited by N. J. Smelser and P. B. Baltes, 7889–90. Oxford: Elsevier.

Dodge, R. 1912. "The Theory and Limitations of Introspection." *American Journal of Psychology* 23: 214–29.

Dunlap, K. 1912. "The Case against Introspection." *Psychological Review* 19: 404–13.

Hirschmann, A. O. 1977. *The Passions and the Interests*. Princeton, NJ: Princeton University Press.

James, H. ed. 1920. *The Letters of William James Edited by His Son, Henry James* 2 vols. Boston, MA: Atlantic Monthly Press.

James, W. 1884. "On Some Omissions of Introspective Psychology." *Mind* 9: 1–26.

_____. 1890. *Principles of Psychology*. New York: Holt.

Joynson, R. B. 1972. "The Return of Mind." *Bulletin of the British Psychological Society* 25: 1–10.

Kroker, K. 2003. "The Progress of Introspection in America, 1896–1938." *Studies in the History and Philosophy of Biology and Biomedical Science* 34: 77–108.

Külpe, O. 1893. *Grundriss der Psychologie. Auf experimenteller Grundlage dargestellt*. Leipzig: Engelmann.

_____. 1895. *Outlines of Psychology. Based Upon the Results of Experimental Investigation*. London: Swan Sonnenschein.

Leahey, T. H. 1992. "The Mythical Revolutions of American Psychology." *American Psychologist* 47: 308–18.

Lieberman, D. A. 1979. "Behaviorism and the Mind: A (Limited) Call for a Return to Introspection." *American Psychologist* 34: 319–33.

Lyons, W. 1986. *The Disappearance of Introspection*. Cambridge, MA: MIT Press.

Malinowski, B. 1926. *Myth in Primitive Psychology*. London: Kegan Paul, Trench & Trubner.

Miller, G. A. 2003. "The Cognitive Revolution: A Historical Perspective." *Trends in Cognitive Sciences* 7: 141–44.

Overgaard, M. 2006. "Editorial: Introspection in Science." *Consciousness and Cognition* 15: 629–33.

Pillsbury, W. B. 1911. *The Essentials of Psychology*. New York: Macmillan.

Radford, J. 1974. "Reflections on Introspection." *American Psychologist* 29: 245–50.

Titchener, E. B. 1909. *Lectures on the Experimental Psychology of the Thought Processes*. New York: Macmillan.

_____. 1912a. "Prolegomena to a Study of Introspection." *American Journal of Psychology* 23: 427–48.

_____. 1912b. "The Schema of Introspection." *American Journal of Psychology* 23: 485–508.

_____. 1914. "Psychology: Science or Technology?" *Popular Science Monthly* 84: 39–51.

Watson, J. B. 1913. "Psychology as the Behaviorist Views It." *Psychological Review* 20: 158–77.

Wilson, F. 1991. "Mill and Comte on the Method of Introspection." *Journal of the History of the Behavioral Sciences* 27: 107–28.

Wundt, W. 1887. "Selbstbeobactung und innere Wahrnehmung." *Philosophische Studien* 4: 292–309.

_____. 1888. "Über Ziele und Wege der Völkerpsychologie." *Philosophische Studien* 4: 1–27.

_____. 1896. *Grundriss der Psychologie.* Leipzig: Engelmann. (Translated into English by C. H. Judd as Wundt, W. 1897. *Outlines of Psychology.* Leipzig: Engelmann.)

_____. 1900–1920. *Völkerpsychologie,* 10 vols. Leipzig: Engelmann.

_____. 1907. "Über Ausfrageexperimente und über die Methoden zur Psychologie des Denkens." *Psychologische Studien* 3: 301–60.

3

A Brief History of Self-Report in American Psychology

Jacy L. Young

Self-observation has been a methodological staple of psychological science since the inception of disciplinary psychology in the latter half of the nineteenth century. While self-observation undertaken within the confines of the psychological laboratory was an important feature of early psychological research, other forms of self-observation were also employed in the early years of the discipline. While Adrian Brock (2012) has ably outlined the history of introspection in his chapter, here I sketch a brief history of self-observation in early American psychology, largely as it occurred outside of the confines of the psychological laboratory. In providing this account, I focus on self-observation as undertaken through self-report measures, which served as a means of undertaking self-observational research en masse. From the earliest questionnaire-based research in the late nineteenth century through to more formal, scaled self-report measures in the twentieth century, the use of paper-based, self-report instruments to collect psychological data has been formative to disciplinary development. The use of self-report measures in early American psychology served as an efficient means of accessing the subjective, inner experiences of a multitude of individuals, providing a needed alternative to the discipline's adoption of experimental methodologies that largely ignored the personal particulars of the mental life of the individual psychological subject. Over the more than a century that has passed since psychology's founding, self-report measures have continued to play much the same role within the discipline.

Why Self-Report Measures?

Self-report measures have a long history in American psychology, but one that is rarely remarked upon. Histories of early American psychology often emphasize the importance of the laboratory for the establishment of psychology as a formal discipline. Psychology's newfound ability to situate itself within the confines of the laboratory, wherein it was possible to measure mental phenomena, was essential to the discipline's claim to the status of a science. Nonetheless, coexistent with the laboratory psychology that emerged in the United States at the end of the nineteenth century was another form of empirical psychology, one based on self-report undertaken en masse. The psychologists who employed self-report measures were engaged in an equally scientific enterprise as those engaged in laboratory research, only they drew upon a different brand of scientific epistemology. Oriented toward the collection of mass quantities of psychological data, psychologists undertaking research with self-report measures adopted what has been termed a taxonomic or natural historical scientific style (Crombie 1994; Hacking 1982; Pickstone 2001), rather than the experimental scientific-style characteristic of laboratory-based research. Within this naturalistic understanding of the scientific enterprise, psychological science involved the collection, analysis, and categorization of data on mental life. It was through the use of self-report measures that such an undertaking was made possible.

As mentioned, for early American psychologists the laboratory served as a means of establishing the discipline as a science, yet not all early American psychologists were content to confine scientific psychology to the realm of the laboratory. The mass collection of psychological data was one methodology adopted by early psychologists as part of efforts to take psychology beyond the laboratory in order to achieve finding of practical significance. One manifestation of such mass data collection were paper-based forms, consisting of lists of questions, that asked individuals to self-report, in an open-ended fashion, their mental experiences. Variously termed, these questionnaires, censuses, topical syllabi, circulars, and blanks, were constructed and circulated by a number of psychologists in order to obtain information on a variety of specific mental phenomena. By far the most sustained use of self-report measures in early American psychology occurred within realm of research related to education, as psychologists sought to contribute to a new science of pedagogy. This applied orientation proved crucial to the discipline's larger success. In part, psychology was able to establish and sustain itself as a discipline because psychologists were able to position themselves as experts within such socially valuable fields as education (see Danziger 1990).

By the twentieth century, the mass collection of data on mental life achieved greater formality with the advent of scaled, self-report measures. Just as earlier measures investigated psychological topics with social relevance, later scaled measures sought to investigate individual attitudes toward subjects of social importance. This shift not only involved a change in the format of such measures, but also a change in orientation. The earliest psychological self-report measures were efforts at understanding the nature of various psychological capacities within particular social groups. Overtime self-report measures—while still gathering psychological information from individuals that was meant to be understood within the context of the aggregate—came to include an increasingly evaluative component. Not only were individuals providing psychological data via self-report, they were also being told something about themselves in the process of completing such measures. Whatever their form, self-report measures allowed, and continue to allow, psychologists to collect information on mental phenomena from a large number of individuals with relative ease. In so doing, self-report measures provide a needed counterpoint to the often-impersonal experimental methods adopted by much of the discipline.

In what follows I describe the move from open-ended, self-report questionnaires in the late nineteenth century to more structured, scaled measures in the early twentieth century United States. First, I discuss the British influence on early American psychology's methodology through the work of Sir Francis Galton (1822–1911) and the mass data collection projects undertaken by psychical researchers. Next, I turn to the extensive program of questionnaire-based research undertaken by Granville Stanley Hall (1844–1924) from the late nineteenth into the twentieth century, much of it conducted on the topic of childhood and carried out in educational settings. I conclude my historical review of self-report measures in psychology with a look at the early twentieth century work of Louis Leon Thurstone (1887–1955) on scaled, self-report measures, before ending with a more general discussion of the role of self-report measures within the discipline.

The British Influence on American Psychology

The most direct influence on the use of self-report in early American psychology is the work of British polymath Francis Galton. In a number of research projects in the latter half of the nineteenth century, Galton employed the questionnaire method as a means of collecting data on specific human characteristics (1883). In doing so, he influenced the methods employed by early American psychologists.

Galton, a cousin of Charles Darwin (1809–1882), is perhaps best known for coining the term "eugenic" (1883, 24) and outlining a corresponding program of better breeding for the improvement of the human race (e.g., 1865; see Kevles 1995). Part and parcel of Galton's concern with the quality of the populace was an interest in individual and group-based differences. One of the methods Galton used to investigate individual differences was the questionnaire. In 1873, he conducted his first questionnaire-based research when he circulated, to members of the Royal Society, a document inquiring into the qualities of English men of science (Galton 1874). This was followed by a questionnaire seeking information on the characteristics of twins (Galton 1883), as well a questionnaire inquiring into individual powers of mental imagery and the mental revival of other sensations (e.g., Galton 1880a, 1880b, 1880c, 1881a, 1881b, 1881c, 1883). This latter questionnaire shortly made its way into American psychology.

Galton's mental imagery questionnaire, titled *Questions on the Visualising and Other Allied Faculties*, began by informing those sitting down to complete it that,

> The object of these Questions is to elicit the degree in which different persons possess the power of seeing images in their mind's eye and of reviving past sensations.
>
> From inquiries I have already made, it appears that remarkable variations exist both in the strength and in the quality of these faculties, and it is highly probable that a statistical inquiry into them will throw light upon more than one psychological problem. (Galton 1883, 378)

Individuals were then instructed as follows:

> Before addressing yourself to any of the Questions on the opposite page, think of some definite object—suppose it is your breakfast-table as you sat down to it this morning—and consider carefully the picture that rises before your mind's eye. (Galton 1883, 378)

Having brought to mind their morning breakfast table, individuals were then asked a series of open-ended questions, including:

1. *Illumination.*—Is the image dim or fairly clear? Is its brightness comparable to that of the actual scene?
2. *Definition.*—Are all the objects pretty well defined at the same time, or is the place of sharpest definition at any one moment more contracted than it is in a real scene?
3. *Colouring.*—Are the colours of the china, of the toast, bread crust, mustard, meat, parsley, or whatever may have been on the table, quite distinct and natural? (Galton 1883, 378)

In all, Galton's questionnaire included fourteen questions. The remaining eleven items left behind the breakfast table scenario and addressed topics such as the visualization of persons, scenery, and numerals. Also included was one multipart item that inquired into an individual's ability to mentally represent light and color as well as other sensations—touch, smell, sound, and taste. For this item, individuals were asked to bring to mind specific objects, "an evenly clouded sky (omitting all landscape), first bright, then gloomy. A thick surrounding haze, first white, then successively blue, yellow, green, and red" (Galton 1883, 380). In responding to these questions individuals were asked to rank their mental representation abilities with respect to these senses as "very faint, faint, fair, good, or vivid and comparable to the actual sensation" (Galton 1883, 379), in addition to commenting more generally on their ability to revive such sensations. The ultimate result of questioning individuals on their abilities to mentally represent sensory experiences in this fashion was a mass of descriptive accounts of mental life.

Outside of his questionnaire-based research, Galton also conducted other psychologically oriented research. In 1884, he established a temporary Anthropometric Laboratory at the International Health Exhibition in London which, following the Exhibition's closure, was moved to a permanent home in the South Kensington Museum. Those willing to pay the three pence price of admission to the anthropometric laboratory were subject to a number of measurements, including a variety of physical measurements, as well as more decidedly psychological measurements of reaction time to visual and auditory stimuli (Sokal 1987). As has been well-documented by historian of science Michael Sokal (1987), Galton's anthropometric studies, through the work of James McKeen Cattell (1860–1944), were of direct influence on the shape of American psychology. Shortly after

Galton established his anthropometric laboratory, he began to correspond with Cattell, who was at the time completing what would be the first doctorate obtained by an American student with Wilhelm Wundt (1832–1920) at the University of Leipzig. With his return to the United States, Cattell brought with him his knowledge of the anthropometric tests developed by Galton (Sokal 1987). Coining the term "mental tests" (Cattell 1890), he added to Galton's existing battery of anthropometric measurements further psychophysical and mental measures.

Using his newly devised series of tests, Cattell tested the students of the institutions at which he was employed from 1890 through to the twentieth century. First, these tests were applied sporadically to students at the University of Pennsylvania and later more systematically to every incoming student to the Columbia School of Mines and Columbia College, later Columbia University. In subjecting a large number of students to a variety of physical and mental tests Cattell sought to use "tests of the senses and faculties in order to determine the condition and progress of students, the relative value of different courses of study, etc." (as quoted in Sokal 1987, 32). This project was only undermined when, at the turn of the twentieth century, Cattell's graduate student Clark Wissler calculated the relationship between the results of Cattell's mental tests and students' academic achievement and found virtually no correlation between the two measures (see Sokal 1987; Wissler 1901).

Among the items eventually included in Cattell's battery of mental tests was a section assessing mental imagery ability taken in part from Galton's earlier questionnaire on the topic (Cattell and Farrand 1896; Galton 1883). For this portion of the test, individuals were presented with a sheet of questions that read,

> Think of your breakfast table as you sat down to it this morning; call up the appearance of the table, the dishes and food on it, the persons present, etc. Then write answers to the following questions:
> (1) Are the outlines of the objects distinct and sharp? . . . .
> (2) Are the colors bright and natural?. . . .
> (3) Where does the image seem to be situated? In the head? Before the eyes? At a distance? . . . . (Cattell and Farrand 1896, 646)

Galton's influence can be clearly felt in these questions, which use very nearly the same breakfast scene prompt as in Galton's earlier visualization questionnaire. Individuals were also asked further questions on mental imagery, ones not taken directly from Galton,

> (1) Can you call to mind better the face or the voice of a friend?. . . .
> (4) Have you ever mistaken a hallucination for a perception, e.g., apparently heard a voice or seen a figure when none was present? If you answer 'yes' describe the experience on the back of this sheet. (Cattell and Farrand 1896, 646)

In speaking of this portion of his set of mental tests Cattell, and his coauthor Livingston Farrand, observed that

> those tests that are of special interest to the psychologist are often ones with which it is difficult to get definite results. The student has had no practice in introspection and even a trained psychologist may find it difficult to fill in such a blank. For this reason we have added to several of the questions proposed by Mr. Galton others admitting of more definite answers. (1896, 646–47)

Recognizing the difficulties associated with untrained introspection, Cattell proposed that these difficulties could be overcome by asking the right questions, in the right manner. Questions into the ability to mentally represent sensory experiences were just one of the psychological measures added to Cattell's battery of anthropometric tests, though the only component added to the series that required individuals to self-report on their conscious experiences.

Cattell was not the only American to take up Galton's research into mental imagery. A decade before Cattell began his program of mental testing, biologist Henry Fairfield Osborn circulated Galton's *Questions on the Visualising and Other Allied Faculties* in the United States. Although Osborn trained as a biologist and would later achieve success as a vertebrate paleontologist, serve as the long-time president of the American Museum of Natural History and gain prominence as an early twentieth-century American eugenicist (Clark 2008; Kevles 1995; Rainger 1991; Regal 2002), early in his professional career he exhibited an interest in the emerging field of scientific psychology. This interest in psychology led him to undertake a questionnaire-based research project on mental imagery in the early 1880s (see McCosh and Osborn 1884; Osborn, 1884a, 1884b, 1884c; Young, in press).

Having completed both his undergraduate and graduate education at the College of New Jersey, later Princeton University, Osborn accepted an appointment as the institution's first professor of biology in 1880. Shortly after taking on this appointment, he demonstrated an interest in the new physiological psychology developing in Germany. At this time both biology and psychology were newly emerging academic disciplines, with indistinct boundaries; for Osborn, delving into psychology was not much of a disciplinary reach (Rainger 1991). While engaging in a number of pedagogical endeavors related to psychology, Osborn also undertook a multiyear research project in the field.

During a period studying in England in 1879, Osborn had met Francis Galton at a Royal Society dinner. The following year, shortly after his return to the United States, Osborn read one of Galton's published reports of his mental imagery research (Galton, F. 1612–1926, H. F. Osborn to Galton, June 14, 1880), in which Galton specifically requested that others collect information on mental imagery (1880b, 1880c). Such a request prompted Osborn to write to Galton,

> If you think it worth your while I will undertake to obtain a number of sets of answers from the most intelligent men and women I know personally or by reputation. They may be interesting in comparison and conjunction with those of your English correspondents. If you have not completed your inferences from the answers already obtained I shall enjoy very much undertaking this small contribution to Psychological service and forwarding the results to you. (Galton, F. 1612–1926, H. F. Osborn to Galton, June 14, 1880)

Galton readily forwarded onto Osborn a copy of his *Questions on the Visualising and Other Allied Faculties,* and Osborn distributed it to students at a number of postsecondary educational institutions in the United States.

Though Osborn initially distributed Galton's questionnaire unaltered, in 1882 he undertook additional research into mental imagery using a new questionnaire. This questionnaire, *Questions on the Visualising Faculties* (Osborn 1882), consisted of some of the same questions as Galton's original questionnaire, most particularly the opening breakfast scene questions. Other items on the questionnaire were either wholly new or altered versions of questions that appeared on Galton's earlier questionnaire. Like Galton's original mental imagery questionnaire, the questions comprising *Questions on the Visualising Faculties* were all open-ended inquiries into individual mental imagery ability and the questionnaire was similarly circulated to college students in the United States. To amass even more information on the topic, Osborn, as Galton had done earlier, solicited responses to some of his mental imagery questions within the pages of scientific periodicals (1884b). Mass data collection of self-reported experiences with mental imagery was of import to Osborn as he speculated,

> In this single branch of visual memory, how much would be gained if we could trace the influences of heredity, of race, of cultivation or neglect,—results such as can be obtained only by pushing our inquiry among large numbers of persons. (1884c, 450)

Ultimately, Osborn's questionnaire-based research into mental imagery was his sole psychological research project. In the mid-1880s his research became decidedly more biologically focused. Despite this, in the early 1890s, Columbia College president Seth Low approached Osborn about taking on the position of professor of physiological psychology at the New York City institution. No longer working in psychology, Osborn turned down the position only to be offered a position as professor of biology at the College, which he accepted along with a joint appointment to the American Museum of Natural History (Rainger 1991). The position as professor of psychology at the institution was given to Cattell, and it was at Columbia that he undertook his extensive program of mental testing.

While the work of Francis Galton was one inspiration for the appearance of self-report measures in American psychology, it was not the only impetus for research of this kind within the discipline. In the case of William James, his self-report-based project was decidedly British in origin, but was not rooted in Galton's work. Though much of James's psychology was speculative and philosophical, he did undertake some empirical research. In the 1880s the British Society for Psychical Research (SPR) circulated a series of questions on the nature of hallucinations and it was this project that James took up in the United States. Though James's interest in psychical and spiritualist phenomena persisted throughout his life, his questionnaire-based research into such was a one-time endeavor.

The American Society for Psychical Research (ASPR), which James helped found in 1884, was initially populated by a number of early psychologists. These included James's student G. Stanley Hall, as well as James Mark Baldwin, Joseph Jastrow, and Christine Ladd-Franklin (Coon 1992). While the interest of most psychologists in this field quickly waned, James's interest in psychical research persisted. At the International Congress of Experimental Psychology, held in Paris in the summer of 1889, he was put in charge of the American leg of a questionnaire-based project on the nature of hallucinations. Acting as the superintendent of the project for the ASPR, James sought information on individual experiences of hallucinations by undertaking a "Census of Hallucinations" (e.g., James 1890a, 292; 1890b, 304; 1986, 56). This investigation was part of the ASPR's larger efforts to scientifically investigate—and more importantly, substantiate—claims of psychical ability that fell outside the accepted range of experience (Coon 1992).

The Census of Hallucinations that James conducted involved the circulation of printed forms consisting of a series of questions on individual experiences of hallucinations, or the lack thereof.[1] In various publications, he solicited help in collecting responses to the questions on hallucinations and described the project's purpose:

> The object of the inquiry is twofold: 1st, to get a mass of facts about hallucinations which may serve as a basis for a scientific study of these phenomena; and 2d, to ascertain approximately the *proportion of persons* who have had such experiences. Until the average frequency of hallucinations in the community is known, it can never be decided whether the so-called "veridical" hallucinations (visions or other "warnings" of the death, etc., of people at a distance) which are so frequently reported, are accidental coincidences or something more. (James 1890a, 292; 1890b, 304)

The mass circulation of questions on the occurrence of hallucinations was to generate information on the prevalence of premonitory visions amongst sane members of the general public (James 1986).

To assess the frequency of hallucinations in the population, James's census asked individuals to response yes or no to the following question,

> Have you ever, when completely awake, had a vivid impression of seeing or being touched by a living being or inanimate object, or of hearing a voice; which impression, so far as you could discover, was not due to any external physical cause? (James 1890a, 292; 1890b, 304; 1986, 58)

Those interested in aiding with the project were sent a formally printed sheet, "Schedule A," on which there was space to record the yes or no responses of twenty-five individuals, as well as the name and address, sex, occupation, and age of the respondents (see James 1986, 58). Presumably the latter demographic information was to be used to determine the specific populations in which hallucinatory experiences occurred with greatest frequency.

In seeking self-reported hallucinatory experiences, both familiarity with such experiences and the lack of such were important. Consequently, in the printed preface that accompanied Schedule A, those collecting data for the census were reminded,

> that the question should be very widely asked and of all sorts of people—not only of those who are thought likely to have had such an experience or those who are thought likely not to have had it. The answer "No" and the answer "Yes" are equally important. (James 1986, 56–57)

The recording of both instances and absences of hallucinatory experiences were crucial to obtaining an accurate estimate of the prevalence of such experiences within the general public. Thus, it was not just the self-reported details of such experiences that were important, but also the relative frequency with which these types of experiences occurred.

Individuals who reported having experienced hallucinations, and thus answered yes to the question on Schedule A, were then asked to complete a longer questionnaire on the nature of their experiences. This form, "Schedule B," consisted of six questions. For example,

1. Please state what you saw or heard or felt, and give the place, date and hour of the experience as nearly as you can.
2. How were you occupied at the time, and were you out of health or in grief or anxiety?
3. Was the impression that of some one whom you were in the habit of seeing, and do you know what he or she was doing at the time? (James 1986, 58)

As in the earlier mental imagery questionnaires constructed and circulated by Galton and Osborn in the 1880s, these questions were all open-ended. Individuals were simply to self-report, in as much detail as possible, their personal experiences with hallucinations. Taken together, these collected accounts of hallucinatory experiences were to provide a complete picture of the nature of hallucinations.

James's plea for aid in conducting a census of hallucinations in the United States was largely successful. His self-report questionnaire-based research on the topic eventually amassed as many as 5,600 responses. Of these, approximately 540 individuals reported having experienced hallucinations and went on to complete the longer questionnaire on the subject (James 1986). Having recently undertaken his own inquiry into hallucinations, James (1895) concluded on the basis of the earlier British inquiry into such that "the most that can be said, so far, in the opinion of the present writer, is this, that the Sidgwick report [on the SPR Census of Hallucinations] affords *a most formidable presumption* that veridical hallucinations are due to something more than chance" (75). This conclusion was not obvious to all however. Cattell (1896) was far more skeptical of the census's results, holding that "when we have an enormous number of cases, and cannot find among them all a single one that is quite conclusive, the very number of cases may be interpreted as an index of the weakness of the evidence" (582). With no readily apparent means of objectively analyzing the descriptive data generated via questionnaire, consensus as to the results of such research was elusive.

The Science of Education and the Self-Report Method

Although Osborn and James both used self-report questionnaires as their method for a single research project, psychologist G. Stanley Hall adopted the questionnaire as his prevailing research methodology. Beginning in the 1880s, Hall undertook research on childhood, and later pedagogy, using questionnaires as his means of gathering data. Open-ended, self-report questionnaires would remain his dominant methodology well into the twentieth century.

In the fall of 1882, Hall conducted his first questionnaire-based research project when he inquired into the contents of children's minds on entering school. The research was inspired by a previous investigation into children's knowledge of their environment undertaken in German schools by the Pedagogical Society of Berlin 1869 and 1874 in which 10,000 children were questioned (Hall 1883, 1893; Ross 1972). Having established a reputation as an educational expert the previous year, through a series of Harvard University-organized lectures on pedagogy before Boston schoolteachers (Ross 1972), Hall was well positioned to undertake such a research project within the city's schools. Through such endeavors, he established himself as a leader in the American Child Study movement, something that would serve him well in his later questionnaire-based research.

To collect information on children's knowledge upon entering school, four Boston kindergarten teachers were recruited for the project and another sixty schoolteachers contributed data. Armed with a questionnaire of 134 items assembled by Hall, the teachers questioned children, three at a time, on their knowledge of various items in their environment. For instance, children were asked if they had ever seen a cow, if they could locate their ribs (and various other body parts), and to identify the current season. In this research project, teachers served as intermediaries between the child and the questionnaire, recording on paper the student's verbal responses to the questionnaire's items, as many children were too young to do so themselves (Hall 1883, 1893). Among Hall's (1893) findings from this project was his observation of the relative paucity of city-reared children's knowledge of the natural world in comparison with country children.

Although Hall initially conducted questionnaire-based research in the early 1880s, he did not conduct further research along these lines until more than a decade later. In 1894, firmly ensconced as president of Clark University, he began a program of questionnaire-based research that would continue for more than two decades (Hall 1924). This research largely revolved around the concerns of child study and investigated, through self-report measures, aspects of the child's mental life and issues related to pedagogy. Such research was to contribute not only to a better understanding of the nature of childhood, but also to an empirically based science of education.

Joined by scores of students of psychology and pedagogy as well as practicing educators, Hall was able to construct, distribute, and assess multitudes of questionnaires over a roughly twenty-year period. Between 1894 and 1906, he and his extended network of students and associates distributed 147 distinct questionnaires, or what he often termed "topical syllabi," on a plethora of topics, including "the early sense of self," "moral education," and "training of teachers" to name but a few (Hall, n.d.). This number would rise to 195 by the time the questionnaire project came to an end in 1915 (Hall 1924). As early on in this questionnaire-based research endeavor as 1896, Hall could assert that in response to the copies of the questionnaires that had been distributed to various individuals, "at least a hundred thousand returns" (184) had been received, with sixty thousand returns received in 1895–1896 alone (Ross 1972). If measured in terms of sheer data amassed, Hall's questionnaire-based project was a momentous success from its very beginning.

Like the questionnaires circulated by Osborn and James, those composed and distributed by Hall and his associates consisted of a series of open-ended questions. In collecting data using these questionnaires, investigators adopted a variety of approaches. Not all of these were self-report based, as some opted to use the questionnaires as a basis for collecting observational data on children. Even the nature of self-report data gathered using the questionnaires varied. As adopted by teachers in normal schools with their adult students, questionnaires were often filled with retrospective accounts of childhood experiences. At other times, it was children themselves who completed the questionnaires (Williams 1896).

When discussing the results of this research no real distinction between these various kinds of reports seems to have been made. Although numerical information was sometimes reported alongside the descriptive findings of a questionnaire, the numerical details of the collected data appeared in only the simplest of forms: as mere counts or as percentages presented in tabular form (e.g., Hall 1883, 1893). A further effort to synthesize the results of such investigations was made by the inclusion of graphs in reports of research results. Still, descriptive accounts of mental life, gathered via questionnaire, received far more attention. For instance, inquiries into children's understanding of lightning included details such as the fact that many children thought lightning to be God "striking many matches at once" or "lighting a gas quick" (Hall 1883, 262). Providing a clear, concise summary of the results of questionnaire research was admittedly difficult (Hall 1924).

In terms of the amount of data generated and the period of time over which it operated, Hall's program of questionnaire research was hugely successful. Still, it attracted a considerable amount of methodological criticism within the discipline. Historian Dorothy Ross (1972), in her biography of Hall, notes that, "the chief strength Hall brought to . . . [the] educational scene, and the first new factor he contributed to it, was the authority of science" (118) but not everyone thought Hall's questionnaire-based psychological science *scientific*. Even Hall (1883) admitted that of the questionnaires completed by educators, which was the de facto source of responses, "many returns . . . are incomplete, careless, or show internal contradictions . . ." (252). Hugo Münsterberg, director of Harvard's psychological laboratory, was far more strident in his criticism. In his view, the work must be done by trained specialists or not at all. That child study which has for its aim only the collection of curiosities about the child, as an end in itself, may be grateful to the nurse who writes down some of the baby's naughty answers or to the teacher who sacrifices half an hour of her lesson to make experiments in the classroom to fill out the blanks that are mailed to her. The students of that scientific child psychology which stands in the service of the general mind study know how every step in the progress of our science was dependent upon the most laborious, patient work of our laboratories and the most subtle and refined methods, and that all this seductive but rude and untrained and untechnical gathering of cheap and vulgar material means a caricature and not an improvement of psychology. (Münsterberg 1898, 115)

A further critique of Hall's method was also offered by E. L. Thorndike (1874–1949) in his biographical memoir of Hall. According to Thorndike (1925), Hall's contributions to psychology were "marred by an apparently extravagant and illegitimate use of the questionnaire method of collecting facts, which, indeed, in the hands of some of Hall's followers, seemed almost a travesty of science" (140). Despite such criticism, he went on to conclude that, "the general effort to learn more of man by studying his actual detailed responses has been very fruitful" (140). Although the method was subject to criticism, there was no denying Hall's project a certain degree of success, if only with respect to its productive capacity.

Self-Report Measures Come of Age

The self-report-based research conducted in American psychology in the late nineteenth century was largely of a descriptive nature. In the research undertaken by Cattell, Osborn, James, and Hall individuals were presented with a series of open-ended questions to which they were to respond at will. The process of organizing the resulting material into a coherent whole was admittedly daunting (Hall 1924). While table and graphs could be employed to visually present data in a more concise manner, it was not until the twentieth century that psychology began to construct more formal self-report measures. In the process, American psychology moved from the mass collection of descriptive data to the collection of data on mental life that was formally scaled. Such a move was largely the result of the work of psychologist Louis Leon (L. L.) Thurstone.

Thurstone's contributions to the theoretical underpinnings of self-report measures began in the 1920s with a series of publications on the scaling of educational and psychological tests (e.g., Thurstone 1925). Among his most significant contributions to the field was his proposal that psychological measurement could be undertaken independent of physical measurement. No longer was it necessary for psychological constructs to correspond to measurements of the physical world in the way of the psychophysics of individuals like Gustav Theodor Fechner (1801–1887) (see Jones 1998; Thurstone 1952). Rather, a psychological scale, independent of scaled physical measurement, could be constructed and used as a means to order self-report data.

To explore such psychological scaling, Thurstone turned to the measurement of social values or attitudes (Thurstone 1928; Thurstone and Chave 1929). According to Thurstone's method, in order to construct a scaled measure of attitudes toward a particular topic, a series of brief, unambiguous statements on the topic, which can be either be endorsed or rejected, are assembled. The statements are then presented to a group of judges who sort the statements into scaled categories along a continuum of favorable to unfavorable statements. Ultimately, scaled values are assigned to each statement. Such values, unknown to those completing a scale, are then used to assess an individual's attitude toward a topic based on their endorsement or rejection of each of these specific statements (see Jones 1998; Thurstone 1928). As Thurstone (1928) asserted, "The essential characteristic of the . . . measurement method is the scale of evenly graduated opinions so arranged that equal steps or intervals on the scale *seem* to most people to represent equally noticeable shifts in attitude" (554). In constructing psychological scales according to the combined judgments of a number of individuals, a scale in which intervals at the very least appeared to be of equidistance could be created. This type psychological scaling, as a method of measuring attitudes based on self-report, was readily adopted by social psychologists, and continues to be used today.

Discussion

Self-report measures, whatever their form, proved an easy way to access the subjective, inner experiences of a multitude of individuals. Yet, this capacity to access such experiences en masse came with certain difficulties. As has been discussed in this chapter, the earliest questionnaire-based research in American psychology faced a problem with respect as to how to condense an overwhelming amount of descriptive data into a concise, coherent whole. The earliest questionnaire research was undertaken at a time in which statistics had yet to overtake the discipline, and was in fact itself only just emerging as a distinct field (see Porter 1988). Without numerical data that could be manipulated statistically, psychologists faced great difficulty explaining the results of their massive research projects in a straightforward manner.

As time progressed, self-report measures came to take on a more structured format, as in the scaled measures produced by Thurstone. These formalized measures allowed psychologists to achieve more meaningful results from their self-report research, as meaning came to be more directly inscribed within the format of such measures. Rather than attempting to synthesize a discordant set of descriptive data into a coherent whole, psychologists created self-report measures that were more purposeful in their construction and in their aim. As a result, it became increasingly easier to deal with the data that resulted from the use of self-report measures, as results fell along particular lines predetermined by the way in which the measure itself was constructed.

A further result of such purposefulness was the increasingly evaluative nature of self-report measures. One route of the development of early self-report measures was toward testing, such as the work of Hall's students Henry Herbert Goddard (1866–1957) and Lewis Terman (1877–1956), while another route of the development of such measures was toward the kind of scaled attitude measures created by Thurstone. Although the latter were less obviously evaluative than the intelligence tests circulated by psychologists such as Goddard and Terman, scaled self-report measures nonetheless provided the individuals completing such measures with a degree of feedback that had not been a part of the open-ended questions that comprised the earliest self-report measures used by psychologists.

In creating measures with more precise content, psychologists circumscribed the kinds of responses that were possible. This not only made the process of understanding the resulting data easier, but they also provided normative information to the psychological subject as to the boundaries of acceptable responses. As a result of these changes in the structure of self-report measures, the aim of such measures was no longer solely to understand the nature of the individuals in particular social groups, but rather to understand a particular individual within the context of some larger aggregate. As a consequence, these types of self-report measures almost certainly had—and continue to have—what Ian Hacking (1995) has termed a looping effect, wherein the very nature of the psychological categories being investigated are altered by the process of investigation. Measuring psychological experience almost always means furthering, deliberately or not, a particular set of norms.

Accessing the subjective, inner psychological experiences of individuals through self-report measures provided a needed counterpoint to the impersonal nature of much psychological research. Yet, such research is not without its difficulties. More structured self-report measures result in more coherent data, but such a structure may more readily influence the psychological subject's self-understanding, by providing cues as to what constitutes normal psychological experience.

Conclusion

As this chapter has outlined, self-report measures have a long history within American psychology. The self-report-based research conducted by early American psychologists in the late nineteenth century was largely descriptive in form. Individuals were presented with open-ended questions on various aspects of mental life and asked to describe their experiences as best as possible. For Galton, Cattell, and Osborn questionnaire-based research took the form of investigations into individual mental imagery ability, while in William James's case, the questionnaire method provided a means of exploring individual experiences with hallucinations. For G. Stanley Hall the questionnaire was a method he was able to employ for decades in his investigations of the nature of the child's mental life and his pedagogical inquiries. It was not until the twentieth century and the work of L. L. Thurstone that self-report measures gained a more structured format in the shape of scaled measures. Common to all these investigations was the view that the mass collection of psychological data on the inner mental life of individuals was an important endeavor. It was through self-report measures that such an undertaking was, and continues to be, possible.

Note

1.   A similar circular of questions on the nature of hallucinations was also prepared for the ASPR three years earlier under the direction of James and Society secretary Richard Hodgson (see James 1986).

References

Brock, A. C. 2012. "The History of Introspection Revisited." In *Self-Observation in the Human Sciences*, edited by J. W. Clegg. New Brunswick, NJ: Transaction Publishers.

Cattell, J. M. 1890. "Mental Tests and Measurements." *Mind* 15, no. 59: 373–81. doi:10.1093/mind/os-XV.59.373.

_____. 1896. "Psychical Research." *Psychological Review* 3: 582–83. doi:10.1037/h0064601.

Cattell, J. M. and Farrand, L. 1896. "Physical and Mental Measurements of the Students of Columbia University." *Psychological Review* 3: 618–48. doi:10.1037/h0070786.

Clark, C. A. 2008. *God – Or Gorilla? Images of Evolution in the Jazz Age.* Baltimore, MD: Johns Hopkins University Press.

Coon, D. J. 1992. "Testing the Limits of Sense and Science: American Experimental Psychologists Combat Spiritualism, 1880–1920." *American Psychologist* 47: 143–51. doi:10.1037/0003-066X.47.2.143.

Crombie, A. C. 1994. *Styles of Scientific Thinking in the European Tradition: The History of Argument and Explanation Especially in the Mathematical and Biomedical Sciences and Arts*, vol. 2. London: Duckworth.

Danziger, K. 1990. *Constructing the Subject.* Cambridge: Cambridge University Press.

Galton, F. 1612–1926. Papers. Francis Galton Papers (152/6B), University College London Archives, London, England.

_____. 1865. "Hereditary Talent and Character." *Macmillan's Magazine* 12: 157–66, 318–27.

_____. 1874. *English Men of Science: Their Nature and Nurture.* London: Macmillan.

_____. 1880a. "Mental Imagery." *Fortnightly Review* 28, no. 165: 312–24.

_____. 1880b. "Statistics of Mental Imagery." *Mind* 5, no. 19: 301–18. doi:10.1093/mind/os-V.19.301.

_____. 1880c. "Visualised Numerals." *Nature* 21, no. 533: 252–56. doi:10.1038/021252a0.

_____. 1881a. "The Visions of Sane Persons." *Fortnightly Review* 29: 729–40.

_____. 1881b. "The Visions of Sane Persons." *Proceedings of the Royal Institution* 9: 644–55.

_____. 1881c. "Visualised Numerals." *The Journal of the Anthropological Institute of Great Britain and Ireland* 10, no. 1881: 85–102. doi:10.2307/2841651.

_____. 1883. *Inquiries into Human Faculty and Its Development.* London: McMillan.

Hacking, I. 1982. "Language, Truth and Reason." In *Rationality and Relativism*, edited by M. Hollis and S. Lukes, 48–66. Cambridge, MA: The MIT Press.

_____. 1995. "The Looping Effects of Human Kinds." In *Causal Cognition: A Multi-Disciplinary Debate*, edited by D. Sperber, D. Premack, and A. J. Premack, 353–83. New York: Oxford University Press.

Hall, G. S. 1883. "The Contents of Children's Minds." *The Princeton Review* (January–June): 249–72.

_____. 1893. *The Contents of Children's Minds on Entering School.* New York: E. L. Kellogg & Co.

_____. 1896. "The Methods, Status, and Prospects of the Child-Study of Today." *Transactions of the Illinois Society for Child Study* 2: 179–91.

_____. 1924. *Life and Confessions of a Psychologist.* New York: D. Appleton.

_____. n.d. Papers. G. Stanley Hall Collection (B1). Clark University Archives, Worcester, MA.

James, W. 1890a. "Letter to the Editor." *The American Journal of Psychology* 3, no. 2: 292. doi:10.2307/1411184.

_____. 1890b. "Census of Hallucinations." *Science* 15, no. 380: 304. doi:10.1126/science.ns-15.380.304.

_____. 1895. "Review of the *Report on the Census of Hallucinations*, by H. Sidgwick, A. Johnson, F. W. H. Myers, F. Podmore, and E. M. Sidgwick." *Psychological Review* 2: 69–75. doi:10.1037/h0068910.

_____. 1986. *Essays in Psychical Research*. Cambridge, MA: Harvard University Press.

Jones, L. V. 1998. "L. L. Thurstone's Vision of Psychology as a Quantitative Rational Science." In *Portraits of Pioneers in Psychology*, edited by G. A. Kimble and M. Wertheimer, vol. 3, 85–102. Washington, DC: American Psychological Association.

Kevles, D. J. 1995. *In the Name of Eugenics: Genetics and the Uses of Human Heredity*. Cambridge, MA: Harvard University Press.

McCosh, J. and Osborn, H. F. 1884. "A Study of the Mind's Chambers of Imagery." *The Princeton Review* no. 1: 50–73.

Münsterberg, H. 1898. "Science and Education." *Educational Review* 16: 105–32.

Osborn, H. F. 1884a. "Illusions of Memory." *The North American Review* 138, no. 330: 476–86.

_____. 1884b. "Illusive Memory." *Science* 3, no. 57: 274. doi:10.1126/science.ns-3.57.274.

_____. 1884c. "Visual Memory." *Journal of Christian Philosophy* 3: 439–50.

Pickstone, J. V. 2001. *Ways of Knowing: A New History of Science, Technology, and Medicine*. Chicago, IL: University of Chicago Press.

Porter, T. 1988. *The Rise of Statistical Thinking, 1820–1900*. Princeton, NJ: Princeton University Press.

Rainger, R. 1991. *An Agenda for Antiquity: Henry Fairfield Osborn & Vertebrate Paleontology at the American Museum of Natural History 1890–1935*. Tuscaloosa, AL: The University of Alabama Press.

Regal, B. 2002. *Henry Fairfield Osborn: Race, and the Search for the Origins of Man*. Hants, UK: Ashgate.

Ross, D. 1972. *G. Stanley Hall: The Psychologist as Prophet*. Chicago, IL: University of Chicago Press.

Sokal, M. 1987. "James McKeen Cattell and Mental Anthropometry: Nineteenth-Century Science and Reform and the Origins of Psychological Testing." In *Psychological Testing and American Society, 1890–1930*, edited by M. Sokal, 21–45. New Brunswick, NJ: Rutgers University Press.

Thorndike, E. L. 1925. "Biographical Memoir of Granville Stanley Hall 1846–1924." *National Academy of Sciences Biographical Memoirs* 12: 133–80.

Thurstone, L. L. 1925. "A Method of Scaling Psychological and Educational Tests." *Journal of Educational Psychology* 16, no. 7: 433–51. doi:10.1037/h0073357.

_____. 1928. "Attitudes Can Be Measured." *The American Journal of Sociology* 33: 529–54. doi:10.1086/214483.

_____. 1952. "L. L. Thurstone." In *A History of Psychology in Autobiography*, edited by E. G. Boring, H. S. Langfeld, H. Werner, and R. M. Yerkes, vol. IV, 295–321. Worcester, MA: Clark University Press.

Thurstone, L. L. and Chave, E. J. 1929. *The Measurement of Attitude: A Psychophysical Method and Some Experiments with a Scale for Measuring Attitude toward the Church.* Chicago, IL: University of Chicago Press.

Williams, L. A. 1896. "How to Collect Data for Studies in Genetic Psychology." *Pedagogical Seminary* 3, no. 3: 419–23.

Wissler, C. 1901. "The Correlation of Mental and Physical Tests." *Psychological Review Monograph Supplement* 3, no. 6: 1–62.

Young, J. L. in press. "The Biologist as Psychologist: Henry Fairfield Osborn's Early Mental Ability Investigations." *Journal of the History of the Behavioral Sciences.* doi: 10.1002/jhbs.21547

4

Introspection and the Myth of Methodological Behaviorism

Alan Costall

> In many spheres of psychology and especially in psychiatry, self-observation, which is usually expressed in words by the subject, is the only kind of observation at our immediate disposal. The patient comes to the psychiatrist and says: "I feel 'sad' and 'gloomy'"; or, "Doctor, I am under a terrible strain—I fear I am going to kill my wife and children." . . . The physician then by a series of skillful questions begins to take the word responses of the patient. These responses, however, are from the physician's standpoint as objective as would be a moving-picture photograph of the subject's activity in weaving a rug or basket. The responses are a part of the record of the subject's way of adjusting to his world. (Watson 1919, 41)

> . . . Lashley told me with a chuckle that when he and Watson would spend an evening together, working out the principles of behaviorism, much of the time would be devoted to introspection. (Jacobson 1973, 14)

There can often be a great gulf between textbook history of science and how science is actually being done. This gulf is not always just the result of ignorance or carelessness on the part of the textbook writers. Textbook history can deliver powerful "origin myths" that reinforce a discipline's "official" ideals and values (Brush 1974).

The identity of modern scientific psychology has been mainly structured around the following three-stage historical narrative:

1. *Introspectionism*: Scientific psychology began as the science of mind, studied by what was then regarded as the direct, and indeed only possible, methodology: introspection.
2. *Behaviorism*: J. B. Watson and his fellow behaviorists rejected the method of introspection, and also consciousness itself as a possible

67

object of scientific inquiry. Psychology was defined as the science of behavior as opposed to mind.

3. *Cognitivism*: The pioneers of modern cognitive psychology restored the mind to psychology as its true object of study, but now based on the methodology developed by the neo-behaviorists rather than introspection.

Here is an early version of this narrative, from Donald Hebb's textbook:

> If Watson's work is seen as [a] house-cleaning operation . . . , its importance becomes clearer. In the first place, he was right about rejecting introspection as a means of obtaining factual evidence; . . . little agreement can be obtained from introspective reports. In 1913 the whole case for mental processes seemed to depend on introspection; if it did, the case was a bad one, and 'mind' had to be discarded from scientific consideration until better evidence could be found . . . *Paradoxically, it was the denial of mental processes that put our knowledge of them on a firm foundation, and from this approach we have learned much more about the mind than was known when it was taken for granted more or less uncritically.* (Hebb 1966, 5–6; emphasis added)

Many of the pioneers of the new cognitivism insisted they were not challenging the *methodology* of the neo-behaviorists (e.g., Miller et al. 1960). Indeed, long after the era of behaviorism, there now exists a wide consensus that the lasting scientific legacy of the behaviorists has been their replacement of introspection by methodological behaviorism:

> The cognitive revolution in psychology was a counter-revolution. The first revolution occurred much earlier when a group of experimental psychologists, influenced by Pavlov and other physiologists, proposed to redefine psychology as the science of behavior. *They argued that mental events are not publicly observable. The only objective evidence available is and must be, behavioral. By changing the subject to the study of behavior, psychology could become an objective science based on scientific laws of behavior.* (Miller 2003, 141–2; emphasis added)

The three-stage history of modern scientific psychology is not just about a sequence of revolutions but also about a grand and conclusive synthesis. It is about the *reconciliation* of the introspectionists' thesis that psychology should be a science of *mind*, and the antithesis proposed by the behaviorists that psychology should instead be a science of *behavior*. Modern psychology claims to have restored the mind to psychology as the object of scientific study, but now on the basis of the only available objective evidence, the study of "behavior."

Modern psychology has hardly lived up to the climax of this historical self-narrative. To the extent that the mind has been restored to modern psychology, it leads a disappointingly shadowy existence. It has been regarded as either predominantly unconscious (Kihlstrom 1987) or else no more than a convenient fiction:

> ... behaviorists argued that a theory of internal structure was not necessary to an understanding of human behavior, and in a sense they may have been right. . . . A theory of internal structure, however, makes understanding human beings much *easier*. (Anderson 2000, 10; emphasis added)

Researchers in the new field of consciousness studies have understandably complained about the failure of modern psychology to address the issue of consciousness. They contrast the "third-person" methods of the experimental psychologists and the "first-person" methods that they regard as appropriate for the study of consciousness (e.g., Chalmers 2004). However, they, in their turn, have largely failed to address the dualism in methodology that is embodied in the official history of modern psychology. As a result, they have left the scientific status of "first-person methods," and even consciousness itself, in doubt. So let us repeat the narrative with the emphasis upon method.

The reasoning runs as follows.

1. Introspection was, as a matter of historical fact, widely tried and tested in the early days of scientific psychology and this method proved to be hopelessly unreliable.
2. The behaviorists, starting with Watson, introduced the only alternative scientific methodology, "methodological behaviorism," a psychology based upon the study of "behavior," where "behavior" is to be understood as mere "colorless movements" rather than meaningful activity (since to attribute meaning to behavior is already to go beyond the only available observable evidence).
3. Although the behaviorists developed a sound scientific methodology, the profound limitation of the behaviorists was either their complete avoidance of theorizing about internal structures, or else their limited theoretical options, most notably, associationism.
4. Modern psychology combined the reductionistic methodology of the behaviorists with the new resources of cognitive theory (notably,

mental rules and representations) and this has proved to be a winning combination.

It is simply taken for granted in mainstream psychology that the mind is "occult" in the sense of hidden (if not also downright weird). However, this assumption does not derive from any principled philosophical commitment to dualism. Most psychologists rightly insist that they are *not* ontological dualists. They are awfully keen to distance themselves from Descartes. It is the three-stage history of scientific psychology itself, however, that enshrines the unexamined *methodological* dualism that modern psychologists have, largely unthinkingly, foisted upon themselves. They simply accepted the official history of psychology as portrayed by the behaviorists, and merely added their own sequel about a cognitive revolution *cum* semi-revolution.

The Myth of Introspectionism

According to Watson's early behaviorist manifestos, psychology had previously been based almost exclusively on the method of introspection, and that method (along with its very object of study) was intrinsically unscientific (Watson 1913a, 1913b). Many of Watson's contemporaries were well aware that Watson was inventing his two-stage history—the replacement of introspectionism by behaviorism—to serve his own cause. Introspection never was the dominant method, nor was it regarded as incompatible with "objective work," such as the measurement of reactions times. This was, after all, the very era of "brass-instruments" psychology. Here is Thorndike complaining about the misleading central message of Watson's textbook, *Behavior: an introduction to comparative psychology* (1914):

> The student is likely, as Watson's book stands, to be left with the impression that mental chemistry—the analysis of conscious states into elements . . .—has been the regular, orthodox thing in human psychology. On the contrary objective methods and results have characterized a very large proportion of the work of recognized psychologists for thirty years. Ebbinghaus' *Memory* and Cattell's studies of reaction-time, for example, are as behaviouristic or objective as Bassett's study of rats or Yerkes' study of frogs. (Thorndike and Herrick 1915, 463)

Somewhat later, Woodworth put Watson firmly in his place:

> Behaviourism, in 1912–1914, was a 'youth movement.' Watson was a young man, and his followers were mostly in the younger generation . . . In their enthusiasm they exaggerated the revolution . . . The actual revolution in psychological research was slight. Objective work continued; introspective work continued. (Woodworth 1931, 62)

Watson's more astute critics pointed out that it was Watson himself who was the dualist, in setting up a stark opposition between body and mind:

> Embedded in the very core of the behaviorist's doctrine is the Platonic distinction between mind and matter; and behaviorism, like Plato, regards the one term as real and the other as illusory. Its very case against dualism is stated in terms of that distinction and is made by the classical metaphysical procedure of reducing the one term to the other. This metaphysical distinction, rather than empirical evidence, is the basis on which behaviorism accepts or rejects data for scientific consideration and on which it forms conceptions for dealing with them. . . . Behaviorism has adopted a metaphysics to end metaphysics. (Heidbreder 1933, 267–68; see also Dewey 1914/1977, 445)

As John Dewey pointed out, the very activity of introspection is not a "private" methodology:

> When the introspectionist thinks he has withdrawn into a wholly private realm of events disparate in kind from other events, made out of mental stuff, he is only turning his attention to his own soliloquy. And soliloquy is the product and reflex of converse with others. . . . If we had not talked with others and they with us, we should never talk to and with ourselves. (Dewey 1925/1958, 170)

In short, introspection is not, after all, a self-enclosed Cartesian methodology. It is a social practice.

The Myth of the Hopeless Unreliability of Introspection

According to the textbooks, and even to several leading historians of psychology, the method of introspection eventually proved to be utterly unreliable. Matters are supposed to have come to a head when the two major "schools" of introspectionism, at Würzburg and Cornell, failed to agree about their findings. Yet, as Brock (1991) has pointed out, this is surely puzzling. If introspectionism really were the hopelessly idiosyncratic and unreliable method that it is still widely claimed to be, how could there have developed collective *schools* of introspectionism, whose members could—at least among themselves—agree about their own methods and findings? Indeed, there seems to have also been reasonably good agreement between the researchers at Würzburg and Cornell in relation to their *findings*. Monson and Hurlburt (1993) examined their laboratory records and concluded that the results obtained by the two groups were substantially the same. Their dispute concerned the interpretation of the results.

The Myth of the Abandonment of Introspection

Again, contrary to the three-stage history, introspection was not abandoned. It has continued to be used in an open way in clinical psychology (Kroker 2003). It has also played an important role within mainstream experimental psychology, even if it has become the method that dare not speak its name (Costall 2006; van Strien 2004; van Strien and Faas 2004). Psychologists have over the years insisted upon a categorical distinction between "introspection" and "self-report." For example, in his textbook of psychology, Hebb, emphatically dismisses introspection as hopelessly subjective, but then goes on to praise the value of self-reports as a "sensitive indicator of what is going on inside the subject" (Hebb 1966, 6). According to Hebb, the *big* difference is that making "verbal reports" (as opposed to "introspecting") involves *nothing but movements*— movements "produced by the chest muscles which control breathing, by changes in the tension of the vocal cords, and by movements of the lips, tongue and jaw" (Hebb 1966, 6)! Somehow, self-observation immediately evades scientific criticism once rebranded as movements of the vocal apparatus or "word responses" (Watson 1924, 42). A mere change of terminology transforms self-observation from utter subjectivism to pure objectivism.

The Myth of Behaviorism

The two most insidious myths embodied in the three-stage history of scientific psychology do not concern introspectionism as such but rather its supposed antithesis, behaviorism—and also *its* apparent antithesis, cognitivism. As I have already explained, modern cognitive psychology is, according to the three-stage history, a *synthesis* of introspectionism and behaviorism—even though modern cognitive psychology is also keen to present itself, at the same time, as a radical "revolutionary" alternative to behaviorism (cf Leahey 1992). There are blatant continuities between the methodology of neobehaviorism and modern cognitivism, such as the commitment to the hypothetical-deductive method and the stimulus-response paradigm. Furthermore, contrary to the three-stage history, most of the neo-behaviorists, with the notable exception of Skinner (1950), were also in the business of explaining their findings by appeal to "internal structures." The most significant continuity, however, concerns the commitment of modern cognitive psychologists— *officially*, though not, I will argue, *in practice* —to methodological behaviorism.

In practice, even the behaviorists were not methodological behaviorists in the sense in which Watson and his followers, when they were being pompous, proclaimed. As Tolman (1932, 6) noted, Watson "dallied with two different notions of behavior, though he himself has not clearly seen how different they are." When Watson was tub-thumping among his scientific peers, he would claim that behavior was no more than mere "physical" movements. When, however, he wished to present behaviorism as of wide human relevance, he could make behavior sound much more interesting: "By response we mean anything the organism does—such as turning toward or away from the light, jumping at a sound, and more highly organized activities such as building a skyscraper, drawing plans, having babies, writing books, and the like" (Watson 1925, 7; see Kitchener 1977, for an extensive review of the different and often ambiguous meanings of "behavior" in the behavioristic literature).

In the actual conduct of their research, the behaviorists were not *really* studying "mere movements" at all. They were studying psychologically meaningful activities, such as rats finding their way through mazes, and cats trying to get out of puzzle-boxes (but see Moore and Stuttard 1979!). Some of the more sophisticated behaviorists were quite explicit about this. Others, notably Tolman, prevaricated (see Still 1987). Skinner also dallied with the term "behavior," but finally came clean: "operant behavior is the very field of purpose and intention. By its nature it is directed towards the future" (Skinner 1974, 61). In short, the behaviorists were hardly "behaviorists" in the reductionist and physicalist sense they are still cracked up to be.

The Three-Stage History as Official Methodology

The rise of cognitive psychology occurred around the time of Thomas Kuhn's influential text, *The structure of scientific revolutions* (1962), and his book may well have also created the very idea of the "cognitive revolution" (see Goodwin 1999, 407). As James Jenkins, one of the pioneers of cognitive psychology, put it, "every one toted

73

around their little copy of Kuhn" (Jenkins 1986, 249). So, given all the hype about revolution, how did the three-stage history of psychology gain such wide currency? After all, the pioneers of cognitive psychology were innovators not only in relation to theory but also in their methodology, including computer simulation, and even reliance upon people's "intuitions" about grammatical structure in relation to Chomskyan psycholinguistics.

There were probably three main reasons. First, the three-stage history conveyed a sense of scientific progression in contrast to the radical discontinuities emphasized by Kuhn, and psychology, given its problematic status among the sciences, could hardly risk presenting itself as undergoing yet another complete upheaval. Second, an explicit commitment to methodological behaviorism would have been politically expedient to the new generation when they were applying for research grants and submitting articles for publication to organizations headed by the prevailing behaviorist elite. Most important, I suspect, was the persistent anxiety among psychologists about the *scientific objectivity* of their methods, and the avoidance of any retreat into the subjectivity of introspectionism.

The cognitive psychologists had reason to be defensive. Whereas the behaviorists' subject matter was (supposedly) "physical" behavior (even if that could include writing books and building skyscrapers!), the subject matter of the cognitive psychologists seemed "distressingly invisible" (Miller et al. 1960, 6). However, the cognitivists soon came to relish the scientific virtues of invisibility. They pointed out that the established sciences are also essentially *sciences of the invisible*. Their favorite example came from physics. Physicists directly study diffraction patterns, but what they are really studying are invisible atomic structures. The crucial difference is that the cognitive psychologists, *through their official commitment to methodological behaviorism*, had created a terminal disjunction between what they claimed to be their evidence and their subject matter.

In practice, of course, reductionistic methodological behaviorism no more corresponds to what cognitivist psychologists have actually been doing in their research than was the case for the behaviorists. Once again, what they have actually been studying are not meaningless, colorless movements, but psychologically meaningful actions.[1] Admittedly, some of the activities studied in many experiments are extremely limited, such as pushing buttons; however, the very *meaning* of these "movements" has already been negotiated with the participants by the investigators when enlisting them into the study and instructing them about what they are *meant* to be doing in the actual study (see Cohn 2008; Costall 2010; Jung 1971; Pierce 1908; Rommetveit 2003; Rosenzweig 1933; Weider 1980). Such "behaviors" are not "mere movements" but meaningful actions from the outset.

Theory of Mind

Over the years, the psychological textbooks have continued to pay lip-service to methodological behaviorism. For a long period, their account of psychological methodology was confined to the initial chapters, and kept quite separate from the later chapters explaining how nonpsychologists—"people"—are supposed to make sense of one another. However, the three-stage history had set up the conditions for a nasty accident just waiting to happen, and by the 1980s it did (see Leudar and Costall 2009).

Proponents of "Theory of Mind" (ToMists) projected the bogus official methodology of modern psychology onto the people they were studying. "People," they claimed, are faced with precisely the same problem facing the research psychologist, of how to infer, "theorize," or in some other way access the existence and nature of beliefs, intentions, or emotions, on the basis of the available evidence: mere physical movements.[2] The ToMists positively relish in the *impossible* difficulty of the problem of knowing other minds they have now created for us all when they set out the *problem*: on the one hand, there is the "peculiarly private nature of mental states" (Leslie 1999, 576), and, on the other, the only available evidence, other people's "movements in space" (Meltzoff et al. 1999, 17). Yet the ToMists always stop at the brink when they present us with their supposed *solutions*.[3] They then proceed as though making psychological sense of other people is not impossible, after all, but just extremely difficult and indirect: "our sensory experience of other people tells us about their movements in space but *does not tell us directly* about their mental states" (Meltzoff et al. 1999, 17; emphasis added).[4]

The Madness of Objectivity

I have been arguing that the official commitment of modern psychology to dualism is not explicit. It has little to do with Descartes. Dualism has been carried over into modern psychology by the official history of psychology created by the behaviorists, and their persuasive myths about both introspectionism and behaviorism.

"Behavior" was not a key scientific term before the rise of behaviorism. There is no entry in Baldwin's extensive *Dictionary of Philosophy and Psychology* (Baldwin 1901). However, by the end of the nineteenth century, it had already become deeply ambiguous. Originally, it referred primarily to how people conduct themselves in polite society, and this meaning is still evident in the term "misbehavior" and the command "behave yourself!" In this sense, its use was restricted to persons. However, "behavior" entered scientific discourse as a metaphor to highlight the lawful nature of *physical processes*. Thus, planets in their orbits "behave themselves" with the regularity with which people conduct themselves—or *should* conduct themselves—in public. There is the original sense, therefore, of behavior as observable, rule-governed, and immediately psychologically meaningful. The derivative sense of behavior retains the properties of observability and regularity, though, in this sense, the regularity is based on scientific laws, rather than social norms.

The myth of methodological behaviorism has been perpetuated in modern psychology by a continuing "dalliance" between these two senses of behavior:

> The confusion of action with movement can often be used to lend credence to [methodological] behaviourism. It is true that we learn about people through their behaviour. This becomes even more true if we include speech in 'behaviour'. But it does not follow that we learn about them through their movements or through their autonomic reactions, or through the chemical processes which their bodies undergo. For the behaviour which we mainly learn from is action, and it only *qua* action that it is revelatory, just as speech tells us little or nothing as a stream of sound, but much as meaningful language. Thus, if we can say that some psychological events are 'inferred' as against 'observed', they are inferred from other psychological events ... So that even if we use 'observed' in the sense of 'not inferred', we cannot say that psychological events are not observed. (Taylor 1964, 50)

As I have already argued, the behaviorists themselves were not methodological behaviorists in the actual conduct of their research. But many of them were deeply attracted to an ideal of scientific objectivity that has come to dominate scientific thinking. According to this "mindless" ideal, subjectivity should be eliminated from the very activity of doing science (see Daston 1992). Watson was certainly enchanted by this ideal. As his former teacher, Harvey Carr insisted "objectivism" would be a more appropriate term for Watson's approach than "behaviorism," because its essence was "not a distinction of subject matter (behavior) but the objective view from which it is studied" (Carr 1915, 309). However, Watson was not only deeply inconsistent in his approach to behavior, but even in his commitment to the ideal of mindless objectivism. Consciousness, as he himself conceded, is "the instrument or tool with which all scientists work" (Watson 1914, 176).

The unthinking distrust of introspection within modern psychology goes hand in hand with the unchallenged prestige of methodological behaviorism. Neither are the result of critical disciplinary reflection, but stem from a dualism of the subjective and the objective that has insinuated itself into psychological thought through a potent historical myth. A dualism of the objective and subjective can seem compelling, even thrilling, when we think of science as *already done* —as a finished structure of facts and theories seemingly independent of us.[5] It is far from compelling, however, once we look upon science as the ongoing, open-ended human practice that it is. We then rediscover the obvious. It is only subjects who can be objective (Macmurray 1961, 28).

Notes

1. There are serious problems, however, with much of experimental psychology. It has become extremely self-enclosed and, in effect, no longer empirical (see Costall 2010).

2. There maybe something more sinister going on here than just reductionism, a "self-destructing instinct for belittling man" (Nietzsche 1887/1967). Take, for example, Gopnik and Meltzoff's (1994, 166) ugly description of people as "bag[s] of skin moving over ground" (cf Weizenbaum 1995).

3. There is a striking similarity between methodological behaviorism and sensationalism. In both cases, the units of analysis are inherently meaningless—bodily movements and atomistic sensations—and were meant to be so by their physicalist proponents. In both cases, these units could never explain the phenomena they were invoked to explain.

4. The ToMists' denial of the impossibility of the problem of other minds that they have created seems to run as follows. It is a kind of "existence proof":

   1. All of us inevitably start out in the position of methodological behaviorists in our dealings with other people.

   2. As a matter of fact, just plain folks do make sense of one another, just as cognitive psychologists are perfectly able to conduct effective psychological research.

3. Therefore, as a matter of plain fact, methodological behaviorism is a viable basis for making psychological sense of others not only in science but also in everyday life.

4. *Quod erat demonstrandum*: We ToMists really cannot be the dualists our critics mischievously claim us to be. The "problem of other minds" we have created is clearly being solved on a routine, daily basis. It does not involve an unbridgeable dualism between body and mind. So forget all the logic mongering!

5. Take Eddington's notorious example of his two tables. The first, as he immediately experiences it, is substantial, and tangible. His second scientific table "is mostly emptiness":

> I need not tell you that modern physics has by delicate test and remorseless logic assured me that my second scientific table is the only one which is really there—wherever 'there' may be." (Eddington 1935, 6; cf Stebbing 1937)

References

Anderson, J. R. 2000. *Cognitive Psychology and Its Implications*, 5th edn. New York: Worth.

Baldwin, J. M. 1901. *The Dictionary of Philosophy and Psychology*. New York: Macmillan.

Brock, A. 1991. "Imageless Thought or Stimulus Error? The Social Construction of Private Experience." In *World Views and Scientific Discipline Formation*, edited by W. R. Woodward and R. S. Cohen, 97–106. Dordrecht: Kluwer Academic Publishers.

Brush, S. G. 1974. "Should the History of Science Be Rated 'X'?" *Science* 183: 1164–72.

Carr, H. A. 1915. "Review of J.B. Watson (1914). Behavior: An Introduction to Comparative Psychology." *Psychological Bulletin* 12: 308–12.

Chalmers, D. J. 2004. *The Cognitive Neurosciences III*. Cambridge, MA: MIT Press.

Cohn, S. 2008. "Making Objective Facts from Intimate Relations: The Case of Neuroscience and Its Entanglements with Volunteers." *History of the Human Sciences* 21, no. 4: 86–103.

Costall, A. 2006. "Introspectionism and the Mythical Origins of Modern Scientific Psychology." *Consciousness and Cognition* 15: 634–54.

_____. 2010. "The Future of Experimental Psychology." *The Psychologist* 23: 1022–23.

Daston, L. 1992. "Objectivity and the Escape from Perspective." *Social Studies of Science* 22: 597–618.

Dewey, J. 1914/1977. "Psychological Doctrine and Philosophical Teaching." In *Dewey and His Critics*, edited by S. Morgenbesser, 439–45. New York: Journal of Philosophy, Inc. (First published in the *Journal of Philosophy, Psychology, and Scientific Methods*, 1914, 11, no. 19).

_____. 1925/1958. *Experience and Nature*. New York: Dover (Based on the Paul Carus lectures of 1925).

Eddington, A. 1935. *The Nature of the Physical World*. London: Dent.

Goodwin, C. J. 1999. *A History of Modern Psychology*. New York: Wiley.

Gopnik, A. and Meltzoff, A. N. 1994. "Minds, Bodies, and Persons: Young Children's Understanding of the Self and Others as Reflected in Imitation and 'Theory of Mind' Research." In *Self-Awareness in Animals and Humans*, edited by S. Parker and R. Mitchell, 166–86. New York: Cambridge University Press.

Heidbreder, E. 1933. *Seven Psychologies*. New York: Century.

Jacobson, E. 1973. "Electrophysiology of Mental Activities and Introduction to the Psychological Process of Thinking." In *Psychophysiology of Thinking*, edited by F. J. McGuigan and R. A. Schoonover, 3–24. New York: Academic Press.

Jenkins, J. J. 1986. "Interview with James J. Jenkins." In *The Cognitive Revolution in Psychology*, edited by B. J. Baars, 239–52. New York: Guilford Press.

Jung, J. 1971. *The Experimenter's Dilemma*. New York: Harper Row.

Kihlstrom, J. F. 1987. "The Cognitive Unconscious." *Science* 237: 1445–52.

Kitchener, R. F. 1977. "Behavior and Behaviorism." *Behaviorism* 5: 11–71.

Kroker, K. 2003. "The Progress of Introspection in America, 1896–1938." *Studies in the History and Philosophy of Biology and Biomedical Science* 34: 77–108.

Kuhn, T. S. 1962. *The Structure of Scientific Revolutions*. Chicago, IL: University of Chicago Press.

Leahey, T. H. 1992. "The Mythical Revolutions of American Psychology." *American Psychologist* 47: 308–18.

Leslie, A. 1999. "Mind, Child's Theory of." In *Concise Routledge Encyclopaedia of Philosophy*, 575–76. London: Routledge.

Leudar, I. and Costall, A. eds. 2009. *Against Theory of Mind*. London: Palgrave Macmillan.

Macmurray, J. 1961. *Persons in Relation*. London: Faber.

Merleau-Ponty, M. 2003. *Nature: Course Notes from the Collège de France*. (Compiled with notes by Dominique Séglard. Translated from the French by Robert Vallier). Evanston, IL: Northwestern University Press.

Miller, G. A. 2003. "The Cognitive Revolution: A Historical Perspective." *Trends in Cognitive Sciences* 7: 141–44.

Miller, G. A., Galanter, E., and Pribram, K. H. 1960. *Plans and the Structure of Behavior*. New York: Holt, Rinehart & Winston.

Monson, C. K. and Hurlburt, R. T. 1993. "A Comment to Suspend the Introspection Controversy: Introspecting Subjects Did Agree about Imageless Thought." In *Sampling Inner Experience in Disturbed Affect*, edited by R. T. Hurlburt, 15–26. New York: Plenum.

Moore, B. R. and Stuttard, S. 1979. "Dr. Guthrie and *Felis domesticus* or: Tripping over the Cat." *Science* 205: 1031–33.

Nietzsche, F. 1887/1967. *On the Genealogy of Morals*. New York: Vintage Books.

Pierce, A. H. 1908. "The Subconscious Again." *The Journal of Philosophy, Psychology, and Scientific Methods* 5, no. 10: 64–271.

Rommetveit, R. 2003. "On the Role of "a Psychology of the Second Person" in Studies of Meaning, Language, and Mind." *Mind, Culture, and Activity* 10, no. 3: 205–18.

Rosenzweig, S. 1933. "The Experimental Situation as a Psychological Problem." *Psychological Review* 40: 337–54.

Skinner, B. F. 1950. "Are Theories of Learning Necessary?" *Psychological Review* 57: 193–216.

_____. 1974. *About Behaviorism*. London: Jonathan Cape, 61.

Stebbing, L. S. 1937. *Philosophy and the Physicists*. London: Methuen.

Still, A. 1987. "Tolman's Perception." In *Cognitive Psychology in Question*, edited by A. Costall and A. Still. Brighton, UK: Harvester Press.

Taylor, C. 1964. *The Explanation of Behaviour*. London: Routledge & Kegan Paul.

Thorndike, E. L. and Herrick, C. J. 1915. "Watson's "Behavior"." *Journal of Animal Behavior* 5: 462–70. (This is in fact two separate reviews)

Tolman, E. C. 1932. *Purposive Behavior in Animals and Men*. New York: Appleton-Century-Crofts.

van Strien, P. J. 2004. "Paris, Leipzig, Danziger, and beyond." In *Rediscovering the History of Psychology*, edited by A. C. Brock, J. Louw, and W. van Hoorn, 75–96. New York: Kluwer.

van Strien, P. J. and Faas, E. 2004. "How Otto Selz became a Forerunner of the Cognitive Revolution." In *The Life Cycle of Psychological Ideas: Understanding Prominence and the Dynamics of Intellectual Change*, edited by T. C. Dalton and R. B. Evans, 175–201. New York: Kluwer Academic/Plenum Publishers.

Watson, J. B. 1913a. "Psychology as the Behaviorist Views It." *Psychological Review* 20: 158–77.

_____. 1913b. "Image and Affection in Behavior." *Journal of Philosophy, Psychology, and Scientific Methods* 10: 421–28.

_____. 1914. *Behavior: An Introduction to Comparative Psychology*. New York: Holt.

_____. 1919. *Psychology from the Standpoint of a Behaviorist*, n. Philadelphia, PA: J. B. Lippincott Company.

_____. 1925. *Behaviorism*. London: Kegan Paul, Trech, Trubner, & Co.

Weider, D. L. 1980. "Behavioristic Operationalism and the Life-World: Chimpanzees and Chimpanzee Researchers in Face-to-Face Interaction." *Sociological Inquiry* 50: 75–103.

Weizenbaum, J. 1995. "The Myth of the Last Metaphor." In *Speaking Minds: Interview with Twenty Eminent Cognitive Scientists*, edited by P. Baumgartner and S. Payr, 249–64. Princeton, NJ: Princeton University Press.

Woodworth, R. S. 1931. *Contemporary Schools of Psychology*. London: Methuen & Co.

Part III

Contemporary Self-Observation: Theory and Practice

5

Language in Self-Observation

Brady Wagoner

The issue of language is at the heart of self-observation. In order for an experience to become scientific data, it has to be expressed in a communicable form. As with all language use, we must presuppose a social practice, in which expressions can be made sense of and evaluated by others (Wittgenstein 1953). The practice of social observation developed out of the protestant cultural tradition, whereby one engaged in private self-scrutiny and self-examination. When this tradition transformed into scientific practice, new languages, social relationships, and roles were simultaneously developed, which in some ways displaced and in other ways extended the existing traditions of self-observation. In either religious or scientific self-observation, knowledge of one's own mind is inseparably intertwined with the institutions in which the activity is performed. As language is an essential feature of institutional life, it is little surprise that the early debates between psychological laboratories about self-observation often revolved around issues of language, description, and expression.

The fact that language is intimately related to the practice of self-observation poses a major challenge for developing adequate methodologies, which I will argue the early introspectionists were not fully aware of. They were guided largely by a dualistic assumption that the mind is inherently individual and private. Beginning with this assumption, however, one wonders how anything can be communicated about inner experience at all! If self-observation is intimately linked to social practices and social institutions, we cannot legitimately claim that it is a purely individual process, but must instead explore it in its social dimensions. In contrast to dualism, I will adopt the functionalist perspective of the American pragmatists and argue that the act of self-observation is essentially a social process. This will be true of *both* its inner-directed observation phase and outer-directed communication phase. Furthermore, we will see that the two phases need to be considered together, as a cycle, if we are to understand the data of self-observation. Rather than condemning self-observation as a method bound to failure, I argue that these dynamics open up novel avenues for pursuing it, which I will illustrate with a study of process-oriented rating scales.

The present chapter is divided into three parts: First, a brief history of the early laboratories using self-observation is given, focusing on how various linguistic practices and social relationships among experimenter and observer shaped their results. Second, I outline an argument for studying mind as it becomes embodied in a public material medium and the influence of others and social institutions on the operation and observation of mind. Finally, I will use ideas developed here to critique and redevelop contemporary psychology's most widely used and perhaps (willfully) least understood method of self-observation, rating scales. The act of rating will be shown to involve a dialogical process of linguistic sense making, and as such the idea that rating scales provide unitary access to some inherently quantifiable mental state will have to be abandoned. Instead, rating scales can be used as tools to explore the context-sensitive dynamics of research participants' meaning making.

Varieties of Laboratory Language

There are many varieties of "self-observation," even among the early laboratories of psychology. Using a single label for them all should not blind us to their diversity. The languages used by different laboratories reflected, or perhaps constructed, these differences in research practice. In this section, I will briefly compare some of the early psychological laboratories, concentrating on how their language use and the practice of self-observation interrelate. Thus, I will not attempt to tell a full narrative history, but rather focus on core themes emerging around the issue of language. Although self-observation has a long history, it will for our purposes be convenient to begin with Wundt, because he initiated a new phase of research practice and set up the restrictions on self-observation, which others would feel compelled to transgress.

Wundt and Why Simple Judgments Are Not so Simple

Wundt sharply distinguished his method of "internal perception" (innere Wahrnehmung) from the traditional notion of "self-observation" (Selbstbeobachtung). This was not mere semantics. It expressed his acceptance of arguments by earlier thinkers against self-observation as a viable scientific method and his strategy for overcoming the problematic. Firstly, it had been argued that scientific method required the subject and object of observation be independent from one another, which was not the case in traditional self-observation. Second, mental events were not reported directly but rather "retrospectively" and thus the data was distorted by memory.

Wundt's solution to these problems was to only accept the data of self-observation when firstly, there was a controllable external stimulus that could be varied at will to produce different experiential effects, and secondly, observers reported their experience *immediately* so as minimize distortions of memory. These conditions could only be achieved in an experimental laboratory. A third major restriction, following from the other two, was on the observer's use of language. Danziger (1980, 247) comments, "the introspective reports (in Wundt's laboratory) were largely limited to judgments of size, intensity, and duration of physical stimuli, supplemented at times by judgments of their simultaneity and succession." In other words, it was not the sensations as such that were described but rather judgments were made about their attributes (Boring 1950).

For instance, to test different sensory thresholds Wundt used the varied distance of two separate points on the skin (a method first used by physiologist Ernst Weber). Observers were to report simply whether they experienced two or one points of stimulation. However, even with this relatively straightforward method, problems crept in. In a study done by Binet (1903) in Paris, instead of asking of judgments of one or two points, he had observers report the sensation qualitatively. In so doing, he found an array of intermediate qualities such as a broad heavy point or bell-shaped point. Were these to count as one or two points? That depended on observers' interpretation of the task and the meaning of one or two points within a social practice.

The Cambridge expedition to the Torres Straight ran into the same problem in using the two-point test to see whether the sensory thresholds of natives were greater than Europeans. The trouble was it is unclear that the people on the Torres Straight interpreted the task in the same way as Europeans. In fact, it is entirely likely that they saw it as a competitive social practice and as such they were more willing to interpret a sensation as two points than they might otherwise be; little did they know winning here really meant losing, in that it confirmed western prejudices about natives as having superior senses and as a result a weaker intellect, given the then widespread assumption that there was a zero-sum relation between the two (see Richards 1998).

It is interesting to note that the question of intermediate forms between one and two points does not arise from inside Wundt's laboratory, but rather from an outsider, i.e., Binet. Wundt's theory stated that the qualitative wholes identified by Binet could be broken down into more elementary sensations, which would then decide the matter between one or two points once and for all. Observers in Wundt's laboratory were taught to automatically decompose wholes into their elementary sensations. To qualify as an observer in Wundt's laboratory one had to have made ten thousand introspective judgments, so as to make judgments more immediately and thus minimize the distorting effect of thought and memory. Thus, observers were acculturated to the particular standards of correctedness of the Leipzig laboratory. This clearly also had the effect of forming the data produced in self-observation towards that laboratory's conventions. In sum, even at this fairly basic level of sensory stimulation, we see that the language of observation is closely linked to what is observed. What one experiences is interrelated with what one is attending to—a fact actually established early on in the introspection debate.

The Würzburg School and the Virtues and Vices of Vague Vocabulary

It was not long before Wundt's restrictions on self-observation were transgressed. Oswald Külpe, one of Wundt's former students, headed an institute of experimental psychology in Würzburg that developed a rather different experimental practice and language for describing the mind. Histories of the Würzburg School usually begin in 1901 with an article published by Mayer and Orth on some of the qualitative and experiential aspects of association. Mayer and Orth (1901) aimed to classify association psychologically, rather than logically, as had previously been done. To do so, they adopted a method, whereby the observer is presented with a word, for which they are to make an association, and then *retrospectively* report on the process and mental content involved in making it.

In the course of their experiments, they claim to have stumbled upon a content of consciousness that did not fit the traditional classifications of sensations, feelings, and images (as used by, for example, Wundt). To handle this new content they invented the untranslatable word *"bewusstseinslagen,"* which nonetheless has been variously translated as "mental set," "posture or attitude of consciousness" (Titchener 1909), "state of consciousness" (Humphrey 1951), "disposition of consciousness" (Mandler and Mandler 1963), and "situation of consciousness" (Kusch 1999). Later that year, Marbe, a collaborator with Mayer and Orth at Würzburg, published a monograph on judgment using a similar retrospective method and language of description. In fact, Marbe restricted his participants' language of reporting to the traditional classifications of mental contents plus *bewusstseinslagen* (Kusch 1999). Neither Mayer and Orth's (1901) nor Marbe's (1901) publication, however, did much with the new concept, beyond identifying it, and the identification itself was purely negative, as *not* an image, sensation, or feeling. Nevertheless, in giving the new content a name, they created an open descriptive concept, which would in turn trigger a generative search for its meaning within the Würzburg School.

The word *bewusstseinslagen* (*Bsl*) soon encompassed all three aspects of the traditional division of mind—i.e., conation, feeling, and cognition. First, against Wundt's associative psychology, they used *Bsl* to conceptualize mind as always actively engaged, goal-directed, or purposive. Second, *Bsl* could be the feelings, which accompany the monitoring of progress toward the task goal. Third, it could be understood cognitively as a kind of "summary feeling"—e.g., Høffding's feeling of familiarity. Given this wide-ranging meaning *Bsl* quickly became ubiquitous in introspective reports. Consider the following examples from Messer's (1905) experiments, in which observers were presented with a stimulus word for which they were to, for example, coordinate a concept or give the first word to come to mind:

> Subject 4: *"Bsl,* containing two thoughts: 1. You have to wait, 2. The coordinated object will come to you." *"Bsl,* for which I can give the thought: that's easy." *"Bsl*: There is a subordinate concept somewhere, but you can't formulate it very easily."
> Subject 6: *"Bsl*: don't say that." *"Bsl,* my father always used to mispronounce that name." *"Bsl*; you could say that at anytime."
> Subject 3: *"Bsl*: Why not think about something else!"
> (Quoted from Mandler 2007, 82)

Others in the Würzburg invented concepts akin to *Bsl* that either supplemented or subsumed it. For example, Ach (1905) developed the even broader concept of "awareness" (*Bewusstheit*) to point to our "immediate knowledge" of a situation, intention, meaning, or action. Messer (1906) and Bühler (1907) went further by relabeling *Bsl* as "thought" (*Gedanke*). Bühler is particularly interesting for our purposes because he not only reformed the theoretical language of the Würzburg School but also encouraged the free use of language by the participants in his experiments. According to him, experimental procedures should be brought closer to everyday life by doing away with complex laboratory equipment and re-conceiving the relation between experimenter and research participant as a naturalistic conversation, where there were no restrictions on the possible uses of language to describe one's experience. This was the exact opposite of Wundt's method and it is little surprise that Wundt was one of the most vehement critics. We will return to this issue in the next section.

Expressions similar to *Bsl* also came to be used outside of Würzburg. The English psychologist Frederic Bartlett, for example, uses the word "attitude" to name "a complex psychological state or process which is hard to describe in more elementary terms" adding that "it is, however, (. . .) very largely a matter of feeling, or affect" (Bartlett 1932, 206–7). Bartlett explicitly points out the similarity between his concept of "attitude" and Würzburg psychologist Betz's (1910) concept of *Einstellung* (Bartlett 1916). Although Bartlett did not use his participants' self-observations as his primary data of analysis, he did carefully attend to them in reconstructing the process by which the primary data (e.g., story reconstructions) was produced. In this way, Bartlett fits his participants' reports (which like Bühler's experiments were expressed in everyday language) into his own theoretical language, and in so doing lumps together a diverse range of expressions, which at first glance do not seem to have much to do with one another—for example, "hesitation," "surprise," "confidence," "repulsion," "exciting," "adventurous," "like I read as a child," and "not English."

In summary, we see that open descriptive concepts can be both enabling and constraining. Coining the word *Bsl* guided the Würzburg to aspects of our experience previously unattended to by psychologists and philosophers. In so doing, they set up a new space of exploration and development. This space should not be thought of as simply an arena waiting to be discovered but rather one that only becomes meaningful within social framework or institution. Psychological phenomena are not *natural kinds* like electrons; they are *human kinds*, which presuppose a background of intelligibility in social practices. Even more, human kinds unlike natural kinds have the potential to feedback into human practices and transform them (Hacking 1995). Thus, our folk conceptions of thought, emotion, and memory guide the way we think, feel, and remember. In this way, new psychological concepts open doors to certain research practices while at the same time closing others. *Bsl* was productive in that it set in motion a novel program of research on thinking, using an innovative new methodology. This is not to say that Würzburg were unconstrained in their use of language. Though Würzburg vocabulary was more permissive than Wundt's laboratory, there was still definite institutional constraint on what and how an experience could be reported.

Holistic Psychology and the Poetics of Description

Unsurprisingly, there was a heated debate between positions adopted by Wundt and the Würzburgers over the contents of consciousness and the appropriate methods for studying psychological phenomena. Titchener, a student of Wundt, adopted Würzburg-like methods (i.e., "systematic introspection") to produce evidence for Wundt's position that imageless thought did not occur. Danziger eloquently describes how this debate transformed into one about the use of language for reporting experience:

> The question of the validity of systematic introspection reports [. . .] becomes a question of the relation between the subjective experiences that form the ultimate data and the verbal form in which they are symbolically expressed. This relationship, however, can take different forms, just as a physical datum can be symbolically represented by a drawing or by verbal description. One might describe the distinguishing parts of the original experience, but then one would inevitably fail to communicate the nature of the experience as a whole; alternatively, one might attempt to convey the quality of the whole experience, but this would usually have to be done metaphorically, and therefore ambiguously, providing no certainty that the experimenter's interpretation corresponded to what had actually been in the subject's mind. While a relatively unambiguous description of elements of experience in a sensationalistic language is possible, it is also irrelevant, for it simply does not give an account of the experience as it existed. On the other hand, verbal messages about actual whole experiences have an expressive, so to say poetic, quality which is effective for purposes of interpersonal communication, but which allows no scientifically certain conclusions to be

drawn about the precise equivalence of what the message evokes in the mind of the listener and what went on in the mind of the reporter. (Danziger 1980, 255–56)

In this section, I will explore the dynamics of holistic and metaphorical language in describing one's experience. After the waning of the Würzburg School in Germany, we find the development of different kinds of holistic vocabularies in Berlin and Leipzig. In Berlin, Gestaltstheorie developed a phenomenological "form" vocabulary, while in Leipzig Ganzheitspsychologie advanced a more metaphorical language. These are differences between both their theoretical and methodological orientations. The Gestalt psychologists used physics as their source of inspiration, while Ganzheit psychologists borrowed more heavily from aesthetics (see Wagoner 2011, for a review). Both schools varied some external stimuli against which a research participant's experience was understood as in Wundt's laboratory. However, unlike Wundt's laboratory experience was described in terms of wholes. For example, by varying the speed in which two points appear Wertheimer demonstrated the phi-phenomenon, whereby we perceive the stationary points as moving. Ganzheit psychologists presented stimuli in suboptimal conditions (e.g., at a distance, very small, for a fraction of a second, or at the periphery of one's vision) and improved those conditions, capturing participants' experience at each step. They showed how perception went beyond the information given, anticipating future forms.

Let us consider a study done by Heinz Werner, who was trained at Leipzig. Werner used a tachistoscope to flash phrases in front of participants at short intervals. Participants had to report what they saw and their accompanying thoughts and feelings at each stimulus exposure. The language they could use was quite open but referred directly to the stimulus presented to them. Consider the following example of a participant who read the tachistoscopically presented phrase "*sanfter Wind*" (gentle wind):

1. "—? Wind." What stood before "wind" feels like an adjective specifying something similar. Definitely not a word defining direction.

2. "—ter Wind." Know now that the word is "heavier" than "warm" . . . somehow more abstract.

3. "—cher Wind." Now it looks more like an adjective-of-direction.

4. "—ter Wind." Now again somehow more concrete, it faces me and looks somewhat like *"weicher Wind"* (soft Wind), but *"ter"* is in my way.

5. Now very clearly: "sanfter Wind." Not at all surprised. I had this actually before in the characteristic feel of the word and the looks of it.

(Werner 1956, 348)

Through this series we can make inferences about the relationship between fully articulated meanings of words (on the left in quotation marks) and "spherical cognition" (on the right). What Werner attempted to capture with this method was exactly the kind of experience that eluded precise description—i.e., the feel of the word. His participant describes it through metaphors (e.g., "heavy" and "warm") and diffuse semantic fields (e.g., adjective-of-direction). Later, Werner in collaboration with Bernie Kaplan developed a method whereby participants expressed their experience in a nonverbal medium (i.e., a line language) to explore nonpropositional aspects of language (Werner and Kaplan 1963) and to help participants articulate their emotions (Kaplan 1955).

James and Bergson had much earlier made arguments for the use of metaphorical expressions to describe one's experience, though both thinkers utilized a nonexperimental method of self-observation. According to them ordinary language misleads us into turning processes into static things. Bergson (1903) even elevated his experiential approach to "metaphysics" as such. Through the "intuitive" grasp of one's own consciousness one came into contact with the "absolute." In order to express this, however, one had to use symbols, which could only "approximate" what was apprehended through intuition. Bergson's strategy was to deploy a number of different metaphors to describe consciousness, always pointing out how they ultimately failed to capture the whole. Yet, they functioned well to sensitize us to certain aspects of our intuitively apprehended experience. Like Bergson, James marveled in the amorphous whole of the mind and called on thinkers to develop rich metaphors that might capture some aspect of it. From James (1890) we have such poetic expressions for experience as "the streaming of consciousness," "the buzzing blooming confusion," and "the fringe of consciousness," which the Würzburgers saw as being akin to their own term *Bsl*. Though it is difficult to pinpoint what exactly James' terms refer to, they are highly suggestive and have inspired generations of psychologists and even stimulated popular culture (with, e.g., the development of the stream of consciousness novel). They are open descriptive concepts that allow us to holistically express our experience as well as guide us in its investigation.

Self-Observation as a Social Process

From the above brief review, we see that there is an intimate relationship between language and the character attributed to experience. I am not suggesting that language determines experience, but rather that there is complex dialectic between the two. Poets and artists as well as psychologists and philosophers have provided us with insightful and novel means of not only expressing, but also, more importantly, observing our own experience. This would not be possible if experience was a purely individual and private matter. Instead, we live in an intersubjectively shared and immanently meaningful world. Humans exist as beings in constant communication with others, through which we come to develop shared perspectives on our experience. This is precisely why works of art and literature are often so illuminating; they teach us both about the particularities of our own life and about aspects of the human condition in general, which we do not usually see simply because we are too close to them in our everyday lives. In this section, we will consider what is involved in this symbolization of experience and how it feeds forward into future experiencing. My starting point for this theoretical discussion is the functionalist perspective of the American pragmatists, whose ideas were later developed by a number of innovative psychologists.

The American pragmatists put forward one of the most powerful critiques of the traditional conceptualization of self-observation, especially Dewey and Mead. Their critique has been generally missed as a result of psychology's history myth, whereby the discipline has progressed in dialectical fashion from the "introspectionists" to "the behaviorists" and finally to their synthesis in "cognitive psychology" (Costall 2006). One of the many things wrong with this story is that Watson's (1913) rather uninteresting arguments are given central place in the advancement of psychology, when in fact more developed critiques of self-observation were made long before him.

For example, Mead (1910) argued that "Other selves in a social environment logically antedate the consciousness of self which introspection analyzes" (179). In other words, the act of self-reflection presupposes social interaction with others. The introspection involves the incorporation of the other into the self. This conceptual move naturalizes the act of self-reflection by showing that it is an outgrowth of a social process. One's own gesture does not initially have meaning for oneself. A dog that shows its teeth or a cat the purrs is expressing an emotion but it is not aware of the meaning of their gesture. The gesture only has meaning for others, which is their response to the gesture—e.g., to fight or run. The establishment of shared meaning requires the existence of stable social institutions with interchangeable social positions (such as buying or selling, talking and listening). Because a vocal gesture can be heard from both sides of a social act in a social practice it takes on a dual meaning and enables the movement from one social perspective to another. I am other from the perspective of another person's perspective. Thus, by taking the social position of the other, through the vocal gesture inside the social act, I can become other to myself (Mead 1934). In short, introspective self-reflection is only possible through a history of interaction with others in social institutions. In Mead's (1910, 179) own words,

> Consciousness could no longer be approached as an island [. . .] It would be approached as experience which is socially as well as physically determined. Introspective self-consciousness would be recognized as a subjective phase, and this subjective phase could no longer be regarded as the source out of which the experience arose. Objective consciousness of selves must precede subjective consciousness, and must continually condition it, if consciousness of meaning itself presupposes the selves as there [. . .] When in the process revealed by introspection we reach the concept of self, we have attained an attitude which we assume not toward our inner feelings, but toward other individuals whose reality was implied even in the inhibitions and reorganizations which characterize this inner consciousness.

Introspective self-consciousness is derivative of consciousness of others and not vice versa. Internal thought here is a form of inner dramatization of social conduct and is thus necessarily bound up with social meanings.

So far the conditions and character of the inner-directed phase of self-observation have been described. Let us at this point consider the outer-directed communication phase, whereby experience becomes the data of scientific analysis. Firstly, it should be made clear that though communication of one's experience has typically been done through the verbal medium in psychology, we can take "language" in a broader sense as any means of establishing intersubjectivity, and may include, e.g., "gesture languages," "picture languages," and "line-languages." For something to count language there must be a differentiation between the perspectives of an *addresser* and *addressee* as well as between the *object* and *symbolic vehicle* used to refer to it (Werner and Kaplan 1963). There is a direct link to Mead's (1934) approach, in which language brings together two perspectives (i.e., *addresser* and *addressee*) taking place within a social act. Objects in Mead's approach are also referred to through some material medium (e.g., the vocal gesture), and thus out of this interaction distinctly *social* objects may emerge, e.g., property. The opposing pairs addressee–addresser and object–symbolic vehicle can be more or less distanced from one another. For example, communication between two people with a long history together has a very different form to one between strangers. In the former case, much can be taken for granted while the latter relies more on widely shared conventions of communication. In communicating we always attune to the perspective of our interlocutor (of course, with varying degrees of success). As a thought experiment, it is interesting to consider what the introspection reports would have looked like if the observer was from one school of psychology (e.g., Würzburg) and the experimenter another (e.g., Leipzig). How would these inter-institutional dynamics affect the data generated there?

The inner-directed phase of self-observation involves reflecting on oneself through the perspective of others and a social institution more generally, while the outer-directed phase involves transforming that experience into a symbolic form understandable within institutional constraints of communication. These two phases are mutual in feeding. The symbolic products of an introspective report can be used as orienting devices in the act of observing one's own experience and what is there observed can find its way back into reports in one expression or another. We saw above how quickly the ambiguous concept *Bsl* quickly became ubiquitous in introspective reports; however, the concept evolved during the history of the Würzburg School, which suggests that the concept was a constraint but not a determinant of experience. It would be interesting to explore how reporting experience (in say one medium, such as drawing versus verbal) affected what was reported in future trails. In one experiment on imagination, Bartlett (1932) presented participants with a series of inkblots and asked them to provide a description of each. He reports a "persistence of attitude" in participants' interpretations—for example, one participant sees "ghosts"; "more ghosts kissing"; "more kissing"; "green ghosts" (Bartlett, 1916, 255). Thus, what is reported in the first instance becomes a constraint on what is observed thereafter.

Experience comes into being and is formed through some material medium. Thus, the strict separation between inner and outer is unjustified. The boundary between the two is mutable. At times, observation of one's experience and communication of it may even coincide, as when we think aloud. Ericsson and Simon (1993) have done a number of ingenious studies on expertise, in which they simply have participants say aloud what they normally say silently to themselves. With this method they can show, for example, the strategies waiters use to organize their memory for orders. In the next section, I will explore how we can transform rating scales into a method sensitive to the above outlined social dynamics of self-observation.

Rethinking Ratings Scales: Triggering a Process of Sense Making

Rating scales are one of the most widely used research methods in contemporary psychology. They provide a quick means of obtaining large quantities of data that can then be interpreted through a statistical analysis. This data, however, is much more problematic than researchers are typically willing to recognize. For rating scales to be valid, we must assume that in making a mark on a scale we are *immediately*, *unitarily*, and *accurately* accessing our mental states, and that these states are *inherently quantifiable* —all very controversial assumptions (Wagoner and Valsiner 2005; see also below). Simply labeling them "self-report" methods rather than "self-observation" or "introspective" methods or by simply attending to the quantitative outcomes of these processes does not overcome the difficulties involved in the practice of self-observation, though it might obscure them in the eyes of the research community. One could without too much difficulty argue that contemporary versions of self-observation, such as rating scales, are in fact much more primitive than those practiced in the first decades of the twentieth century: By using naïve observers, who have only a minimal social relation to the experimenter, and by only attending to static outcomes of the rating process, the data produced is much more ambiguous than in early introspective methods.

In this section, I will draw on a study I conducted with Jaan Valsiner (Wagoner and Valsiner 2005) to disambiguate rating scale data by focusing on the process by which the data is produced rather than the quantitative outcome of this process. Rating scales normally encourage research participants to *speed up* the process of rating with endless pages of a boring questionnaire, which participants try to get through as quickly as possible. Our method, by contrast, was a process-oriented approach. To observe it we *slowed down* the process of rating and focused our analysis on the dynamics therein. In our study observers were presented with a picture of an attractive member of the opposite sex, which they were to rate on multiple dimensions—e.g., attractiveness, approachable, likeable, etc. In the questionnaire, participants were first to make their rating and then immediately explain how they arrived at the mark in a space provided directly below the scale. Thus, the research strategy was similar to that of the Würzburg School.

Consider the following female's rating for "approachable" (Wagoner and Valsiner 2005, 203)—the arrows and divisions are made by the researchers to help the reader attend to certain aspects of the participant's text:

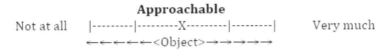

Approachable

Not at all |--------|---------X---------|---------| Very much
                ←−←−←−←−<Object>→−→−→−→−→

In the inquiry into the subject's rationale of putting the marker in the middle, we get:

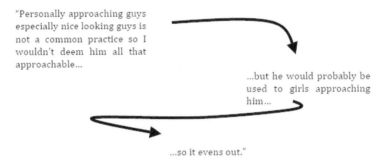

"Personally approaching guys especially nice looking guys is not a common practice so I wouldn't deem him all that approachable...

...but he would probably be used to girls approaching him...

...so it evens out."

We see that making a rating does not involve an immediate or unitary access to some internal mental state. Instead, an elaborated *process* of sense making is involved. The participant relates to the object of rating (i.e., the picture of a man) through the linguistic category of "approachable." The category does not directly map onto some hypothetical internal state, but is rather an internally negotiated intersubjective relation. In other words, "approachable" can only be made sense of in a co-inhabited and immanently meaningful world. Although the subject is engaged in what might be called an "internal" process, the process itself involves imagining public scenarios that would count as "approachable" within ordinary language. In so doing, she identifies two rather different and opposing scenarios: in the first, she imagines herself approaching a nice-looking guy, while the second is a more abstract use of "approachable" as a category to describe the man on his own terms, taking herself out of the picture. Both meanings of "approachable" are *grammatically* correct (to use Wittgenstein's phrase) in ordinary language.

This ambiguity in the meaning of "approachable" as this participant relates to the picture generates a dialogical tension (represented by the <object> with arrows to the left and right of it), which traditional rating scales that only look at the quantitative outcome would be entirely blind to. They would assume a rating in the middle of the scale is the outcome of a neutral response. However, here we see that in fact it represents two forces pulling in opposite directions. It is the interplay between these two parts (phases) that produces the "3," rather than a single state. In focusing on the *process* of constructing an intersubjectively meaningful rating over the *outcome*, we come to see that a multiplicity of meanings and forces are at work for a single unitary rating. In short, by *slowing down* the process and by building in space for meaningful elaboration in order to access these constructive dynamics of rating, we see that there is much more to rating than is normally assumed. Let us take another example to further illustrate this point:

Courteous

Not at all |---------|---------|----X----|---------| Very much

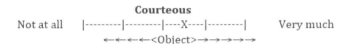

In the inquiry into the subject's rationale of putting the mark just right of the middle, we get:

"I can see this guy holding doors for the ladies and buying flowers for his girl, etc. which is courteous/nice...

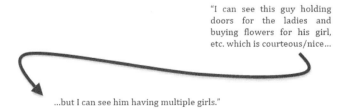

...but I can see him having multiple girls."

Again, there is striving to situate the category and object of rating in an intersubjectively meaningful world, leading the subject to imagine two opposing scenarios, both of which are grammatically correct uses of "courteous." As above, the switch of perspectives is easily identifiable with the use of the word "but." Interestingly, although the two uses of "courteous" are conflicting when viewed from a meta-level (as we force participants to do with the rating task), they coexist without confusion in everyday life, and as we see here they can easily flow into each other in thought. Of course, the researcher can try to fixate language but he or she cannot fix observers' sense making. Rigorously designed rating scales will include a test phase to minimize the problem of the openness of word meaning, rewording their questions accordingly. However, language is inherently open and ambiguous. Words do not fit things in a one-to-one relation. Therefore, researcher's efforts to fix the meaning of words and their relation to judgments can only ever be partial. Instead of hiding these complexities behind quantitative scores and aggregate statistics, methods of self-observation need to bring them to the fore if they are to count as rigorous scientific methods. Otherwise, the meaning of the numbers on a scale will remain entirely obscure. Moreover, ignoring the question of participants' meaning allows researchers to talk as if a certain experimental manipulation *caused* participants to think in a certain way (as indicated by a rating scale score). The above examples illustrate that participants enter a space of reasons or norms when they fill out a rating scale. Thus, the category of cause is inappropriate here; instead, participants *negotiate* meaning. As such we need to adopt a discourse of mediation in the place of causality (see e.g., Moghaddam 2006).

Conclusion

In this chapter, I have argued that the practice of self-observation should be developed along functionalist lines of thought rather than in dualistic terms. Using early debates about in self-observation as our case study, we saw that the data produced was intertwined with the institutions (with their varied practices, social roles, and languages) within which it occurs. An expression of experience is a social relation because (1) it is made possible by being a coinhabitant of an intersubjectively shared world and (2) it carries with it the potential to attune others to some aspect of human experience. In the remaining space, I will sum up some of the key take-away points of this chapter:

1. One gets different results on the two-point test depending on the degree of permissiveness in language used to report the scores and more broadly the institution in which the reporting occurs. Thus, there were differing results between laboratories in Leipzig, Paris, and Torres Straight.

2. Open descriptive concepts (such as *Bsl* or the "stream of consciousness") can be generative of productive new research directions. This points to the fact that psychological concepts are not *natural kinds* but rather *human kinds*, which once created feedback into social practices and experience.

3. Debates over self-observation turned into discussions about the appropriate scientific language to express experience—either sensationalist or holistic language. The former is restrictive but relatively clear, while the latter opens up psychology to new dimensions of mind but is at the same time more ambiguous.

4. Self-observation is not a purely individual act. Instead, it presupposes interaction with others in stable social institutions. The inner phase of self-observation involves taking the perspective of others toward one's self. The outer-directed phase requires expressing that experience in publically accessible symbol. Both phases are social—thus they are not as separate as they might first appear and may even coincide using methods like the "think-aloud protocol."

5. Traditional rating scales can be transformed into instruments for capturing the dynamics of meaning making. From the examples given here we see that making a rating involves thinking of public scenarios in which to ground the rating. Thus, rather than providing access to some unitary mental state, ratings are make like creative self-dialogues taking place within an intersubjectively shared and imminently meaningful world.

References

Ach, N. 1905. *Über die Willenstätigkeit und das Denken.* Göttingen: Vandenhoeck, Diss. Würzburg.

Bartlett, F. C. 1916a. "Transformations Arising from Repeated Representation: A Contribution towards an Experimental Study of the Process of Conventionalisation." Fellowship Dissertation, St. John's College, Cambridge.

_____. 1916b. "An Experimental Study of Some Problems of Perceiving and Imagining." *British Journal of Psychology* 8: 222–66.

_____. 1932. *Remembering: A Study in Experimental and Social Psychology.* Cambridge: Cambridge University Press.

Betz, W. 1910. "Vorstellung and Einstellung: I. Über Wiedererkennen." *Archiv für die gesamte Psychologie* 17: 266–96.

Bergson, H. 1903/1999. *Introduction to Metaphysics.* Indianapolis, IN: Hackett Publishing Company.

Binet, A. 1903. *L'etude expérimentale de l'intelligence.* Paris: Schleicher.

Boring, E. G. 1950. *A History of Experimental Psychology*. New York: Appleton-Century-Crofts.

Bühler, K. 1907. "Tasachen und Probleme zu einer Psychologie der Denkvorgänge, I: Über Gedanken." *Archiv für die Gesamte Psychologie* 9: 297–365.

Costall, A. 2006. "'Introspection' and the Mythical Origins of Scientific Psychology." *Consciousness and Cognition* 15, no. 4: 634–54.

Danziger, K. 1980. "History of Introspection Reconsidered." *Journal of the History of the Behavioral Sciences* 16, no. 3: 241–62.

Ericsson, K. A. and Simon, H. 1993. *Protocol Analysis: Verbal Reports as Data*. Cambridge, MA: MIT Press.

Hacking, I. 1995. "The Looping Effect of Human Kinds." In *Causal Cognition: A Multidisciplinary Approach*, edited by D. Sperber, D. Premack, and A.J. Premack, 351–83. Oxford: Oxford University Press.

Humphrey, G. 1951. *Thinking: An Introduction to Its Experimental Psychology*. New York: Wiley.

Kaplan, B. 1955. "Some Psychological Methods for the Investigation of Expressive Language." In *On Expressive Language*, edited by H. Werner. Worcester, MA: Clark University Press.

Kusch, M. 1999. *Psychological Knowledge: A Social History and Philosophy*. London: Routledge.

Mandler, G. 2007. *A History of Modern Experimental Psychology: From James and Wundt to Cognitive Science*. Cambridge, MA: MIT Press.

Mandler, J. M. and Mandler, G. 1964. *Thinking: From Association to Gestalt*. New York: Wiley.

Marbe, K. 1901. *Experimentell-psychologische Untersuchungen über das Urteil: Eine Einleitung in die Logik*. Leipzig: Engelmann.

Mayer, A. and Orth, J. 1901. "Zur qualitativen Untersuchung der Association." *Zeitshrift für Psychologie* 26: 1–13.

Mead, G. H. 1910. "What Social Objects Must Psychology Presuppose?" *Journal of Philosophy, Psychology, and Scientific Methods* 7: 174–80.

_____. 1934. *Mind, Self and Society*. Chicago, IL: Chicago University Press.

Messer, A. 1906. "Experimentell-psychologische Untersuchungen über das Denken." *Archiv für die Gesamte Psychologie* 8: 1–224.

Moghaddam, F. M. 2006. "Performance Capacity and Performance Style: Looking Back and Moving Forward in Psychology." *Theory and Psychology* 16: 840–46.

Richards, G. 1998. "Getting a Result: The Expedition's Psychological Research 1898–1913." In *Cambridge and the Torres Strait: Centenary Essays on the 1898 Anthropological Expedition*, edited by A. Herle and S. Rouse. Cambridge: Cambridge University Press.

Titchener, E. B. 1909. *Lectures on the Experimental Psychology of Thought Processes*. New York: Macmillan.

Valsiner, J. 2003. "Beyond Social Representations: A Theory of Enablement." *Papers on Social Representations* 12: 7.1–7.16. (Retrieved March 2005, from http://www. psr.jku.at).

Wagoner, B. 2011. "What Happened to Holism?" *Psychological Studies* 56, no. 3: 318–24.

Wagoner, B. and Valsiner, J. 2005. "Rating Tasks in Psychology: From a Static Ontology to a Dialogical Synthesis of Meaning." In *Contemporary Theorizing in Psychology: Global Perspectives*, edited by A. Gülerce, I. Steauble, A. Hofmeister, G. Saunders and J. Kaye, 197–213. Toronto: Captus Press.

Watson, J. B. 1913. "Psychology as a Behaviorist Views It." *Psychological Review* 20: 158–77.

Werner, H. 1956. "Microgenesis and Aphasia." *Journal of Abnormal Social Psychology* 52: 347–53.

Werner, H. and Kaplan, B. 1963. *Symbol Formation: An Organismic-Developmental Approach to Language and the Expression of Thought.* Hillsdale, IN: Lawrence Erlbaum Associates.

Wittgenstein, L. 1953. *Philosophical Investigations.* Oxford: Blackwell.

6

Confronting the Challenges of Observing Inner Experience: The Descriptive Experience Sampling Method

Christopher L. Heavey

If one wishes to study private, first-person experiences that present themselves directly to a person, what we call inner experience, one should consider the challenges inherent in such a task (Hurlburt et al. 2006; Hurlburt 2011a). Perhaps the most fundamental challenge facing those wishing to understand inner experience is that it is private, directly accessible to only one person. Thus, there are no easy methods available for calibration of reports of experience, no easy pathways to independently confirm measurements. A report about experience must originate from an individual who has direct access to her own inner experience but no direct access to the inner experiences of anyone else. This presents challenges with, among other things, the shaping of the language used to convey the experiences (Hurlburt and Heavey 2001; Skinner 1974). As a result, substantial care is required to develop a shared understanding of the descriptions of these private experiences. For example, what precisely is the experience of anxiety or happiness? These words and the descriptions that contain them cannot be presumed to have a shared meaning between the person using them to describe an experience and the person attempting to apprehend that experience.

In addition to the challenge of communicating about inner experience, inner experience appears to be evanescent, both in the sense of often being fleeting and in the sense of being fragile or easily disturbed. Thus, one must consider carefully how any attempt to capture or apprehend inner experience affects the experience. Hurlburt (Hurlburt 2009, 2011b; Hurlburt and Akhter 2006) uses the term "pristine inner experience" to describe naturally occurring inner experiences that is directly present in awareness before "it is disturbed by any attempt at apprehension or introspection" (Hurlburt 2009, 157). Pristine inner experience is what populates our normal waking consciousness as we go about our lives. The delicate and fleeting nature of pristine inner experience means that any attempt to study it will impact it to some degree. This is true both in terms of the setting in which pristine inner experience is studied and the manner in which it is studied. The further from our natural daily environment and the more disruptive the method of accessing the inner experience, the more we likely we will be to disrupt pristine inner experience. Attention to these issues may increase the likelihood that the impacts will be acceptably small.

The person to whom the inner experience is directly observable also has a host of limitations as an observer. First among these may be that the observer has beliefs about the nature of his or her inner experiences. People over time develop beliefs about their own pristine inner experiences. In the vast majority of cases, these beliefs are not the result of careful, systematic observations and scientifically adequate generalizations. In other words, people are casual theory builders and most will come to any investigation of their pristine inner experience with self-theories well developed and ready to be deployed. Accessing these theories should not be confused with an investigation of pristine inner experience. We call these types of theories presuppositions (Hurlburt and Heavey 2006a, Chapter 10; Hurlburt and Schwitzgebel 2011) to highlight the fact that they are generally so woven into the fabric of people's thinking that they are typically beyond consideration. Because of the deep-seated and typically invisible nature of presuppositions, any adequate method for investigating inner experience must be prepared to identify, confront, and minimize their impact (Hurlburt 2011a; Hurlburt and Heavey 2006a; Hurlburt and Raymond 2011; Hurlburt and Schwitzgebel 2011).

Investigators will also bring their own presuppositions about inner experience to any investigation. The investigator's presuppositions are probably at least as pernicious as those of the subject given the likelihood that they will inhabit the fabric of the investigation and all of its procedures. The investigator's presuppositions are likely to be reflected not just in any hypotheses or predictions but also in questions asked, the procedures used, and the examination of the resulting data.

Often investigators set out to confirm their presuppositions about the nature of inner experience rather than to learn from the data. Moreover, subjects are unlikely to be in a position to resist or even recognize the investigator's presuppositions given the novelty of the investigative situation. A simple example of this dynamic is when the investigator asks, "What are you feeling?" This question presumes the subject is feeling something. Subjects typically will answer this question by reporting a feeling, particularly if the question is accompanied by a checklist of possible feeling (e.g., Watson et al. 1988). Our investigations (Heavey and Hurlburt 2008), however, suggest the most common answer to this question as it pertains to pristine inner experience should be "nothing," as subjects experience feelings as part of pristine inner experience only about a quarter of the time.

Any method intending to observe inner experience must also confront the inherent limitations in the memory of the subject. The evanescent nature of inner experience means that we must try to stabilize inner experience in memory long enough to observe it. Thus, researchers must be cognizant of limitations in both the capacity and the duration of memory. If inner experience is complex, limitations in the capacity of memory may make it difficult for observers to retain more than a brief moment of it. The rapid decay of memory, particularly if sensory memory is involved (Atkinson and Shiffrin 1968), indicate that time is potentially a critical factor if high-fidelity observations are the goal. One should be skeptical of highly retrospective reports about inner experience or reports about inner experience over substantial lengths of time.

One potential exception to the strictures of memory on investigations of inner experience is think-aloud procedures (e.g., Davison et al. 1995) in which experience is reported in real time, as it occurs. However, with think-aloud procedures, the strictures of memory are replaced by three other potentially more damaging limitations. First, pristine inner experience may be severely disrupted by the parallel process of reporting it aloud as it unfolds. Second, the strictures imposed by communication bandwidth limit the complexity of the unfolding experience that might be conveyed by a think-aloud procedure. Third, the very definition of "think aloud" implies, perhaps incorrectly, that thinking is verbal and therefore can be easily externalized.

Finally, even if all of the above challenges are confronted, we are still left with the issue of the reporting of the pristine inner experiences.

In addition to the nontrivial difficulty of shaping language about private experiences mentioned earlier, we remain at the mercy of the subjects' motivation to provide high-fidelity accounts of their inherently personal, private inner experience. Thus, investigators should carefully consider the environment they create and the motivations in play within subjects that may potentially impact their reports.

Descriptive Experience Sampling

Hurlburt (1990, 1993, 2011a) developed the Descriptive Experience (DES) method to attempt to obtain high-fidelity reports of inner experiences in full acceptance of those challenges inherent in the task. At the outset it is important to note that accepting the challenges inherent in the task provides no guarantee of overcoming them. Thus, the DES method should be understood as providing the possibility of obtaining high-fidelity apprehensions of the inner experience. Despite that being the case, DES does involve specific procedures and guidance designed to maximize the likelihood of revealing inner experience in high fidelity. Space does not permit a full explication of either the procedures or their rationale. Readers interested in a more complete account should see Hurlburt and Heavey (2006a), Hurlburt and Akhter (2006), and Hurlburt (2011a).

A DES subject is given a pocket-sized random beeper, an earphone, and a small notepad to carry with her as she goes about her everyday activities. Thus, samples of pristine inner experience are collected where they occur, in the subject's everyday natural environment. The beeper is set to beep randomly as a way of working against selection bias by the subject and/or the investigator. The subject hears the beep through the earphone. The beep is designed to have a fast rise time, making it quickly detectable. The earphone keeps the beep private, thus not disturbing the external environment or provoking inquiry from others that would distract the subject from focusing on her ongoing inner experience. The subject is instructed to jot down notes about whatever was present in her experience at the last undisturbed moment before the beep, which DES calls the moment of the beep. She is asked to jot down notes as soon as possible after the beep to preserve as much as possible her recollection of the ongoing inner experience. This procedure is intended to minimize retrospection and correspondingly decrease the demands placed on the subject's memory. Although some degree of retrospection is occurring, it is typically in the realm of seconds (rather than the hours or days of other methods). The subject is asked to repeat this sequence of going about her everyday activities, beep sounding, and jotting down notes about her ongoing experience at the moment of the beep about six times. The subject is told that the notes will be for her private use to assist her memory. This allows the subject to use her notes in whatever way best helps her to preserve her apprehension of her experience rather than worrying about the investigators' reactions to the notes. Except for the instruction to note whatever was ongoing in experience, subjects are not told what to write or even what type of inner experience to expect or focus on at the moment of the beep. This is a central aspect of keeping the process open-beginninged and battling the presuppositions of the investigators.

Another important aspect of the initial instructions to DES subjects is that they are asked to serve as coinvestigators in the exploration of their inner experience and, as such, they have equal control over the process. This shared control includes the genuine request for input and feedback about the process as it unfolds based on the view that the subject may have unique insights into how best to explore her inner experience. It also includes explicit discussion of the right to decline to discuss any moment of experience. The intent here is to establish a partnership aimed at uncovering the truth of the subject's inner experience. In this partnership both sides play vital roles, the subject with exclusive access to the experience and the investigator with a method and skills potentially able to reveal the experience in high fidelity. The partners must rely on each other and trust is a critical component of the alliance. Essentially the contract is to work together to reveal the subject's inner experience with the understanding that, should the subject not want to reveal any aspect of a moment of her inner experience, she should explicitly decline to discuss that moment rather than avoid the sensitive aspects of it—the whole truth or nothing, either of which is fine with the investigator.

The subject also retains the right to keep all of the discussions about her inner experience private until she explicitly agrees otherwise. Thus the subject can decide, even after the conclusion of the investigations, to withhold her consent to release or publish descriptions of her inner experience. This is done to give the subject the greatest possible sense of control over the process and to respect her privacy at all points. Sometimes a subject is reluctant to reveal her private experience; the revocable consent allows her to test the water, knowing that she can change her mind later.

After collecting about six moments of her experience, the subject participates in an "expositional" interview. The expositional interview is scheduled soon after the collection of moments of experience, no more than twenty-four hours later. During the expositional interview the coinvestigators work together toward a high-fidelity apprehension of the subject's inner experience at each sampled moment. As described in Hurlburt and Akhter (2006) and Hurlburt and Heavey (2006a), the investigator focuses the interview entirely on answering one fundamental question, *What, if anything, was ongoing in your inner experience at the moment of the beep?* There are several important dimensions of this question. First, it is "open-beginninged," meaning that it does not presume anything, including that there was something ongoing in experience at all. The intention is to allow the subject complete latitude to report on her experience without a priori guidance or limitation. Each investigation is a new foray into unknown territory with the possibility that what is found never has been encountered before. The investigator begins with a structured method but a blank slate regarding what may be revealed.

Other important aspects of the intention represented in this question are "ongoing in your experience" and "at the moment of the beep" (Hurlburt and Akhter 2006; Hurlburt and Heavey 2006a). "Ongoing in experience" keeps the focus on what is directly present to the subject. Beliefs, attitudes, judgments and the like are of interest only if they happen to be ongoingly present in experience at the moment of the beep, a rare occurrence. However, subjects often have to be taught to exclude these types of events from consideration (unless they were directly present). Statements such as, "I always . . ." or "When I . . . , I . . ." are cues that the conversation has strayed from that which was observed as being directly present in experience at that moment.

The continual focus on the moment of the beep, insisting on discussing only the pristine experience that was ongoing when the beep sounded, also helps to undermine the tendency to let beliefs and other presuppositions steer the discussion away from randomly selected pristine inner experience. A subject is often motivated to tell investigators about some particular aspect of her inner experience; it may be what she thinks is special or interesting about herself, or what is consistent with her own theories about her inner experience, etc. Whatever the motivation, anything other than a focus on what was ongoing at the moment of the beep moves the discussion away from pristine inner experience and increases the risk of contamination of reports by presuppositions.

Focusing on the inner experience present at the moment of the beep also limits the demands placed on memory, particularly if the pristine inner experience was complex or multifaceted. The subject also can use her notes, hopefully recorded shortly after the beep, to reawaken her recollection of her ongoing pristine inner experience. DES accepts that the beep disturbs the ongoing experience to some extent, and that even with notes taken shortly after the beep, the recollection will be a somewhat degraded version of the original experience. High-fidelity apprehensions are the goal; perfection is beyond reach.

In addition to these more relatively straightforward intentions of the fundamental question (What, if anything, was ongoing in your experience at the moment of the beep?), high levels of effort and skill are often required to obtain high-fidelity apprehensions of the moments of inner experience (see Hurlburt 2011a; Hurlburt and Akhter 2006; Hurlburt and Heavey 2006a). Subjects are rarely skilled observers of their pristine inner experience. Thus, subjects must be taught to examine their inner experience carefully, to explore the nooks and crannies of their pristine inner experience to discover what might be present, to focus in precisely on the moment of the beep and to exclude that which was not actually ongoingly present in experience. Additionally, the subject and investigator have to work, sometimes painstakingly, to develop the skills and language to communicate about the (possibly) unique inner experience of the subject. What does each word mean? Does it mean the same thing to the subject as it does to the investigator? How can that be established and other possible interpretations ruled out? What is the fullest extent to which the inner experience can be described? Were there aspects that were present but defy description? When has the edge of what can be described been reached, where going further would cross into speculation or confabulation? These are difficult questions, often challenging or impossible to resolve for a specific moment, but the struggle with these questions conveys the intention that the goal is a high-fidelity apprehension of the pristine inner experience and they encourage the subject to hone her skills at observing her pristine inner experience.

One can easily imagine a novice and well-intentioned but nonetheless insufficient application of the DES procedures. A subject collects six moments of experience, comes into expositional interview and is asked the fundamental question: *What, if anything was ongoing in your experience at the moment of the beep?* The subject responds: "I was reading a book" or perhaps "I was feeling depressed" or perhaps "I was talking with my friend." The investigator then repeats the question for each of the subsequent moments and the interview is over a few minutes later. These are probably not high-fidelity apprehensions of moments of inner experience.

In this scenario, the investigator has not worked diligently to understand precisely what the subject means by words such as "depressed"; he has not tried to understand what the experience of reading was like for this subject at this precise moment or what was ongoing in her experience when she was "talking with her friend." The investigator has not helped the subject to be a careful observer of her inner experience, not ensured that she was reporting only about experience ongoing at the moment of the beep. Our experience suggests that a subject would probably be quite content with such a demonstrably inadequate interview, would not recognize that she has not described her experience with fidelity. A subject does not have a basis for determining what is and what is not a high-fidelity apprehension of a moment of their inner experience until she has been trained to apprehend her own inner experience in high fidelity.

Finally, the entire process of collecting moments of experience with the beeper and conducting an expositional interview is repeated iteratively (Hurlburt 2009, 2011a; Hurlburt and Akhter 2006), ideally with incremental improvement during each subsequent cycle. The iterative nature of the process is critical. Few subjects are skilled observers of their pristine inner experience at the outset. Therefore, subjects need to develop their skills at observing their inner experience and communicating about it. These skills are developed through practice and the shaping interactions of the expositional interview combined with repeated practice. In other words, it is not enough to simply repeat the apprehending process without some type of skill-building feedback such as that which comes through repeated expositional interviews. Questionnaires, for example, are often administered repeatedly, but that by itself does not build skill. The iterative nature of DES also allows the investigator to build his own skill in apprehending the experience of the unique subject who appears before him. As coinvestigators, the subject and investigator attempt to learn to communicate effectively about the subject's inner experience. When important aspects of the pristine experience are unclear, they potentially can be explored during a subsequent interview through contrasts with similar or different moments of experience that have previously been discussed. Over time, an increasingly faithful apprehension of the subject's inner experience may emerge.

The typical result of a DES investigation is an idiographic characterization of an individual's inner experience. After each expositional interview the investigators prepare a written description of each moment of inner experience. These descriptions aid the investigators later in developing an idiographic characterization of the salient aspects of the subject's pristine inner experience. These characterizations can then be compared to determine the extent to which there are commonalities or differences across subjects, including those sharing a common characteristic such as a psychiatric diagnosis.

The intention in this chapter has been to describe how the features of the DES method are designed to address the challenges inherent in the task of obtaining high-fidelity apprehensions of inner experience. Despite this, as was stated at the outset, success cannot be assured and, in fact, the results will inevitably be less than perfect. Each investigation is its own foray into uncertain territory with unique constellations of the fundamental challenges of exploring inner experience, the outcome unknowable in advance. More concretely, each investigation depends on the skills of the investigator(s) and subject(s) as they unfold and interrelate in the specifics of the real interactions. Thus, even a skilled investigator using a method such as DES is not assured of success, though his chances are better than those of an unskilled investigator or someone using a method not suited to the task. A sports metaphor is perhaps instructive, where the skills and efforts of subject and researcher, necessarily coinvestigators if there is any hope of success, are pitted against the challenges inherent in the task as they apply in that unique situation, at that unique time. Where this metaphor falls short is that it is unlikely that the outcome will be as clear as provided in an actual sporting event, with a definite score and clear success or failure. Partial success is possible and at the conclusion of the investigation the degree of success is likely at least partially obscured from the participants. What is at issue is the degree to which it falls short and the relative advantages and disadvantages of using this method compared to other available methods.

Strengths of DES include its focus on randomly chosen, real moments of pristine inner experience; its ecological validity in that it seeks pristine experience where it occurs, in the everyday goings on of subjects; its explicit attempts to fight against the distorting effects of presuppositions; its efforts to minimize the demands on memory, including retrospection, and to clarify the meaning of the language used to convey reports of inner experience; and its open-beginninged nature which allows the possibility of discovering the unexpected and helps to check the influences of the investigator's presuppositions.

These strengths must be weighed against its drawback. DES requires substantial skill and practice on the part of the investigator, meaning, among other things, the work cannot be done primarily by relatively lower-skilled research assistants. It is very time intensive for both investigators and subjects, leading to small sample sizes. The qualitative nature of DES also makes it less transparent than many other methods. It is difficult for outsiders to know the full nature of the interactions with subjects, leaving open the possibility of bias or other distortions being introduced by researchers. Thus, there is no easy way to validate DES results. Hurlburt and Heavey (2002) showed that interviews can be reliable, but ultimately they only established that they themselves, as two particular investigators, produced largely the same results; that does not guarantee that others would be able to do so or that they would be able to do so with all populations. Hurlburt and Schwitzgebel (2007) produced a transcript of one complete set of subject interviews and debated the validity of the procedures and results, again showing that it can be a valid procedure. But neither of these studies transfers directly to other researchers in the way the validation of a self-report questionnaire does.

Finally, DES is a method for exploring pristine experience, experience which presents itself directly to the person in ongoing awareness. There may well be other important features of consciousness that are not part of pristine experience. There certainly are many important cognitive processes that occur outside of pristine experience (e.g., Wilson 2002). Mental activity occurring outside of pristine experience is beyond the reach of DES.

Given this constellation of strengths and weaknesses, DES may be well suited to some task but not others. Heavey et al. (2010) compared the appropriate use of DES to the use of scouts in the army; scouts are a small number of well-trained individuals suited for surveying the battlefield before the majority of the troops are brought in. The notion is that DES is well suited to explore the unknown, to survey the landscape of pristine inner experience, providing reports of what is found but accepting that these reports will need to be validated by others using complementary methods.

Comparison of DES to Related Methods

As we have seen, DES can be said to be a beeper-driven qualitative/phenomenological method. It may be useful to contrast DES with some other methods that use beepers and with some other qualitative phenomenological methods. Besides DES, there are in current use two main methods that use beepers with the aim to capture aspects of experience, the Experience Sampling Method (ESM; Csikizentmihalyi and Larson 1987) and Ecological Momentary Assessment (EMA; Stone and Shiffman 1994). Although ESM and EMA have some differences (e.g., EMA collects more diverse information and uses more flexible measures than does ESM, whereas ESM collects more information about context and co-occurring events), they can be grouped together for purposes of comparing to DES. By using random beepers to cue subjects to pay attention to their ongoing experience as they go about their normal daily activities, and by asking subjects to report on the spot (thus minimizing retrospectiveness), these methods share with DES an emphasis on the ecological validity of observations. However, these methods differ from DES by asking subjects to respond to pre-determined questions about their experience, typically using Likert scales. This reporting format steers away from an exclusive focus on pristine experience, does not allow the discovery of new phenomenon, and does not allow for the shaping of language used to describe private experiences. Additionally, these methods are not meaningfully iterative because, even though their questionnaires are completed on repeated occasions, no training occurs between administrations. Finally, there is little discussion or effort within these methods devoted to the bracketing or presuppositions.

There are many methods that are called "qualitative" or "phenomenological." DES has been compared and contrasted with five of them: Giorgi's phenomenological psychology (1975, 1989, 1997), Kvale's (1996) InterView method, Petitmengin's (2006) explicitation method, van Manen's (1990) hermeneutic phenomenological inquiry, and Moustakas's (1994) human science research. Broadly speaking, these methods employ interviews aimed at apprehending inner experience. Hurlburt and Heavey (2006a, Chapter 12) compared DES to Giorgi's phenomenological psychology (1975, 1989, 1997) and Kvale's (1996) InterView method. Hurlburt and Akhter (2006) and Hurlburt (2011b) compared DES to Petitmengin's (2006) qualitative interview method. Heavey et al. (2010) compared DES to van Manen's (1990) hermeneutic phenomenological inquiry and Moustakas's (1994) human science research. Hurlburt credits Giorgi, Husserl (1960), and other phenomenological psychologists for providing an important foundation for the development of DES, particularly in emphasizing "the importance of description, the mistrust of theory, and the value of bracketing presuppositions" (Hurlburt and Heavey, 2006a, 204).

However, DES diverges from phenomenological psychology (for our purposes these five methods can be grouped together) in important ways. First, DES does not define the target or topic of the investigation (beyond seeking pristine inner experience) in advance. In contrast, the typical phenomenological investigation identifies the subject area a priori. For example, Giorgi (1975, 1989) set out to investigate the experience of learning, asking subjects to describe an experience when they experienced learning. Beginning with a predetermined focus or type of experience increases the risk that presuppositions will invade reports of experience.

Second, phenomenological methods allow highly retrospective reports, often about experiences that occurred months or years in the past. Because phenomenological investigations seek a predefined type of experience (e.g., learning), they ask subjects to search their memory for an instance of that specific type of experience and then to report on it. This is fundamentally different from DES which asks subjects to attempt to capture a precisely identified moment of experience as it is occurring.

Third, phenomenological methods do not explore experience as it is occurring in its natural environment. DES emphasizes the importance of disturbing pristine experience as little as possible. Thus, subjects go about their normal daily activities and observe their ongoing experience (when cued by the beep) in that context. Phenomenological psychology interviews subjects about experiences that were not observed carefully when and where they occurred, but rather are reconstructed from some distant vantage point in a different context and setting.

Fourth, the minimally retrospective and iterative nature of DES allow it to consider the actual inner experience as the starting point for the investigation rather than the reports of the experience which are considered the starting point for phenomenological investigations (Hurlburt and Heavey 2006a). This is a subtle but important point. DES seeks to improve the reports by keeping subjects in touch with the experienced moment as much as possible and through iterative training. Thus, subjects are often able to consult their memory and improve or modify their reports during the interview. Although modified reports may be more suspect due to the potentially biasing effect of the interview, the iterative nature of DES allows subjects to improve their observations and apprehensions over time (Hurlburt 2009). The highly retrospective, noniterative nature of the reports in phenomenological investigations makes this much less feasible.

Finally, DES does not seek essences or use techniques such as free imaginative variation to discover essential features of objects or experiences (Giorgi 1997), nor does it seek the meaning of experiences (Kvale 1996). DES instead seeks to apprehend all that is present in specific moments of experience and then to build an understanding of the salient characteristics of the inner experience of one individual through an examination of many as-complete-as-possible moments of experience. In other words, DES does not ask the subject to do anything more than assist in the process of apprehending randomly selected moments of pristine inner experience. Derivative understandings or conclusions are then built up from these repeated as-true-as-possible observations.

A Few DES Findings

When DES is used to survey the landscape of pristine inner experience, what has been found? Hurlburt (1990, 1993) performed the first in-depth observations using DES. He worked with people suffering from various mental illnesses as well as healthy subjects, producing idiographic characterizations of the inner experience of each person. These characterizations contained a number of unexpected observations. For example, Hurlburt (1990) observed that his schizophrenic subjects had clear emotional inner experience despite "affective flattening" (aka blunted affect) being a diagnostic symptom of the disorder:

> Our samples force us to make the distinction more clearly between the inner experience and the outward expression. Our schizophrenic subjects simply did *not* have blunted inner emotional experience. On the contrary, their emotional experiences were quite clear to them; they were easily capable of describing the nuances and discriminations of their inner emotional experiences; and the range of such emotions was quite varied. (Hurlburt 1990, 254, italics in original)

In fact, Hurlburt observed that some of his schizophrenic subjects' emotional experiences were *hyper*-clear. Subsequent research using a variety of other methods has supported Hurlburt's (1990) observation that despite outward appearances to the contrary, schizophrenic subjects have frequent emotional experience, sometimes even more frequent than nonschizophrenic subjects (Kring 1999). The hyperclarity of schizophrenic emotion has yet to be explored outside of DES.

Hurlburt's (1990, 1993) early DES studies also began to define the frequent phenomena of inner experience. Some of these phenomena have been long been believed to be common in inner experience, phenomena such as inner seeing (aka mental images), inner speaking, and feelings. Others have not been commonly recognized. For example, Hurlburt (1990; Hurlburt and Akhter 2008) identified the phenomenon of unsymbolized thinking: the experience of thinking some particular, definite thought without the awareness of that thought's being represented in words, images, or any other symbols (Hurlburt and Heavey 2006b). Hurlburt (1993; Hurlburt et al. 2009) identified the phenomenon sensory awareness: a sensory experience (itch, hotness, pressure, visual taking-in, hearing) that is itself a primary theme or focus for the subject (Hurlburt and Heavey 2006b). Hurlburt and Heavey (2002) showed that the presence of these five most frequent phenomena of inner experience (i.e., inner seeing, inner speaking, feelings, unsymbolized thinking, and sensory awareness) could be coded reliably; Heavey and Hurlburt (2008) found that each of these five common phenomena were present in about one quarter of sampled moments. This collection of studies has begun the process of describing the landscape of inner experience. In doing they have elaborated many of the details of commonly recognized aspects of inner experience and also identified phenomena that are common in inner experience but largely unrecognized (e.g., unsymbolized thinking and sensory awareness). The fact that these common phenomena could remain so infrequently recognized attests to the importance of using a careful method such as DES to observe inner experience.

The longest running and most well-developed of these investigations into a group sharing a common external characteristic is the series of investigations Hurlburt and his students have done with women suffering from bulimia nervosa (Doucette 1992; Doucette and Hurlburt 1993a, 1993b; Jones-Forrester 2006, 2009; Hurlburt 1993). Hurlburt and Jones-Forrester (2011) review this collection of studies, describing the discovery of, among other things, "fragmented multiplicity" in the inner experience of all of the bulimic women. Fragment multiplicity is the experience of many simultaneously ongoing experiences, often

ten or more. Descriptions of moments of inner experience containing fragmented multiplicity are striking:

> Jessica was in class and was directly experiencing about 10 simultaneous, chaotic unworded thought/feelings. These experiences were in her head, were all jumbled together so that none was clearly differentiable or separable. Jessica knew them to be related to the day's activities: her paper is due, about the final exam, wanting her teacher to shut up, wanting the class to be over, realizing that she was going to be late to her sampling appointment, wanting to leave the class. These experiences were neither thoughts nor feelings, or perhaps were both thoughts and feelings, or were somewhere between thoughts and feelings, and were apprehended as simultaneous experiences; that is, it was *not* one thought with 10 aspects or ten thoughts quickly in a row. All of these thought/feelings were apprehended to be in her head except the wanting to leave the class, which involved an undifferentiated bodily urge to get up and go as well as a cognitive wanting to leave. Simultaneously, Jessica was feeling a complex nervousness/worry/anxiety that was also undifferentiated but contained all three aspects (nervousness, worry, and anxiety); this feeling included a bodily sensation of her stomach's turning upside down. She also was seeing her teacher in the front of the room. (Hurlburt and Jones-Forrester 2011, 30, italics in original)

Before these DES studies, the existence of fragmented multiplicity in the inner experience of bulimic women was unknown, despite the fact that it was present in all of their subjects with a minimum frequency of above 40 percent of sampled moments. How could this be? Without using a method well suited to the challenges inherent in exploring inner experience, neither subjects nor researchers are likely have a clear apprehension of inner experience. If in fact inner experience is important, more investigations of pristine inner experience using a method well suited to the task are needed.

Note

I would like to thank Russell Hurlburt for his comments on this paper.

References

Atkinson, R. C. and Shiffrin, R. M. 1968. "Human Memory: A Proposed System and Its Control Processes." In *The Psychology of Learning and Motivation*, vol. 2, edited by K. W. Spence and J. T. Spence, 89–195. New York: Academic Press.

Csikizentmihalyi, M. and Larson, R. 1987. "Validity and Reliability of the Experience-Sampling Method." *Journal of Nervous & Mental Disease* 175: 526–36.

Davison, G. C., Navarre, S. G., and Vogel, R. S. 1995. "The Articulated Thoughts in Simulated Situations Paradigm: A Think-Aloud Approach to Cognitive Assessment." *Current Directions in Psychological Science* 4: 29–33.

Doucette, S. 1992. "Sampling the Inner Experience of Bulimic and Other Individuals." Unpublished master's thesis, University of Nevada, Las Vegas.

Doucette, S. and Hurlburt, R. T. 1993a. "A Bulimic Junior High School Teacher." In *Sampling Inner Experience in Disturbed Affect*, edited by R. T. Hurlburt, 139–52. New York: Plenum Press.

_____. 1993b. "Inner Experience in Bulimia." In *Sampling Inner Experience in Disturbed Affect*, edited by R. T. Hurlburt, 153–63. New York: Plenum Press.

Giorgi, A. 1975. "An Application of Phenomenological Method in Psychology." In *Duquesne Studies in Phenomenological Psychology, II*, edited by A. Giorgi, C. Fischer, and E. Murray, 82–103. Pittsburgh, PA: Duquesne University Press.

_____. 1989. "Learning and Memory from the Perspective of Phenomenological Psychology." In *Existential-Phenomenological Perspectives in Psychology*, edited by R. S. Valle and S. Halling, 99–112. New York: Plenum Press.

_____. 1997. "The Theory, Practice, and Evaluation of the Phenomenological Method as a Qualitative Research Procedure." *Journal of Phenomenological Psychology* 28: 181–205.

Heavey, C. L. and Hurlburt, R. T. 2008. "The Phenomena of Inner Experience." *Consciousness and Cognition* 17: 798–810.

Heavey, C. L., Hurlburt, R. T., and Lefforge, N. L. 2010. "Descriptive Experience Sampling: A Method for Exploring Momentary Inner Experience." *Qualitative Research in Psychology*, 7: 345–68.

Hurlburt, R. T. 1990. *Sampling Normal and Schizophrenic Inner Experience*. New York: Plenum Press.

_____. 1993. *Sampling Inner Experience in Disturbed Affect*. New York: Plenum Press.

_____. 2009. "Iteratively Apprehending Pristine Inner Experience." *Journal of Consciousness Studies* 16: 156–88.

_____. 2011a. *Investigating Pristine Inner Experience: Moments of Truth*. New York: Cambridge University Press.

_____. 2011b. "Descriptive Experience Sampling, the Explicitation Interview, and Pristine Experience: In Response to Froese, Gould, & Seth." *Journal of Consciousness Studies* 18, no. 2: 65–78.

Hurlburt, R. T. and Akhter, S. A. 2006. "The Descriptive Experience Sampling Method." *Phenomenology and the Cognitive Sciences* 5: 271–301.

_____. 2008. "Unsymbolized Thinking." *Consciousness and Cognition* 17: 1364–74.

Hurlburt, R. T. and Heavey, C. L. 2001. "Telling What We Know: Describing Inner Experience." *Trends in Cognitive Sciences* 5: 400–403.

_____. 2002. "Interobserver Reliability of Descriptive Experience Sampling." *Cognitive Therapy and Research* 26: 135–42.

_____. 2006a. *Exploring Inner Experience: The Descriptive Experience Sampling Method*. Philadelphia, PA: John Benjamins Publishing.

_____. 2006b. *Descriptive Experience Sampling Codebook Manual of Terminology*. http://faculty.unlv.edu/hurlburt/codebook.html (accessed May 12, 2011).

Hurlburt, R. T., Heavey, C. L., and Bensaheb, A. 2009. "Sensory Awareness." *Journal of Consciousness Studies* 16: 231–51.

Hurlburt, R. T., Heavey, C. L. and Seibert, T. 2006. "Psychological Science's Prescriptions for Accurate Reports about Inner Experience." In *Exploring Inner Experience: The Descriptive Experience Sampling Method,* edited by R. T. Hurlburt and C. L. Heavey, 41–60. Amsterdam: John Benjamins Publishing.

Hurlburt, R. T. and Jones-Forrester, S. 2011. "Fragment Experience in Bulimia Nervosa." In *Investigating Pristine Inner Experience: Moments of Truth,* edited by R. T. Hurlburt, 28–48. New York: Cambridge University Press.

Hurlburt, R. T. and Raymond, N. 2011. "Agency: A Case Study in Bracketing Presuppositions." *Journal of Consciousness Studies* 18: 295–305.

Hurlburt, R. T. and Schwitzgebel, E. 2007. *Describing Inner Experience.* Cambridge, MA: MIT Press.

_____. 2011. "Presuppositions and Background Assumptions." *Journal of Consciousness Studies* 18: 206–33.

Husserl, E. 1960. *Cartesian Meditations: An Introduction to Phenomenology,* trans. D. Cairns. The Hague: Martinus Nijhoff.

Jones-Forrester, S. 2006. "Inner Experience in Bulimia." Unpublished master's thesis, University of Nevada, Las Vegas.

_____. 2009. "Descriptive Experience Sampling of Individuals with Bulimia Nervosa." Unpublished doctoral dissertation, University of Nevada, Las Vegas.

Kring, A. 1999. "Emotions in Schizophrenia." *Current Directions* 8: 160–63.

Kvale, S. 1996. *InterViews: An Introduction to Qualitative Research and Interviewing.* Thousand Oaks, CA: Sage.

Moustakas, C. 1994. *Phenomenological Research Methods.* Thousand Oaks, CA: Sage.

Petitmengin, C. 2006. "Describing One's Subjective Experience in the Second Person: An Interview Method for the Science of Consciousness." *Phenomenology and the Cognitive Sciences* 5: 229–69.

Skinner, B. F. 1974. *About Behaviorism.* New York: Vintage Press.

Stone, A. A. and Shiffman, S. 1994. "Ecological Momentary Assessment (EMA) in Behavioral Medicine." *Annals of Behavioral Medicine* 16: 199–202.

van Manen, M. 1990. *Researching Lived Experience: Human Science for an Action Sensitive Pedagogy.* New York: State University of New York Press.

Watson, D., Clark, L. A., and Tellegen, A. 1988. "Development and Validation of Brief Measure of Positive and Negative Affect: The PANAS Scales." *Journal of Personality and Social Psychology* 54: 1063–70.

Wilson, T. D. 2002. *Strangers to Ourselves: Discovering the Adaptive Unconscious.* Cambridge, MA: Harvard University Press.

7

Multimodal Introspection Theory

Stephen Gould

I have written about introspection and related processes for many years on a very personal level, i.e., grounding what I write and theorize about on my own experience. Here, I demonstrate my experiential approach which includes introspective thought exercises that all readers may try. In this experiential process, we can consider different modes and approaches to introspection and self-observation which challenge established paradigms and suggest that they are defined too narrowly, hence, Multimodal Introspection Theory. In particular, I add nonconceptual consciousness which is perhaps best addressed and engaged via meditative introspection.

Much of consumer research has failed to describe many experiential aspects of my own consumer behavior, especially the everyday dynamics of my pervasive, self-perceived vital energy

—Gould 1991a, 194

I have written about, researched and practiced introspection as an academic for a very long time, on the order of decades. Reflexively the process has not only has advanced my own conceptions and understandings of what introspection is and can be but also has evolved my own self-understanding and insight. Thus, there is an experiential element of practice or praxis as I called it in Gould (1991a) which at the same time is grounded in theory, both a priori as in traditional, experimental research, and more emergently, as in more phenomenological and poststructural perspectives. It is also informed by Eastern meditation and yogic practices from Tibet, India, China and elsewhere. In detailing these aspects, I am aiming at a minimum, to map perspectives on introspection and hopefully more, to provide a coherent if necessarily incomplete theoretical framing which I call Multimodal

Introspection Theory. There are many modes of introspection based on how it is done, including conceptually and nonconceptually, among other perspectives.

In many respects, there are two histories interacting here: the history of introspection (e.g., James 1918; Wheeler 1923) and my personal history of applying it. To some degree my own personal introspection reflects the former but in many respects it grew up independently as I drew on my meditation experiences for much of my development. At times, these two converge in a hermeneutic of going back forth between the two in informing my own thinking and further development of introspection. There are also cultural factors as I mingle East and West in ways that are inextricably tied to my own development and perspectives. I know this may be problematic for many as it is hard for many to break out of the Western mindset enough to grasp the Eastern mindset though this is evolving culturally in what I regard as a positive way. It is not to say that one mindset is correct and another is not but it is to say that to understand what I do with introspection it helps to reflect both Eastern and Western perspectives. In particular, since I have been a meditator for something on the order of forty years, I am able to draw on experience which some have suggested may enable a person to be more skillful in self-observation and introspection (Hurlburt and Heavey 2001).

I have even written of my personal history with introspective research and how people reacted to the introspections and experiences I was relating (Gould 2008a). While as might be expected I recount the controversies surrounding my work, the really important thing for me to is how I took all the critiques and points made and fed them into my introspective stream of consciousness, deepening and enriching it. For example, being compelled to deal with the issues addressed by Nisbett and Wilson (1977) as raised by Wallendorf and Brucks (1993) in relation to my own work led to me further refine the issues of consciousness and to consider the liminality between consciousness and the unconscious so as to reflect on what I could and could not know. Also this gave me a further perspective on training the mind to further observe in ways I might not have thought of before and to extend the introspective project. I do not make claims about this way or that as being the answer to the boundaries of the conscious and unconscious but instead pose ways to explore these issues. In this, I am informed by the scientific approach which is always self-challenging but also by poststructuralism and even deconstruction where meanings are contextual, not fixed, and inherently uncoiling like a snake to reveal nothing being held in its coils.

To account for my approach to introspection in this chapter, I consider different modes or dimensions of introspection as constituting a theoretical or paradigmatic multimodal introspection framework. I first lay out the basic approach I take in defining introspection across disciplines, that is, narrative versus metacognitive introspection. Next, following primarily a metacognitive approach, I ask what can I know and consider basic introspective thought exercises as a tool for such understanding. Following my development of this approach, I consider the idea of the phenomenal versus epiphenomenal in terms of what may seem phenomenal or important to one introspector may not seem so to another. Then, I lay the groundwork for developing multimodal introspective theory and insight by considering hypothesis-testing versus grounded theory introspection. In this context, I then consider extrospective versus introspective observation as well as embodiment. After that, I more fully develop a model for what we can introspect. Going further, I consider a few applications before finally offering some conclusions.

Narrative versus Metacognitive Introspection

I have suggested that introspection has two major disciplinary aspects (Gould 2006). Thus, because of my personal and academic experience reflecting different streams of research, I have accordingly framed introspection in terms of two approaches (Gould 2006, 2008a, 2008b, 2012): (1) narrative introspection which reflects a more qualitative, interpretive approach and (2) metacognitive introspection which encompasses the more experimental, psychological approach. Narrative introspection is the telling of one's own story in one's own words. For example, I can tell you about something that happened to me which may bear on some theoretical topic or even in the work of some characterized as mainly atheoretical, at least in terms of having a priori or deductive hypotheses though maybe having implications of some sort (Brown 2006). The narrative approach has autobiographic aspects in which one tells a story about oneself. It is also sometimes applied from a cultural or ethnographic perspective and called autoethnography (Gould 2012).

Metacognitive introspection involves the following of one's own thoughts, emotions, and sensations. The latter is perhaps more familiar to psychologists since it is the raw material of most scientific psychological research. Not that narrative is unfamiliar to psychologists, especially phenomenological psychologists, but the telling of stories is often a topic for cultural anthropologists, among others. While in some cases it is useful to separate these two, it may also be useful to link them in ways that are not generally done. For example, I can follow my thoughts and feelings over a long period of time and at the same time show how they reflect my story or construct it. Or perhaps most tellingly for thinking about self-observational processes in relation to consciousness and nonconsciousness, introspection with deliberation is a narrative, even if short-lived or moment-to-moment. As described in the metacognitive literature, for instance, there are linked and path-dependent implicit and explicit processes (cf. Dienes and Perner 2002). We become conscious that we became aware step by step, including steps back from consciousness. Then as we become more and more aware, we tell ourselves a story about what we observed (e.g., I saw the table; I observed a thought.). This perspective will be developed further below.

In producing a reflexive focus on one's own awareness and thus self-observing with the metacognitive eye, we can potentially assess and detect whether there are different modes of introspection akin to various modes of perception, including sensory, cognitive, and affective. These can be even more finely grained. For example, the sensory mode can include the usual senses plus proprioception and interoception, as well as an often ignored dimension, our perceived vital energy (Gould 1991a, 1991b, 1993, 1995). We can investigate these modes in terms of such topics as explicit versus implicit aspects and biasing cognitive interferences, and explore where each mode of perception leads in the mind (i.e., whether introspecting constitutes one end point or many).

What Can I Know?

Following Nisbett and Wilson (1977), there has been a trend to critique the conscious-knowing mind which has only been extended by advances in cognitive neuroscience. I do not argue against limits on that mind but instead try to develop what those limits might be and how to best understand them. For example, I may as I have done train myself to be aware of my inner cognitive, affective, and sensory workings in ways that experimental lab work with students cannot possibly capture. Cognitive neuroscience work on mediation, for instance, differentiates experienced mediators from novices or nonmediators (e.g., Manna et al. 2010). What I am suggesting is that one can become a more sensitive introspective instrument; indeed I have personally spent most of my adult life to achieve this goal though I have defined it in terms of meditative introspection or other related terms. While I believe this idea applies to everyone, it is likely that some people will still be better at introspection than others or certainly that individual differences will apply.

One approach to exploring the boundaries of introspective and self-observational processes I have used in my academic writing (Gould 1995a, 1995b, 2006, 2008a, 2008b, 2012), as well as my personal life, applies introspective thought exercises. In deriving these exercises, I am informed mainly by my own direct experience with Eastern meditative practices and such related writings as the work of Tulku (1977) and Norbu (1999). A major contribution of these exercises is to go beyond the state of the field in which academic researchers study or investigate introspection and self-observation for the most part in the abstract in terms of what subjects other than the researcher reveal about themselves. The upshot of this is that what is thought to be ostensibly scientific is only partly so because it ignores evidence solely available to an informed researcher, i.e., his or her own thoughts. While there certainly may be shortcomings as well as advantages to such an approach, such as a small N and accessibility biases of privileging one's own mind, it allows for a rich longitudinal following of one's own awareness in its myriad manifestations and perhaps even more crucial, a training and development of one's own metacognitive mind so as to become more conscious of previously undetectable, nonconscious material. Furthermore, the exercises allow for the possibility of sharing introspective experiences to varying degrees in terms of the substance and methods applied.

While this approach is suggestive of the excavation approach which Wilson and Dunn (2004) critique in terms of ever being able to introspect unconscious material (i.e., digging deeper and then detecting something unconscious), I would indicate that they do not approach the limits of what can be detected because they are not considering various meditative and nonconceptual approaches which work with these "undetectable" processes. This is not to say that there is nothing that is undetectable, just that the boundaries of what can be detected are hardly challenged in traditional approaches such as that of Wilson and Dunn (2004). For example, when I observe various meditative states which I can only call here "nonconceptual conscious trance," I tread on some boundary condition in which yes I excavated but which I also invoked, provoked, and brought up to my mind. Based on these types of experiences, I have created exercises that anyone can try.

I actually introspect these exercises and offer them for others to try so as to make my ideas clear experientially as well as conceptually. It also provides for an expansion beyond thought to watching feelings and sensations as related to thought. In this regard such exercises provide a basis of discursive or "talking" points for further theoretical development and thought unlike any other research tool. We all self-observe and hopefully somewhere along the line we inform our research and draw on it in further discourse and community development. Here, I present a basic introspective thought exercise derived from meditative techniques which you the reader can try and which will form the basis for further development below. I start with watching our thoughts. Then later in the chapter we build on this approach to further develop introspective theory and insight.

Basic Thought-Watching Exercise. Watch your thoughts as they arise. Make no effort to govern them or be attached to their content. Just notice them arising. You can do this for as long as you like. You might try an alternative to focus on your breath, watching your breath as it goes in and out. Also you can do this as a longitudinal experience so as to break it up but also to become more familiar with it as a kind of training. People often meditate on their thoughts and/or breath as a regular practice.

There is also the idea of the watcher self, that is, the self that watches the watching or introspecting self. Try taking a step back and watch who is watching your thoughts. Often this may seem like an infinite regress of watching selves. You can explore that way at times or just simplify with one self watching your watching mind. You might also tie this in as an exercise to what Josipovic (2010, 1120) refers to as "subject-observing-object." Does thinking about oneself as subject and object constitute the same process as the watcher self, especially with infinite regress or not? Suggestive of later discussion in this chapter, is there something beyond this dualistic view such as no self to be found?

You can try the same thing with emotions and sensations. Focus on them and watch how they go. Do you become more familiar with them than you were before? Do you detect them in ways you previously did not? Do you detect sensations and emotions or emotional qualities you did not before? Does this correspond to embodied self-reflexivity

(Pagis 2009) in which you engage in a hermeneutic exchange with yourself? Does this meaning of your perceptions change with this perspective?

This exercise is the basis for further explorations of what we can introspect and for investigating self-observational processes. Hopefully, you have begun to see and experience that metacognitively knowing is a process rather than an end-point. It is constantly in flux. In the next section, with this exercise in mind and drawing on my own personal experience with it, I will suggest how we can model what we introspect.

Modeling What Can We Introspect

Echoing earlier work by Nisbett and Wilson (1977) and others, Wilson and Dunn (2004) frame the discussion of introspection in terms self-knowledge and what one could or could not detect. They further surmise the opposition of a Freudian architectural metaphor for digging down deeper into consciousness versus "The more contemporary view . . . that the vast adaptive unconscious is dissociated from conscious awareness and can never be directly viewed via introspection" (505; cf. Epstein 1994 on the cognitive unconscious). I realize that applying this framing, I have a different view that first requires me to deconstruct the view of Wilson and Dunn. It would be difficult to counter the view that there is much that is unconscious, implicit, and undetectable by introspection in everyday consciousness. In fact, I have no intent to do that—I find the evidence for that premise quite strong though as I argue above there is training one can do to become a better introspector and more aware of seemingly nonconscious material, including meditative training which is not considered by Wilson and Dunn. However, we really need to understand what introspection and self-knowledge mean.

Introspection and self-knowledge as used by Wilson and Dunn, among others, refer to conceptual mind. Can conceptual mind detect the many unconscious effects that research says it cannot? No, because these are two different orders of function, defined, for instance, as the rational versus experiential systems view (Epstein 1994). Thus, when Wilson and Dunn argue that introspection as they frame it is a conscious-conceptual process, it can only detect like phenomena. So it is likely true that it cannot detect unconscious or most, if not all less conscious phenomena. Likewise, self-knowledge as they discuss it has similar problems since it is enchained in conceptualization. However,

127

framing the issue in this conceptual way ignores what I call meditative introspection involving nonconceptual mind.

It is instructive in this regard, for instance, that Schooler (2011) has directly linked introspection to contemplative practices, albeit only in acknowledgment of a relationship and not by addressing nonconceptuality. It is also useful to note that like ideas, including nondual awareness, also open awareness, open presence or nonconceptual awareness, have been advanced (Josipovic 2010; Kohenevikov et al. 2009; Lutz et al. 2007). This means that introspection of this type might detect phenomena that the more conceptual mind, even one engaged in conceptual forms of meditation (e.g., imagining or visualizing something with attention) would not. Likewise, self-knowledge might be expanded to fuller, more spacious boundaries in which less conscious phenomena are detected and brought to awareness. But this is without conception or intentional direction though conceptual readings of what is happening will occur. For example, Travis and Shear (2010) discuss a prior study of TM mediators who in response to a question to describe their experiences like they were describing the taste of a strawberry reported on something akin to, if not being nondual awareness while admittedly skirting the boundaries of the conceptual and nonconceptual. Consider the following exercise to illustrate.

Meditative Exercise. As an exercise you might try this with or without formal meditation. Sit quietly and observe. Then at points observe or describe what you experienced as akin to tasting a strawberry. By the way it is hard to describe the taste of a strawberry, isn't it? Then going further sit and observe aspects of the three themes reported by Travis and Shear (2010): absence of space, absence of time, and absence of bodily sense. Try describing each of these. For instance, what does the absence of space entail? No self? No boundaries? What remains? Is there still a you? Or something akin to you but not you?

I am suggesting therefore something quite different from other understandings and practices of introspection—it is nonconceptual consciousness which is the key element while it is conceptual consciousness which interferes with or blocks insight. This may rise to constitute a different paradigm from the usual consciousness/nonconsciousness one. In this case, we need to consider what the nature of the relationship is among at least three modes of mind: (1) conceptual consciousness, (2) nonconsciousness, and (3) nonconceptual consciousness. For instance, one idea is that consciousness is cognitive, about something and explicitly held in mind. Nonconsciousness may be held in mind to varying degrees but is implicit and below the level of consciousness. Nonconceptual consciousness reflects some elements of both perhaps in that it involves explicit awareness but not in the usual conceptual sense. For example, I experience my body in space without thinking about it or translating it to my conscious mind—I taste the strawberry. This could be said to be nonconscious or less conscious in that there is no conceptual awareness, but it is not unconscious. For our minds schooled in the two-way notion of consciousness, this is an alien idea, almost unfathomable.

As a paramorphic, intellectual idea, it can certainly be understood. But as an everyday experience, it is less recognizable, if it is perceived at all. Even if perceived, it may also be seen as epiphenomenal—what do we do with it? Yet, since it is an accessible element of some forms of meditation, we need to consider it if we want to develop full theories of consciousness and introspection. There is an element where we statically describe introspective processes and we dynamically experience them. This might be likened in certain aspects to research in decision making where decisions vary by whether they are made from descriptions or experiences (Hertwig et al. 2004). To be sure both modes may have their biases or misleading effects but to ignore the experiential mode is to miss much that may have relevance to understanding introspection.

The architectural digging metaphor might be retooled as well since digging here may mean digging into processes by applying meditative means that penetrate into less and or completely nonconceptual material. The tools for such digging may be many from using a random shovel to see what is there to a more laser-like tool with a sharp focus for detecting phenomena. By the "random shovel" I mean paying attention or be called to attention by some signal in the midst of everyday life (e.g., Hurlburt and Heavey 2001). A more laser-like tool might be developed by moving away from notions of continuity to noting perceptions on a moment-to-moment basis such as discussed by Engler (2003). In this regard, things come and go, thereby passing by in ways that we can regard the unconscious and conscious mind in ways that are more discontinuous and suspend at least some dimensions of conscious blocking.

The architectural model as characterized by Wilson and Dunn (2004) may have its limitations but at the same time the best excavations suggested by it remain to be done, at least in academic research. The view here is that Wilson and Dunn are no doubt correct about many aspects of the unconscious not being susceptible to "conscious introspection" but we need to be a bit circumspect in how we apply such terminologies and methods. There are things that are undreamed of in their formulation that are perhaps capable of being revealed with a different approach. Just as consciousness may interfere with judgment as some research suggests (e.g., Wilson and Dunn 2004) so a misunderstanding of consciousness and introspection may interfere with comprehending their possibilities.

We need to consider the translation process which goes on between the nonconceptual and conceptual minds (Epstein 1994; Schultheiss and Brunstein 1999). To some degree some meditative practices do take given cues as signs of some less conscious process. In this case, the conceptualizing of any practice becomes like a finger pointing out something but it is not the actual thing. Another metaphor is a reflection of an object in water or a mirror; again it is not the object itself. For instance, if I practice visualizing a meditational deity as is done in Buddhism and it appears more clearly and vividly, then I must be doing something right. The original image I may see in a picture points to my visualization. This is also akin to hypotheses-driven introspection in that I had some idea of what I wanted do and then tested whether I could do it. But then suppose I meditate and see some things I have never seen before such as lights or visions. Maybe again I am doing something right, but the translation is not quite the same as in the first case. Here, depending on what I thought beforehand, I have a more grounded theory introspection in terms of being more open-ended in what I set out to do.

Pagis (2009, 265) suggests that reflexivity grounded in meditation is not discursive but involves self-knowledge which "is anchored in bodily sensations." Along these lines she distinguishes discursive self-reflexivity (involving language) from embodied reflexivity (feeling the body). Her work (Pagis 2009, 2010) is a move in the direction I would like us to consider: as in her quotes from Damasio (1999) and others (Pagis 2009), she looks to other intervening nonverbal, somatic levels which register reflexively in some manner of consciousness and may not require verbalization. This I would suggest involves some sort of presence and attention often applied in meditation though it may not be necessary to be in a meditative state or at least a formal one to engage in this presence. A difference here is that what she reports is largely retrospective. Here, we can explore this presence, somatic or otherwise, through experiential introspective exercises in our own online, real-time dimension. We can approach the theoretical question of whether we can archeologically dig into some further aspects of consciousness/unconsciousness or whether everything that is apparently hidden to consciousness is all hidden or to the contrary is at least somewhat capable of being revealed. Consider the next section where we can weigh what is epiphenomenal or phenomenal, for instance.

The Epiphenomenal versus Phenomenal

What one experiences as happening and meaningful, i.e., phenomenal, may be seen by others either to not happen or be a meaningless part of experience, i.e., epiphenomenal. For example, if I see lights as visions am I seeing something that has no meaning apart from brain physiology or am I seeing something meaningful in terms of yogic or meditational experience? Contextual framing in terms of experience and culture makes a difference in this regard and people have different views of what matter is and the material world (Gould 1992). I have found that this is a crucial issue for all social science research, especially regarding introspection and self-observation, since many, if not all theories are grounded in embodiment and there are different sensibilities with respect to that embodiment. I feel embodied in my vital energy and related channels, for instance, and find that how I work with these is virtually ignored in most researcher venues. Still, a person may still be able to understand the experience as described though she may not experience it herself directly (Gould 1991a; Thompson 1990). At least, that would constitute an intellectualized paramorphic starting point for inquiry. Then perhaps through experiential thought exercises one might be able to develop some experiential insight. If one continues over time for many of the phenomena, one might deepen this experience.

Phenomenological–Epiphenomenological Exercise. Going back to basic watching, watch your sensations and energy level. Notice how a feeling corresponds to a bodily locale(s). Beyond watching, try sending warm energy to different locales. What do you experience? Is this something meaningful or is it just something we are noticing here. Can it be used to heal your body or mind in some way? I would suggest it can but you must develop the context yourself to make it a meaningful phenomenon for you. I can describe how I use such strands of this exercise in my own life but it is up to you if interested to take it to that level for yourself. Otherwise, it is merely epiphenomenal. You might even experience some of the same energy feelings or sensations but they may have no meaning to you. They are "real," that is, you can notice them if you are made aware but without the context, they are as nothing to you. If there is a sound in the forest but no one is there to hear it, the proverbial claim is that it is not a sound. In the present case, you might even "hear" it (feel it) but still attach no meaning to it.

The importance of this epiphenomenal–phenomenal issue cannot be underestimated. Indeed, I expect recognition of this issue to constitute a greater research and social trend and theme over our lifetimes and beyond. I believe it is because much research stops where some individuals might begin in terms of awareness and consciousness, especially those who meditate. Thus, the very limits of introspection as posed in the history of Western research might have been stymied by a lack of meditative and related awareness tools to work with. It is difficult for me to imagine writing and introspecting the way I do without meditative training and perspective. This could turn solipsistic except that much of what I am saying is backed by a broad cultural paradigm in Asia where centuries of inner development of awareness has held sway. This is constituted in practices of mediation, outer and inner yogas, lucid dreaming, healing practices, and more where inner experiences are obtained that otherwise would not be possible or even perceived as possible. Western thought, science, and practice are now recognizing at least of these phenomena which bodes well for further theoretical development. At a minimum, some formerly epiphenomenal matters (e.g., lucid dreams, various meditative states) are coming to be recognized as meaningful phenomena. In the next section, I further explore how these and other introspective matters might be investigated.

Hypothesis-Testing versus Grounded Theory Introspection

To apply what we have explored thus far in terms of modeling introspective processes and what I have touched on earlier, I posit two general forms of research introspection which can be applied: (1) hypothesis-testing introspection and (2) grounded theory introspection. Hypothesis-testing introspection means that the researcher deductively has a hypothesis that she wants to test on herself. This is akin to the scientific method though many might still take issue with the validity of it. An interesting analogous example concerning self-observation comes from Roberts (2004) who engaged in self-experimentation. Not only is his work of singular interest in its own right but the accompanying published comments on it serve to illustrate the issues of validity many might raise (cf. Gould 1995a). Grounded theory introspection means that the researcher watches what happens introspectively and then inductively reflecting upon it builds theory. Grounded theory research is an approach often employed in qualitative research in which theory is constructed from the grounded observations made by a researcher. It shares with the deductive method in its usual application, the quality of being extrospective (or outwardly focused—see also the next section) though perhaps a bit more recognition might be given by at least some researchers to the "subjective" but necessary involvement of the researcher in everything from the data collection process to data analysis and interpretation.

The process by which these all come together usually involves a hermeneutic in which the researcher goes back and forth between various interpretive elements, including the data, one's own interpretations, and prior research and thought. While I pose both of these types of introspection for consideration, this is not to say they are fixed, separate entities but instead may be used together in various combinations and fashions. One simple way might be to try hypothesis-testing introspection and then as it manifests, observe elements that emerge. These emergent elements might be likened to a grounded theory introspection process since they were not necessarily conceived beforehand. Consider the following exercise.

Intended Hypothesis Testing Thoughts versus Grounded Thoughts Exercise. As an exercise, play with watching thoughts as consciously versus unconsciously determined phenomena. Ask yourself and notice when thoughts emerge, how they do so, and how you may explicitly intend or not intend them (i.e., think them into consciousness versus just watch them). Focus on something intentionally such as a visualization or a problem to solve. Notice how you can change versus how thoughts arise on their own in relation to it. Try and focus your thought as much as possible on that problem or visualization. What seems to be explicit or implicit as you are thinking? Can you let these thoughts go and observe in a nonconceptual way? This does not mean necessarily to attempt to block thoughts though that can be a useful part of this exercise to try at times. Rather observe and let thoughts go without being distracted by them. This is hard to do but worth exploring for theoretical insight and constitutes a grounded theory approach in which concepts eventually emerge in your translating mind (translating experience into concepts however imperfect that might be) that may well differ from your and our prior understandings.

Embodiment and Introspective versus Extrospective Observation

Further theoretical insight can be gained by examining whether and how we focus inwardly introspectively or outwardly extrospectively as another aspect of both one's own personal psychology and also our collective academic researcher stance (Gould 1993). Let us explore the first personal aspect as an exercise.

Extrospective–Introspective Exercise. Notice your focus inward or outward as a matter of course. This involves inductive grounded theory introspection in that you observe without intention or direction though you may see patterns and/or reach conclusions based on these introspections. You can try this sitting and reflecting or as you go through the day. For instance, do you focus more on your surroundings, the people around you or your own feelings, and/or thoughts? When does one or the other aspect seem to command more of your attention? Do the boundaries between you and the outer world blur?

Now work more intentionally. This can be more deductive hypothesis-driven introspection in which you have certain ideas about what might happen and then see if they do (e.g., observing situations, conducting research). The emergent aspects may be more inductive so the boundaries between inductive and deductive may blur. Focus inwardly or outwardly one at a time by choice and intentional direction.

Regarding research stance, it is apparent reflecting on introspection and its history that the stance taken is extrospective and away from the researcher. The idea is that science needs to be free of the subjective observer, i.e., being objective and partialing out the researcher. We can deconstruct this view from several points of view. For instance, there are various formulations of the psychophysiological, embodied, and grounded dimensions of cognition. Here, compare a simulated experience to an actual experience. Following Barsalou (2008), such simulations are said to be partial recreations at best with biases in their construction. Let us follow this further.

Extending the Extrospective–Introspective Perspective Exercise. Look at the scene or something, in particular, in front of you. Stare intently. Then close your eyes. Notice how much similar or different that after image is to what you saw. Then a little later (eyes open or closed) try recreating that image in your mind. Again, notice how similar or different that image is to both the actual image and the after image. Try changing it as well. How does changing it affect your perception of it?

Is the object really internal or external (i.e., external to your mind or other parts of it)? Admittedly, there may be difficulties in doing this but play with it and adjust accordingly.

That exercise assumed that the extrospective view, i.e., looking outward and then seeing what registered in the mind, is the dominant perspective at least in terms of experience. But suppose now what amounts to simulation in the prior exercise is actually the experience. It has an introspective focus from the beginning.

The Inner as Extrospective. Focus on and feel some part of your body. For example, you can focus on your head, heart area, stomach, or genital region to name but a few places. For now you just feel that area. Perhaps you could also visualize something there such as light if you wish. Now notice what it is like to engage in extrospective-outward versus introspective-inward focus. Look outside at the world with your eyes completely open. Observe what you see, feel, smell, and hear. Now with eyes still open focus inwardly. Again, observe what you see, feel, smell, and hear. How do the two experiences compare? Finally in this exercise, close your eyes and observe what you see, feel, smell, and hear. How is this experience similar to or different from the other two? Try introspecting or thinking under these different conditions. How clear is your thinking? How much is cognitively overloaded or unclear?

Playing introspectively with our mind this way allows us to ponder the extent of embodied embedded cognition in which body and external world contribute to cognition along with the brain (van Dijk et al. 2008; cf. Barsalou 2008 on grounded cognition). We may in fact speak of embodied embedded introspection in which the extrospective perceptions and senses of the external world interact with our body–mind continuum as we introspect. Indeed, can we determine the boundaries where introspection and extrospection begin and end? This expands our notion of introspection beyond the amodal mental–brain aspect to many other dimensions.

A Few Related Issues and Applications Informed by Introspection

The view of introspection given in this chapter may allow for the investigation of a number of issues in ways that had not been considered before. Here to illustrate I consider: introspecting on the self, introspection as a tool for self-fashioning and development, and the controversy over thinking aloud.

What Is the Self? The self is a central construct in psychology. Introspection can help us to deconstruct this construct so as to further to penetrate its meaning and what it is. Building in part on earlier introspective thought exercises such as that involving the watcher self, I pose a traditional Buddhist exercise which introspectively deals with the self or no-self. In my adaptation of it, I consider issues of explicitness and implicitness. We assume a self. Buddhists argue there is a conventional self which we label and recognize in everyday life. This self is functional—I am Steve and people everyday deal with me that way. It is not ignorable because it has real consequences. We experience and we take action. However, let us examine further and see what the self is.

What Is the Self Exercise? When we look introspectively and explicitly, we are following a Buddhist practice: look for the self in all parts of our bodies and mind. Is the self in our heart for instance? Is it in our arms? Is it in our minds? Is the self to be found in the whole of us? Nowhere do find something that we can inherently identify as self. It is neither the parts nor the sum of its parts. Try focusing on these questions one at a time. A similar approach can be applied to other people and objects. The self is empty and does not exist inherently or in any "real" way. This is the Buddhist traditional approach and follows an explicit path as well in that we are searching our consciousness of what we are and seeing if there is anything we can label as self.

What about an implicit self? You can observe if something like this operates. When you have dreams, for instance, you are the center of most, if not all of them. We automatically speak of I or me most of the time. Does this mean we have an automatic self? Is this a real self or can it be deconstructed like the more explicit self? How is this self constructed in the first place? Do we automatically construct a self which as we develop, we reflexively translate into conceptualization and language? That is, does this phenomenon of centering on whomever or whatever we are or seem to be only arise as a self in conceptualization? We could apply IAT methods to show how the self or at least awareness of what we perceive as self arises automatically in response to any number of cues? But does this mean the self is not constructed or is it merely another form of construction? What is the watcher self in this context? Is there an abstraction such that if we took this self-centering phenomenon and placed it in different contexts, cultures, or situations, we could then specify whether it would be the same or different?

Introspection as a Tool for Self-Fashioning and Development. Thus far we have considered introspection and related practices as aspects of being or becoming self-aware. This implies that we can discover what is already there to be aware of if we only could. However, a further stage seems possible. This involves self-fashioning or working with one's mind to develop oneself and produce a new phenomenology in one's life in very conscious ways as a way of self-realization (Gould and Stinerock 1992). For example, I might observe my thinking and feeling in various locales or situations and try not only to observe it but transform the whole experience. Thus, I might watch how a person or movie energizes or enervates me and use that experience to learn to self-regulate my energy. Recent work with exercises in positive psychology has a few encouraging echoes of this (e.g., Schueller 2010), but that is still largely rooted in conceptual-centered mind and does not at least as yet embrace the fuller perspective of energetic or meditative introspection. This means for me that working with the mind through various introspective and meditative processes such as mindfulness, one can enhance or change one's own mind, both physically and mentally. The physical is perhaps the more astonishing but nonetheless research such as that provided by Hözel et al. (2011) has shown that mindfulness meditation increases gray matter density in the brain. When we consider embodied embedded cognition or embodied embedded introspection, this may expand our sense of it.

Through meditative introspection, I feel like a different person, one transformed. I feel a spaciousness and calm that I relate very specifically to watching my mind, calming it when necessary. An important point is that this is a chronic process. Not only does it involve training and experience but there are synergistic effects that other research approaches may not uncover because they generally cannot follow people longitudinally in this way. I have metacognitively engaged in meditative introspection everyday for many years and then have narratively observed myself and now tell my story to you. In this process, I both introspect as a practice of self-fashioning and I introspect and observe this practice as a research discipline. While the former is more important and dominant, the two intersect in ever-evolving synergies. When I take a research stance, it provides an informing and framing perspective on my practice.

Thinking Aloud. Thinking aloud has recently been treated as a controversial topic in relation to introspection. Schooler (2011) lays out how thinking aloud has introspective properties while Ericsson and

Fox (2011) claim that it is a different method from introspection. The issue turns on reactivity. Defining introspection as reactivity (changes in accuracy of performance as they define it) or at least as necessarily involving it is a limiting way to characterize it. For example, to say that planning or explaining something in thinking aloud rules out introspection as Ericsson and Fox do labors under the misapprehension of what introspection is from the start. I will not repeat Schooler's objections with which I mostly agree in questioning whether thinking aloud or all of it is nonreactive. (I would also reiterate his linking of the introspection-talking aloud domain to contemplative practices which is of course where I develop my introspective insight to begin with.)

But I will go further to suggest considering monitoring processes in which one watches what one is thinking and saying along a continuum of reactivity from none to total or some such. These processes of monitoring and thinking aloud will go on simultaneously. Whether and how such monitoring changes what is said is an open question and whether they are entirely different or shared modes of activity is also of interest. But such monitoring can be thought of as similar to watching thoughts in a grounded theory way without changing them or at least attempting to change them. Deductive or hypothesis-testing introspection is more akin to reactivity. However, further and similar to the idea of inchoate thoughts posed by Schooler, there are subtle processes which may be going on. For example, there is a self speaking and a watcher self watching or monitoring what is happening. There may be more or less consciousness, implicitness, or automaticity involved, but it can be and may be tracked by the person thinking aloud. I am going to hazard offering an introspective thought exercise which all of us concerned with this issue might try and then see what we conclude. This exercise combines introspection and thinking aloud together in one formulation.

Thinking Aloud and Introspection Exercise. One approach might be to try introspecting by watching your thoughts and then thinking aloud about them. This in a way is a variation on the old saw that observing something such as your mind changes it, as Schooler also alludes to with respect to William James. See if it does. Who or what monitors your thoughts when you say them? Does the process make you inattentive or do you become hypnotized so you speak your thoughts without watching? Is there a monitor or watcher self that is always or most of the time present? Does it capture inchoate cognitions and feelings?

Again ask yourself and notice when thoughts emerge, how they do so and how you may explicitly intend or not intend them (i.e., think them into consciousness versus just watching them). What seems to be explicit or implicit as you continue thinking aloud or just thinking?

Now let us consider some variations such as someone else being present or you record speaking aloud for yourself or someone else to listen to. Does this change your reactivity? Does impression management or self-consciousness enter in at some level such as in the form of the watcher self? This part of the exercise is particularly important since thinking aloud is a research tool conducted with subject and researcher. How do the two (thinking aloud alone and with or for another) differ assuming they do? How does the watching or monitoring process work?

Before we reach any conclusions about thinking loud and introspection, we should explore in this way. Watching thoughts may provide a specific way to apply or test thinking aloud. In this case, we can move beyond ourselves as research introspectors to conducting larger research studies of multiple subjects combining introspection and thinking aloud in various designs and formats. I also want to speak to the issue of the ineffable raised in the debate of Ericsson and Fox versus Schooler. In my application of introspection as being nonconceptual as well as conceptual (involving thought as in standard definitions of introspection), I find that the ineffable can be introspected, it just may not be verbalized but one is nonetheless aware of it. I would conclude therefore that while the focus on reactivity in this debate may have its uses, awareness may be the central point. To what degree is a person thinking aloud aware and what are they aware of?

Related, for instance, is the issue of hypnotic states which I find may be related to thinking aloud. I have been hypnotized and also often observe hypnotic or trance-like states in which my conscious awareness slips. But this does not necessarily mean that introspection or thought watching are not in play, at least for many trance-like states. For example, what about chanting a mantra out loud as is common in many Asian meditation practices? One may experience varying degrees of awareness or trance-like states. I have experienced such things in my own mediation practice. For instance, I may be more or less conscious of saying the mantra or I may be more or less conscious of the feelings they induce or I may be more or less conscious of the mantra's words, syllables or letters or I may get something akin to "high." Perhaps everyday singing might be explored in this regard as well.

The point is that there are many stages (e.g., inchoate, well formed, cf. Schooler's discussion of transitory aspects) and states of introspected or metacognitive awareness that should not be ignored. Nor is my formulation of the problem to ignore the implicit side of things which Ericsson and Fox seem to be getting at. Rather I think there is a complex network of implicit and explicit processes all occurring simultaneously which need to be explicated and explored. Thus, I also think that Ericsson and Fox's (2011) linking of thinking-aloud data to psychophysiological tools such as latencies, functional magnetic resonance imaging, or heart rate is largely, if not completely misleading. To the degree that thinking aloud involves "pure" nonconsciousness if indeed it does at all, they may have a point, but I find much more compelling the links of talking aloud to such consciousness inducing or altering tools (methods if you will) as hypnosis, meditation, mantra chanting, and in fact anything that induces flow states. These much better allow for the joint consideration of implicit and explicit processes. Joint use of psychological and consciousness altering tools would also be very useful, provided the research does not operate in a reductionist, nonexperiential mode.

Finally as shown in this discussion of thinking aloud and introspecting, I suspect that theorizing and exploring this way, our understanding of these two seemingly separate approaches, thinking aloud and introspection, will change quite a bit. Moreover, this method of watching thoughts and other self-phenomena such as feelings and the "ineffable" may serve as a model for other controversies involving introspection and (non)consciousness as well. Bringing actual introspection into introspective processes could be most useful.

Conclusions

In this chapter, I pose applications of introspection which while reflecting the past history of its use in Western psychology, also represent the implications of my personal encounters with it. Many of these fall in many respects outside that Western domain as often constituted and derive in many respects from Eastern (Asian) psychology. Because of this enlarged perspective I have often claimed at least to myself that I was more scientific than those who called themselves scientists in terms of scientific method because their observational limitations were always apparent to me. The main aspect of this perspective is that introspection and, in particular, reflections on consciousness and the unconscious, are not mere paramorphic representations or abstractions but instead involve my very real experiences with meditation and related psychophysiological tools such as yoga and chi gung. This is not to say that there could not be such representations, but that in the holistic experience of consciousness, its dynamic nature and ever-evolving nature problematizes any fixed notions even as our closure-oriented, research mind seeks them. This is not unlike the research into effects of introspection where it is thought to interfere with self-insight or effective decisions (Nisbett and Wilson 1977; Wilson and Dunn 2004). However, it may be important to consider what we are introspecting. If we limit ourselves to the current paradigm, we may miss some important elements of introspective extensions of consciousness.

Introspection also should not be regarded as amodal, but instead has many modes, types, or subtypes that may be considered. As noted out at the outset, I label this phenomenon, Multimodal Introspection Theory. Elsewhere I have described Consumer Introspection Theory (Gould 2012) which developed introspection in terms of a host of interdisciplinary methods which also included various autoethnographic approaches. Here, I want to emphasize more the psychological modes of introspection though not excluding the others. The most important modal distinction I consider is conceptual versus nonconceptual introspection. There are also modes of activity, based on a grounded theory versus hypothesis-driven approaches, such as monitoring and watching versus intending some mind process. Also there are embodied and sensory as well as thought dimensions so that introspecting on the body and mind may be different. Consider the interoceptive and proprioceptive senses for instance. When I consider extrospection versus introspection, one might also think of embodied embedded cognition or what I develop into embodied embedded introspection. For example, cultural neurophenomenology might speak to issues of how neuroscience, culture, and personal experience as introspected might function to inform our understanding of consciousness (Laughlin and Throop 2006). Everything from cognitive neuroscience to thought exercises may allow us to consider these different forms of introspection and the ways they function, whether similarly or differently.

Thus, I have tried in this chapter to establish a different footing for introspection and self-observation, one grounded in a variety of thought, embodied and meditative experiences which attempt to plumb the depths of conscious and unconscious processes. This constitutes a dynamic exercise, one which is meant to provide a path for further theoretical development and study, rather than one grounded in a fixed, paramorphic framework. One major facet of this dynamic is that based on my own introspective experiences I have suggested ways for others to engage with them and over time comment on and study them in their own way. This is meant to be a hermeneutic, revelatory endeavor in which we go back and forth among each other and with others outside our immediate circle(s) to investigate what we are finding and saying.

References

Barsalou, L. W. 2008. "Grounded Cognition." *Annual Review of Psychology* 59: 617–45.

Brown, S. 2006. "Autobiography." In *Handbook of Qualitative Methods in Marketing*, edited by R. W. Belk, 440–52. Cheltenham, UK: Edward Elgar Publishing Limited.

Damasio, A. 1999. *The Feeling of What Happens: Body and Emotion in the Making of Consciousness.* San Diego, CA: Harcourt.

Dienes, Z. and Perner, J. 2002. "The Metacognitive Implications of the Implicit-Explicit Distinction." In *Metacognition: Process, Function and Use*, edited by P. Chambres, M. Izaute, and P. -J. Marescaux, 171–89. Boston, MA: Kluwer Academic Publishers.

Engler, J. 2003. "Being Somebody and Being Nobody: A Reexamination of the Understanding of Self in Psychoanalysis and Buddhism." In *Psychoanalysis and Buddhism: An Unfolding Dialogue*, edited by J. D. Safran, 35–79. Somerville, MA: Wisdom Publications.

Epstein, S. 1994. "Integration of the Cognitive and Psychodynamic Unconscious." *American Psychologist* 49: 709–24.

Ericsson, K. A. and Fox, M. 2011. "Thinking Aloud Is Not a Form of Introspection but a Qualitatively Different Methodology: Reply to Schooler (2011)." *Psychological Bulletin* 137: 351–54.

Gould, S. J. 1991a. "The Self-Manipulation of My Pervasive, Perceived Vital Energy through Product Use: An Introspective-Praxis Perspective." *Journal of Consumer Research* 18: 194–207.

_____. 1991b. "An Asian Approach to the Understanding of Consumer Energy, Drives and States." In *Research in Consumer Behavior*, vol. 5, edited by E. C. Hirschman, 33–59. Greenwich, CT: JAI.

_____. 1992. "Consumer Materialism as a Multilevel and Individual Difference Phenomenon: An Asian-Based Perspective." In *Meaning, Measure, and Morality of Materialism*, edited by F. Rudmin and M. Richins, 57–62. Provo, UT: Association for Consumer Research.

_____. 1993. "Introspective versus Extrospective Perspectives in Consumer Research: A Matter of Focus." In *Marketing Theory and Applications*, vol. 4, edited by R. Varadarajan and B. Jaworski, 199–200. Chicago, IL: American Marketing Association.

_____. 1995a. "Researcher Introspection as a Method in Consumer Research: Applications, Issues and Implications." *Journal of Consumer Research* 21: 719–22.

_____. 1995b. "The Buddhist Perspective on Business Ethics: Experiential Exercises for Exploration and Practice." *Journal of Business Ethics* 14: 63–70.

_____. 2006. "Unpacking the Many Faces of Introspective Consciousness: A Metacognitive-Poststructuralist Exercise." In *Handbook of Qualitative Research Methods in Marketing*, edited by R. W. Belk, 186–97. Cheltenham, UK: Edward Elgar Publishing Limited.

_____. 2008a. "An Introspective Genealogy of My Introspective Genealogy." *Marketing Theory* 8: 407–24.

_____. 2008b. "Introspection as Critical Marketing Thought, Critical Marketing Thought as Introspection." In *Critical Marketing: Issues in Contemporary Marketing*, edited by M. Tadajewski and D. Brownlie, 311–28. Chichester, UK: John Wiley & Sons.

_____. 2012. "The Emergence of Consumer Introspection Theory (CIT): Introduction to a *JBR* Special Issue." *Journal of Business Research* 65: 453–60.

Gould, S. J. and Stinerock, R. N. 1992. "Self-Fashioning Oneself Cross-Culturally: Consumption as the Determined and the Determining." In *Advances in Consumer Research*, vol. 19, edited by J. Sherry and B. Sternthal, 857–60. Provo, UT: Association for Consumer Research.

Hertwig, R., Barron, G., Weber, E. U., and Erev, I. 2004. "Decisions from Experience and the Effect of Rare Events in Risky Choice." *Psychological Science* 15: 534–39.

Hözel, B. K., Carmody, J., Vangel, M., Congleton, C., Yerramsetti, S. M., Tim Gard, T., and Lazar, S. W. 2011. "Mindfulness Practice Leads to Increases in Regional Brain Gray Matter Density." *Psychiatry Research: Neuroimaging* 191: 36–43.

Hurlburt, R. T. and Heavey, C. L. 2001. "Telling What We Know: Describing Inner Experience." *Trends in Cognitive Science* 5: 400–403.

James, W. 1918. *The Principles of Psychology*. New York: Holt.

Josipovic, Z. 2010. "Duality and Nonduality in Meditation Research." *Consciousness and Cognition* 19: 1119–21.

Kohenevikov, M., Louchakova, O., Josipovic, Z., and Motes, M. A. 2009. "The Enhancement of Visuospatial Processing Efficiency through Buddhist Deity Meditation." *Psychological Science* 20: 645–53.

Laughlin, C. D. and Throop, C. J. 2006. "Cultural Neurophenomenology: Integrating Experience, Culture and Reality through Fisher Information." *Culture & Psychology* 12: 305–37.

Lutz, A., Brefczynski-Lewis, J., Johnstone, T., and Davidson, R. J. 2008. "Regulation of the Neural Circuitry of Emotion by Compassion Meditation: Effects of Meditative Expertise." *PLoS One* 26: e1897.

Manna, A., Raffone, A., Perrucci, M. G., Nardo, D., Ferretti, A., Tartaro, A., Londei, A., Del Gratta, C., Belardinelli, M. O., and Romani, G. L. 2010. "Neural Correlates of Focused Attention and Cognitive Monitoring in Meditation." *Brain Research Bulletin* 82: 46–56.

Nisbett, R. E. and Wilson, T. D. 1977. "Telling More Than We Can Know: Verbal Reports on Mental Processes." *Psychological Review* 84: 231–59.

Norbu, N. C. 1999. *The Crystal and the Way of Light: Sutra, Tantra and Dzogchen*. Ithaca, NY: Snow Lion Publications.

Pagis, M. 2009. "Embodied Self-Reflexivity." *Social Psychology Quarterly* 72: 265–83.

_____. 2010. "From Abstract Concepts to Experiential Knowledge: Embodying Enlightenment in a Meditation Center." *Qualitative Sociology* 33: 469–89.

Roberts, S. 2004. "Self-Experimentation as a Source of New Ideas: Examples about Sleep, Mood, Health, and Weight." *Behavioral and Brain Sciences* 27: 227–62.

Schooler, J. W. 2011. "Introspecting in the Spirit of William James: Comment on Fox, Ericsson, and Best (2011)." *Psychological Bulletin* 137: 345–50.

Schueller, S. M. 2010. "Preferences for Positive Psychology Exercises." *The Journal of Positive Psychology* 5: 192–203.

Schultheiss, O. C. and Brunstein, J. C. 1999. "Goal Imagery: Bridging the Gap between Implicit Motives and Explicit Goals." *Journal of Personality* 67: 1–38.

Thompson, C. J. 1990. "Eureka! and Other Tests of Significance: A New Look at Evaluating Interpretive Research." In *Advances in Consumer Research*, edited by M. E. Goldberg, G. Gorn and R. W. Pollay, 25–30. Provo, UT: Association for Consumer Research.

Travis, F. and Shear, J. 2010. "Reply to Josipovic: Duality and Non-duality in Meditation Research." *Consciousness and Cognition* 19: 1122–23.

Tulku, T. 1977. *Time, Space and Knowledge: A New Vision of Reality*. Berkeley, CA: Dharma Publishing.

van Dijk, J., Kerkhofs, R., van Rooij, I., and Haselager, P. 2008. Can There Be Such a Thing as Embodied Embedded Cognitive Neuroscience?" *Theory & Psychology* 18: 297–316.

Wallendorf, M. and Brucks, M. 1993. "Introspection in Consumer Behavior: Implementation and Implications." *Journal of Consumer Research* 20: 339–59.

Wheeler, R. H. 1923. "Introspection and Behavior." *Psychological Review* 30: 103–15.

Wilson, T. D. and Dunn, E. W. 2004. Self-Knowledge: Its Limits, Value, and Potential for Improvement." *Annual Review of Psychology* 55: 493–518.

Part IV

Self-Observation in the Phenomenological Traditions

8

A Conceptual History of Self-Observation in the Phenomenological Tradition: Brentano, Husserl, and Heidegger

Edwin E. Gantt and Jeffrey L. Thayne

In this chapter, we will explore some of the ways in which self-observation has been historically conceptualized in the phenomenological tradition of philosophy and psychology. Although often rejected by mainstream psychological researchers, perhaps due to a misguided association with the introspectionism of Wundt and Titchner, self-observation has long been defended as a viable method for understanding the psychological reality of human life. Indeed, perhaps the central hallmark of psychological research in the phenomenological tradition—despite the often striking variations in the specific methods that researchers in the tradition have employed—has been its unwavering commitment to self-understanding through carefully attentive and critically reflexive self-observation.

In order to better grasp exactly how self-observation has been conceptualized and what it has meant (and continues to mean) in the phenomenological tradition, then, we will provide a brief survey of the work of three major contributors to the contemporary phenomenological understanding of self-observation: Franz Brentano, Edmund Husserl, and Martin Heidegger. As such, we are not presenting an exhaustive historical account of the various innovations, implementations, or even the findings of research in philosophy and psychology that has been conducted from a phenomenological perspective.

Rather, our analysis will center on (1) the philosophical origins of later phenomenological thinking about self-observation as articulated in the work of Franz Brentano, (2) the formalization of phenomenology as a distinct philosophical movement, and consequent justification of self-observation as an epistemologically viable approach to the study of consciousness and meaning, by Edmund Husserl, and, finally, (3) the radical reconceptualization of phenomenology (and, therefore, self-observation) as a fundamentally existential-hermeneutic enterprise in the work of Martin Heidegger.[1] The principle aim of this chapter is to help clarify the rationale behind the phenomenological tradition's widely noted conceptually and methodologically heterogenous approach to self-observation as a vehicle of psychological research.

What Is Phenomenology?

Though admittedly difficult to define in manner that will meet with universal agreement,[2] in its most general sense, phenomenology is "the study of human experience and the way things present themselves to us in and through such experience" (Sokolowski 2000, 2). As such, the phenomenological approach, Keen (1975) states, "seeks to meet phenomena on their own terms and not to press them into the mold of preconceptions" (41). Thus, rather than measuring the behavior of human beings as exhibited in controlled laboratory environments, or interpreting the unconscious interplay of inferred psychic entities, or tracking the mechanical operations of complex cognitive information processing systems, as do many researchers in mainstream psychology, phenomenological psychologists seek to study the meaningful experience of human beings as encountered and reported by them in the course of everyday living (see, e.g., Fuller 1990; Giorgi and Giorgi 2008; Kruger 1988; Smith and Osborn 2008).

As a species of applied phenomenological philosophy, phenomenological psychology concerns itself with "the world as we encounter it in everyday experience, the world in which we pursue our goals and objectives, the scene of all our activities" (Fuller 1990, 24). The world, in this phenomenological sense, consists of "all items and objects which present themselves in prescientific experience and as they present themselves prior to their scientific interpretation in the specific modern sense" (Gurwitsch 1974, 17). Accordingly, phenomenology attends to "the world of everyday meanings, the world of malls, tulips, and lakes" (Fuller 1990, 24). Thus, Keen (1975) argues, "phenomenological psychology seeks to articulate explicitly the implicit structure and meaning of human experience. In order to carry out this task, we must describe experience" (19). And, he continues, "in trying to describe the overall structure of experience we must look to experience itself. . . . This lived experience must be our guide in understanding other people and what things mean to them" (Keen 1975, 21). In its most general sense, then, phenomenology reflects a basic philosophical commitment to phenomena as they appear in experience, in all of their contextual specificity and experiential variability.

For these reasons, phenomenological psychologists have traditionally relied on self-reports and first-person observations about meaningful experience. That is, phenomenological psychologists have typically employed qualitative rather than quantitative approaches in gathering their data, most often by inviting participants to engage with them in a critically reflective dialogue about very specific sorts of experiences that the participants have had. This research dialogue usually occurs in the context of extensive and probing face-to-face interviews, but can also include critical analysis of one's own experience, collecting and analyzing the written narrative accounts of others, and/or participating in cooperative groups wherein researchers and participants collaboratively examine both their own experiences and the research process itself (see, e.g., Fischer 2006; Halling et al. 1994; Kvale and Brinkmann 2009; Pollio et al. 1997). Whatever the specific parameters of the methodological approach taken, research participants are invited to describe their experience as it is experienced and in as much detail as possible, with particular attention paid to the temporal unfolding of the experience in its social and physical context. A wide variety of common human experiences have been studied in this way. For example: the experience of being criminally victimized (Wertz 1985), feeling alone (Barrell 1997), forgiving another person (Halling et al. 2006), being joyful (Robbins 2006), being bored with life (Bargdill 2000), experiencing oneself as beautiful (Rao and Churchill 2004), being artistically creative (Nelson and Rawlings 2007), and living with chronic pain (Smith and Osborn 2007).

Researchers analyze the accounts they are given in a phenomenological way; that is, in a way that strives to be as faithful and remain as close to the phenomenon as it presents itself as is possible while nonetheless articulating its meaning in an explicit, rigorous, and systematic fashion. As Keen (1975) explains, "The behavior that we observe in others is always interpreted by us in some way. . . . By interpreting it phenomenologically, we are expanding what we already do in everyday experience by making it explicit. We are using our natural interpretations in more disciplined form" (27). "The goal of every [phenomenological] technique," he continues, "is to help the phenomenon reveal itself more completely than it does in ordinary experience" (Keen 1975, 21). Lived experience, Keen (1975) further points out:

> is already understood . . . but only implicitly. . . . To take lived experience, even in its most trivial and commonplace form, and to operate on it with phenomenological reduction, imaginative variation, and interpretation is to embark on an exciting adventure, at the conclusion of which we are more conscious, more astutely attuned to life, more understanding of ourselves and others, less constricted by conventions, and less plagued by inexplicable moods. (44–45)

In other words, a phenomenological approach in psychology is one that seeks to provide insight into the meaning of actual lived experience through a process of self-observation and careful reflection, such that we can come to better understand, grasp, and engage that meaning and appreciate its impact on our daily lives.

Brentano: Self-Observation and the Roots of the Phenomenological Tradition

In order to fully appreciate the central role that self-observational methods have played in phenomenological psychology's attempts to investigate and articulate the meanings of everyday lived experience, it is important that we understand the thinking of those who have contributed most to its historical and contemporary formulations and practices. While there are a number of thinkers with whom one could begin in tracing the origins of phenomenological thought in psychology—Nietzsche, Kierkegaard, Kant, Hegel, and even St. Augustine are all possible candidates—most accounts begin with the pioneering work of the German psychologist and philosopher, Franz Brentano. Indeed, while Husserl is usually held to be the father of phenomenology (see, e.g., Moran 2000; Sokolowski 2000; Spiegelberg 1994), at least one author has somewhat playfully described Brentano as the "grandfather of phenomenology" (Tymieniecka 2002). Husserl's early thinking in both philosophy and psychology were profoundly shaped by what he learned while studying under Brentano while at the University of Vienna between the years of 1884 and 1886, and then the following year with one of Brentano's previous students, Carl Stumpf. Although Brentano himself never claimed to be a phenomenologist, per se—and even greeted the rise of the phenomenological movement under Husserl with bewilderment and dismay—because his influence on Husserl's thinking was so significant, Brentano is nonetheless widely considered one of the most important forerunners of the phenomenological enterprise, both in philosophy and psychology (Spiegelberg 1994).

Brentano was born at Marienberg am Rhein, Germany, on January 16, 1838. He studied philosophy and theology at the universities of Munich, Würzburg, Berlin, and Münster, and displayed a special interest in Aristotlean and scholastic philosophy. His dissertation was entitled *On the Manifold Sense of Being in Aristotle,* a work that eventually proved to be an important influence on the young Martin Heidegger. Brentano was ordained a Catholic priest and member of the Jesuit Order just prior to completing his Habilitation and securing a lectureship at the University of Würzburg. While at Würzburg he supervised the work of the philosopher Carl Stumpf, who proved to be one of his most dedicated and careful students. Brentano's influence flowed through Stumpf to impact a number of other thinkers, including Husserl, the highly influential phenomenological psychologist Aron Gurwitsch, and even William James.[3] In 1874, Brentano published his major work, *Psychology from an Empirical Standpoint* and began teaching at the University of Vienna. During his time as a professor at the University of Vienna from 1874 to 1895, Brentano attracted a number of brilliant students in addition to Husserl: Alexius Meinong, Sigmund Freud, Alois Höfler, Christian von Ehrenfels, Oskar Kraus, Franz Hillebrand, and Tomáš Masaryk (later the first president of Czechoslovakia). Brentano died in Zurich, Switzerland, on March 17, 1917.

Brentano deliberately set out to articulate a vision of "psychology from an empirical standpoint" that was quite distinct from the behavioral, physiological, and introspectionist approaches that were becoming increasingly popular in his day. Brentano (1995a) believed that psychology was the study of "people's inner life . . . that is, the part of life which is captured in inner perception" (3). His system is often termed "act psychology" because of its foundational rejection of "the exclusive alignment of scientific psychology with physiology" and its assertion that "a truly empirical psychology will discover that experience is forward looking, active, manipulative, and intentional" (Viney and King 2003, 235). That is to say, "while the physical sciences study *objects,* for Brentano the fundamental units of psychological analysis are *acts* that always refer to or 'contain' an object" (Fancher 1996, 370–71; italics in the original). To employ a modern-day metaphor that Brentano would likely have been willing to accept, psychology from the empirical standpoint is the attempt to place a sort of video camera into the individual's mind to allow the psychologist to see precisely what the person herself experiences as she experiences it, to observe individual experience from the inside and share the first-person perspective of the individual in some fundamental and systematic way.

In this context, Brentano often referred to this sort of work as descriptive psychology, or psychognostics (Brentano 1995; see also Tymieniecka 2002). "By phenomena," he wrote, "[I understand] that which is perceived by us," because phenomena are "objects of inner perception" (Brentano 1995a, 137). By inner perception, Brentano meant "the immediate awareness of our own psychological phenomena, of our joys or desires, our sadness or rage" (Spiegelberg 1994, 35–36). A psychology devoted to the world of "inner perception" is, then, a psychology concerned with describing what people experience from the first-person perspective in the active engagement between consciousness and the world of external objects, and not one that is concerned primarily (or even necessarily) with how or why people behave the way they do. While inner perception as "immediate awareness of our own psychological phenomena" is, of course, constrained by the immediate present, such awareness can nonetheless be accessed for study by the scientific mind, Brentano claimed, if we focus retrospectively on the immediate past and the flow of events as they were experienced. Contrary to "inner observation," or the practice of experimental introspection found in the work of Wundt and others, where the researcher seeks to identify mental states and catalogue their contents in what is fundamentally a static manner, Brentano's descriptive psychology relies on "report[ing] our perception of the flow of events and their effects" (Viney and King 2003, 237). Wundtian introspection, Brentano argued, cannot help but distort the phenomena under study because we cannot observe our own mental states while we are occupying them. As McCall (1983) points out, Brentano "rejected outright Wundt's contention that having an idea and being conscious of an idea are one and the same. On the contrary, we do not and cannot comprehend clearly an idea in the act of having it" (38). He continues:

> We cannot stand outside our ideas, feelings, and other mental acts and observe them as we would physical events. At most, we can

train ourselves to recall clearly our experiences immediately after we had them. Reconstruction must take the place of self-observation, introspection become retrospection. (38–39)

We can, however, "retrospect about those things that just took place and the things that preceded them and the perceived consequences" and we can "know about the inner state of others through verbal reports and behavior" (Viney and King 2003, 237). Indeed, Brentano maintained that careful study of behavior, even in terms of involuntary physical responses such as blushing or crying, is often our most reliable guide to the events and meanings of inner life (see Brentano 1995a, 1995b).

Brentano (1995a) argued that not only was psychology a study of first-person experience, it "aims at exhaustively determining (if possible) the elements of human consciousness and the ways in which they are connected" (3). In much the same way that water is composed of hydrogen and oxygen atoms, Brentano believed that all human perception is a composite of smaller, more basic components. He claimed, therefore, that the ultimate aim of psychological research to be:

> nothing other than to provide us with a general conception of the entire realm of human consciousness. It does this by listing fully the basic components out of which everything internally perceived by humans is composed, and by enumerating the ways in which these components can be connected. (Brentano 1995a, 4)

In essence, Brentano wished to document how "atoms" of perception combine to form the variety of experiences that we encounter in our daily lives. Further, he maintained that there was a parallel between his plan for a descriptive psychology and the intellectual aims of the natural sciences generally. For example, in his masterpiece, *Psychology from an Empirical Standpoint*, he wrote:

> just as the natural sciences study the properties and laws of physical bodies, which are the objects of our external perception, psychology is the science which studies the properties and laws of the soul, which we discover within ourselves directly by means of inner perception, and which we infer, by analogy, to exist in others. (Brentano 1995b, 4)

Clearly, Brentano believed that a careful and rigorous observation of inner perception could reveal these basic components of experience, as well as the manner in which they were constituted in the activity of consciousness.

Brentano trained a number of other young researchers (whom he termed "psychognosts") to carefully observe their "inner perception," and developed extensive guidelines to ensure the rigor and reliability of their work. First, according to Brentano (1995a), the psychognost must experience; that is, his "inner perception must register . . . a wealth of facts of human consciousness if he is not to lack the material necessary for his investigations" (32). Next, the psychognost must then note (i.e., become conscious of) relevant experiences "and their essential parts" (34). Third, the psychognost must then express the noted experience "in some language or other" so as to communicate it to other researchers in such a way that "they too will have permanent knowledge of it" (67). This process of communicating experience as carefully and rigorously as possible Brentano (1995a) referred to as "fixing" (see 66–73).

Once the noted experience had been properly fixed in the minds of each of the researchers and all were in agreement that the experience had been adequately understood by all, they then moved to inductively generalize the essence of the psychognost's experiences and describe them in terms of universal laws of human perception and experience (see 73–76). The fifth step in the methodological process, Brentano states, is that "the psychognost must intuitively grasp the general laws wherever the necessity or impossibility of unifying certain elements becomes clear through the concepts themselves" (75). Finally, "the psychognost has to make deductive use of what he gained in one way or another (inductively or intuitively) from the general laws" (76). In the end, Brentano believed that psychology, through the careful attentions of inner perception, could yield certain (what he termed "apodictic") knowledge and identify the universal laws that governed psychological life. It was in this sense that he understood his project for a descriptive psychology as being in line with that of all the other natural sciences.

Husserl: Self-Observation and the Commencement of the Phenomenological Tradition

Perhaps the most famous of Brentano's students while he was at the University of Vienna—with the possible exception of Freud[4]—was Edmund Husserl. Edmund Gustav Albrecht Husserl was born on April 8, 1859, in Prossnitz, Moravia (now part of the Czech Republic).

Although born into a Jewish family, the second of four children, he asked to be baptized as a Lutheran in 1886. In 1884, he began attending Brentano's lectures at the University of Vienna and was so impressed with his teacher that he decided to dedicate his life to philosophy. Husserl's focus during his time of study in Vienna with Brentano was to "find psychological foundations for a philosophy of arithmetic" (Spiegelberg 1972, 7). Indeed, Husserl was originally a mathematician and wrote a mathematical dissertation under the twin tutelage of Karl Weierstrass and Leopold Kronecker, both very eminent mathematicians of the day.[5] At Vienna, Husserl mastered the techniques (both experimental and logical) that Brentano had developed and used them to describe and catalogue the inner experience of counting, adding, and performing other arithmetic functions. While working with Brentano, Husserl considered himself a descriptive psychologist, and, concomitantly, a descriptive phenomenologist. For a time, Husserl planned to employ Brentano's methods of descriptive psychology to prove that arithmetic could be derived from psychological foundations. Eventually, however, Husserl came to pursue a philosophical agenda that diverged significantly from the one envisioned by his teacher.

While Husserl maintained that his philosophical project was the development of an "a priori psychology of our inner experiences designed to describe its essential features" (Spiegelberg 1972, 11), his vision of the scope and content of that project far surpassed what could be found in Brentano. According to McCormick (1981), for example, Husserl saw phenomenology as "a philosophical enquiry into the invariant . . . features of pure . . . consciousness" (162). In some ways, Husserl tried to distance himself from the newly founded discipline of psychology and to establish his work as a uniquely philosophical enterprise. Just as Brentano had attempted to document the "atoms" of perceptual experience, Husserl attempted to document the essential, underlying structures of conscious experience. While Brentano's psychognosy was limited to the documentation of the inner experience of perception in the acts of consciousness, Husserl expanded his work to elucidate the constitution of meaning in that experience. Husserl believed that the constitution of meaning in consciousness was just as much a part of conscious experience as any of those elements of perception that Brentano had held to exist in consciousness. Furthermore, according to Spiegelberg (1994), Husserl "recognized [that] the world of logical structures [w]as something apart from mere psychological acts" (62). In other words, Husserl believed that phenomenology ought to be about something more than merely describing the psychological experience of the various events of consciousness. Rather, phenomenological research was meant to penetrate the experience of consciousness and the appearances found therein to arrive at the essential structures of experience itself.

To accomplish this end, Husserl sought to dissolve the distinction between the "I" of consciousness and the world of objects, perhaps by taking Brentano's concept of intentionality even more seriously that Brentano himself had. For Husserl, and for most subsequent phenomenologists (both in philosophy and psychology), the concepts of inner perception and introspection, as originally characterized by Brentano and Wundt, are not conceptually defensible. Husserl's phenomenological project, unlike Wundtian introspection and Brentano's descriptive psychology, was not an attempt to peer into the "black box of the mind," "get a look inside the self," or "observe directly what the self is and does" while remaining aloof from consciousness itself, as some superficial summaries might claim. Rather, Husserl sought to focus on the way in which subject and object are inextricably connected, constituting and being constituted by one another, through the event of meaning wherein experience can be grasped in a holistic manner.

According to Husserl, the self as intentional consciousness cannot be understood or even conceived independent or apart from the relationship it shares with the objects of consciousness (i.e., meanings). "In perceiving," write phenomenological psychologists Churchill and Wertz (2001), "a perceiver relates to the perceived; for example, water is presented to the thirsty person as a drink, whereas it is presented to the dishwashing person as a cleaner. These are *objectively experienced meanings* of the water" (249; italics in the original). "Intentionality," they continue, "is a relational phenomenon, wherein consciousness and object together constitute one irreducible totality" (249–50). Thus, while Husserl certainly adopted some of the techniques and some of the terminology first introduced by Brentano, he shifted his attention away from "inner perception" (as Brentano had described it) and toward explicating the structures of meaning that constitute the inescapable grounds of lived experience in all its many varieties. From Husserl onward, then, self-observation has been generally understood by phenomenologists as a form of careful and critical reflection on experience as experienced. To the extent that self-observation is taken to mean "looking inwards" at the (more or less Cartesian) mind, its contents, and/or processes, it has been rejected by phenomenologists for relying too heavily on an inadequate conception of intentionality and the nature of consciousness.

Husserl suggested an important distinction, and one not readily discernable in the work of Brentano, between the empirical ego and the transcendental ego. This distinction reflected not an instance of Husserl stealing a concept wholesale from his predecessor, Immanuel Kant, or the simple assertion of the existence of two divergent entities constituting a fundamentally bifurcated self: the embodied ego located in space and time and the deeper, more foundational ego that exists in some way independent of physical and historical being, and, as such, grounds rationality, awareness, and all other manner of mental capacity. Rather, for Husserl, there is "a marvelous ambiguity to the ego: on the one hand, it is an ordinary part of the world, one of the many things that inhabit it. . . . [and] on the other hand, this very same self can also be played off against the world: it is the center of disclosure to whom the world and everything in it manifest themselves" (Sokolowski 2000, 112). This ambiguity of the ego lies in the way in which it is both a part of the world and can stand over against the world. When we take the self to be one among many things in the world, we are approaching the self in terms of what Husserl (1999) called the empirical ego.

When Husserl spoke of the "transcendental ego," however, he was addressing that aspect of intentional consciousness that stands out from the world and is not simply one more thing among many, but that which reveals us to be the agents of our intentional life, responsible for judgment, the source of analytic understanding, and the recipient of a world of meanings. "The empirical and the transcendental ego," Sokolowski (2000) writes, "are not two entities; they are one and the same being, but considered in two ways" (113). However, it is not just our consideration of the ego in two ways that grounds this distinction between the empirical and the transcendental ego, but that the ego itself exists in a double manner. As Sokolowski (2000) states, "We can consider it in this dual way only because it enjoys the kind of being that allows it to be so considered. . . . Even as transcendental, the ego's intentional character requires that it have things and a world correlated with itself. The ego and the world are moments to one another" (113).

For Husserl, and many later phenomenological psychologists, it is only because intentional consciousness is unitary in nature—even as it exhibits an ambiguous duality—that scientific inquiry into the phenomena of lived experience can even take place. It is, according to

Husserl (1977, 1983), only because of our ability to directly experience the world in terms of the meanings that are presented to us via the intentional stance of consciousness *and* our ability to stand out from ourselves while critically reflecting on those meanings (and the "structuredness" of lived experience that they reveal) that we are able to engage the subject matter of psychological investigation in a scientifically viable and productive manner. Phenomenological psychology, along these Husserlian lines, therefore, seeks to articulate the ways in which consciousness is fundamentally intentional and dynamic. The principle task of such a psychology is to fully explore the meanings of lived experience as those meanings are manifest in consciousness, independent of any philosophical presuppositions about the possible origins of those meanings.

A task such as this, however, demands a careful and critically reflective self-observational approach, wherein the various strata of consciousness, including both active and passive elements, are revealed and, thereby, the essential relationships among them can be exhibited. According to Husserl, this was to be accomplished by first "bracketing" (i.e., setting aside or suspending for analytic purposes) our various presuppositions about how the world operates and about the ontological status objects may or may not have outside of our consciousness of them. We must, Husserl (1983) argued, set aside "the natural attitude" (i.e., the way in which we commonly understand ourselves and the world from the perspectives of both everyday cultural life and the more formal accounts of natural science) in order to avoid the distorting influence it can have on our capacity to fruitfully engage the meaningfulness of lived experience as experienced. Husserl maintained that only by suspending our assumptions about the external world, as well as our individual biases, could we successfully achieve contact with the essences underlying experience that were the focus of phenomenological investigation.

Once the abstract prejudices of natural science and philosophy have been set aside, as well as the pre-reflective assumptions of common sense, we are then ready "to recollect our own experiences and to empathically enter and reflect on the lived world of other persons in order to apprehend the meanings of the world as they are given to the first-person point of view" (Wertz 2005, 168). In this way, the perceived *as* perceived can be "described solely on its own grounds and merits, without any reference to an extra-phenomenal reality" (Gurwitsch 1966, 105). Through a process of imaginative variation, the phenomenological psychologist is now able to engage not only her own original sphere of experience in an unbiased and open manner, but can also enter into a space of intuition that permits access to the experiences of others (see Husserl 1954, 254). In this process the researcher holds the phenomenon under investigation in her imagination as she develops examples of similar experiences through imaging the phenomenon from as many varied perspectives as possible. This method of variation ultimately leads the researcher to a description of the invariant or essential structures (i.e., those features without which it would not exist) of the phenomenon of interest. Husserl (1954) identified this intimate and immediate focus on experience as manifest in consciousness "the phenomenological psychological reduction" (236) because the investigative field of interest is "reduced" to the realm of the psychological. "This presence of the psychological," Wertz (2005) argues, "allows the investigator to reflectively describe the meanings and psychological performances of lived-through situations" (168).

This reflective description of meaning as experienced directly in the acts of consciousness is by its very nature a personal one. "The student of phenomenology," Fuller (1990) writes, "must become personally engaged in the phenomena being described, must indeed become a student of the phenomena, of 'the things themselves'" (28). In this sense, all phenomenological psychological research is self-observational in nature. That is, unlike the psychological researcher committed to the natural science project of identifying and measuring the causal impact of externally located variables on the behavior of human organisms, the phenomenologist is committed to the careful explication of the contours and essential structures of a shared lifeworld and its events of meaning. Because the lifeworld constitutes a shared space of meanings, the phenomenologist's research into the experiences of others is always in profound ways self-observational, self-referential, and self-illuminating.

As the phenomenological researcher attends carefully to meaning as it is experienced in consciousness, the epistemological distance between knower and known, so much a hallmark of the natural scientific approach to psychological inquiry, collapses. This collapse of epistemological distance helps the phenomenologist to personally access the world of common experience and meaning through a process of intuitional empathy. Indeed, as Fuller (1990) argues, for the phenomenological psychologist to be successful, "there needs to occur a sense of realization of what is being described, a sense of personal identification with the description being offered" (Fuller 1990, 28). "The phenomena," Fuller (1990) maintains, "must come to be felt in its living immediacy – for it is precisely this immediacy of life, this living flux, that phenomenology is after" (28). Thus, phenomenological psychology, he continues, is "an approach to meaning events, then, that requires interested parties to become personally involved in the work undertaken, checking out every description proposed, every claim that a phenomenon has been brought to a self-display, against firsthand experiences of their own" (Fuller 1990, 28). Phenomenological psychological research in this Husserlian vein, then, is "descriptive, uses the phenomenological reductions, investigates the intentional relationship between persons and situations, and provides knowledge of psychological essences (that is, the structures of meaning immanent in human experience) through imaginative variation" (Wertz 2005, 170; see also Giorgi 1989).

Heidegger: The Turn to Existential Phenomenology

Martin Heidegger is widely regarded as one of the two most important philosophical figures of the twentieth century.[6] Indeed, many regard his major work, *Being and Time*, as "without question an enduring a philosophical masterpiece on a par with Kant's *Critique of Pure Reason* and Hegel's *Phenomenology of Spirit*" (Moran 2000, 192). Heidegger was born on September 26, 1889, in Messkirch, Germany. Raised as a Roman Catholic, early on he anticipated a career in the Church but later chose to study theology at the University of Freiburg. In 1911, he switched to philosophy and completed his doctoral thesis on psychologism in 1914 and wrote his Habilitation on the doctrine of categories and meanings in the work of the medieval philosopher Dun Scotus. Following service in the military during World War I, Heidegger returned to Freiburg to serve as a salaried senior assistant to Husserl. Heidegger obtained a professorship at the University of Marburg in 1923 and remained there until he was selected to be Husserl's successor at the University of Freiburg following the publication of *Being and Time*.[7] He continued to lecture at Freiburg until 1967. Heidegger died on May 26, 1976, and was buried in the Messkirch cemetery, his nephew serving as sexton—a position his father had held when he was young.

Although a careful and engaged student of Husserl,[8] Heidegger clearly parted ways with his mentor over the meaning of phenomenology, its methods, and its ultimate aims. Husserl sought to explicate the foundations of a transcendental phenomenology—or an all-encompassing philosophical framework to ground the claims and practices of not only phenomenological psychology but all of science as well—whereby the essential structures of the lifeworld could be described from the viewpoint of a detached observer. Heidegger, on the other hand, laid the foundations for what is commonly termed "existential phenomenology" or "hermeneutic phenomenology," an approach in which it is maintained that the observer can never separate himself from the interpretive world of his historical and social engagements. "Martin Heidegger," Fuller (1990) writes, "has given intentionality in particular and phenomenology in general a concrete and historical possibility oriented, *existential* orientation" (43).

Heidegger effectively shifted phenomenology's focus from individual consciousness and its apprehension of meanings in the context of the lifeworld to Dasein, or "being-in-the-world," as the nexus of those social, physical, and historical relationships that human beings inhabit and in which they exist as the beings they are. In so doing, Heidegger also shifted phenomenology's focus from the earlier epistemological concerns that had animated Husserl's thinking to the articulation of the ontological grounds for addressing the question of being (Schacht 1972).[9] With his 1927 publication of *Being and Time*, Heidegger raised the question of the meaning of being and argued that both the question and its answer, far from being merely an esoteric matter, were profoundly relevant to human self-understanding. What Heidegger understood was that "in order to ask about the meaning of Being, we must first inquire into the nature of the particular being who is doing the questioning: man. Thus, the question of the meaning of Being is intimately related to the question of the meaning of man's, or as Heidegger puts it, *Dasein's* Being" (Hoeller 1988, 3). The German word "dasein" means "existence" (literally, "there being"), and Heidegger employs the term in a technical sense to designate that particular being (i.e., human beings) who not only asks the question of the meaning of being but for whom the question has particular significance.

The principle concern of Husserlian phenomenology lay with describing the structures and processes of perception, intentionality, and consciousness, and with securing an epistemological vantage point from which to ground science. Heidegger, in contrast, was more animated by the "ontological question of existence itself, and with the practical activities and relationships which we are caught up in, and through which the world appears to us, and is made meaningful"

161

(Smith et al. 2009, 16–17). Thus, Heidegger sought to ground the phenomenological project in what might be called a "world-centric" perspective. The concept of Dasein as fundamentally being-in-the-world "affords the embodied, intentional actor a range of physically-grounded (what is possible) and intersubjectively-grounded (what is meaningful) options" (Smith et al. 2009, 17). In fact, Spiegelberg (1994) maintains that "Possibly the most important structural characteristic considered in hermeneutic phenomenology is being-in-the-world (*In-der-Welt-sein*)" (387). The concept of world, as Heidegger articulated it, was not merely a term referring to the mathematical or dimensional space of natural science, a space that is populated solely by quantifiable physical objects which are either at rest or in motion, and which are solely subject to the impelling or inhibiting power of natural forces and laws. Rather, the world is that referential totality of meanings and relationships (physical, social, historical, moral, etc.) in which we find ourselves thoroughly and inescapably enmeshed, and toward which we exhibit a fundamental preoccupation and concern. "Meanings exist," Fuller (1990) explains, "in a network of references to one another. This network in its totality . . . is what Heidegger calls *world*" (43; italics in the original).

For Heidegger, Dasein as being-in-the-world was also equally and primordially being-with others. Heidegger argued that as human beings we are neither primordially instantiated as private Cartesian egos nor as individual Husserlian consciousnesses intending a world of meaning. Rather, he maintained that selfhood requires the existence of others with whom one shares a world and with whom one is able to engage one's own selfhood. "The world of Dasein is a *with-world* [*Mitwelt*]," Heidegger (1927) wrote, "Being-in is *Being-with* Others" (155, italics in the original). It is important to understand, however, that by "Others" Heidegger (1962) did not mean "everyone else but me – those over against whom the "I" stands out. They are rather those from whom, for the most part, one does *not* distinguish oneself – those among whom one is too" (154). Thus, the being-in-the-world as being-with others of Dasein signifies the fundamentally "shared, overlapping and relational nature of our engagement in the world" (Smith et al. 2009, 17). On the Heideggerian account, then, "to be *someone* is necessarily to be *with other someones*" (Fuller 1990, 50). And to truly be-with others in a genuinely shared world, there can be no fundamental ontological distinctions between self and other and world. "There is," Merleau-ponty (1962) says, echoing Heidegger, "no inner man, man is in the world, and only in the world does he know himself" (xi).

In *Being and Time*, Heidegger identified two basic modes of Dasein's engagement in the world: the present-at-hand and the ready-to-hand. By the present-at-hand mode of engagement, Heidegger meant to draw our attention the common ways in which we approach and understand the world in an abstract, reflective, and detached manner. In the present-at-hand mode, we take-up the world of history, culture, personal experience and meaningful relationships as essentially derivative, secondary, or not entirely real—as though they are merely the byproducts of some other underlying rational order or causal process. In this mode, Dasein and its world of meaningful relationships become objects of study and abstract reflection as presumably "rational beings contemplate and experiment with reality as though it were separate from them" (Slife and Williams 1995, 84). The present-at-hand mode of engagement intimates that the world is in fact composed of two distinct "worlds": the subjective (or internal) and the objective (or external). The subjective is the "inner world of the person, consisting primarily of an individual's consciousness and rationality;" while the objective is the "world of things or beings they really exist, independent of our subjective thoughts" (Slife and Williams 1995, 84). The Western intellectual tradition, Heidegger claimed, had consistently privileged the present-at-hand mode of engagement, its metaphysical presuppositions, epistemological assumptions, and the narrow and misleading accounts of persons and world such a mode of engagement invites.

The ready-to-hand mode, however, signifies the practical understanding reflected in our everyday active engagement in the world with others and things, and, as such, is prior to any abstract explanations or rational theorizing. As a phenomenologist, Heidegger argued that in our everyday engagement in the world of meaningful activities and relationships we do not experience the world as a separate objective entity or collection of entities external to us. Rather, we experience the world in its meaningful and textured immediateness, as "ready" (to hand) because the world is prepared for us, welcomes us, entices us, and is where we dwell and that to which we are submitted. In other words, it is "the world and its meanings, and not some inner self and its cultivation, [that] are Dasein's possibility, that to which Dasein always and already is given over" (Fuller 1990, 52). In a sense, then, we are fused with the world and it is an extension of our bodies and our purposes, though we are seldom fully aware of this fusion and its intimacy. We are, in most cases, much too absorbed in what we are doing and attempting to accomplish in the world to attend sufficiently to our own immersion in the world. Thus, we take-up (to us an Heideggerian example) the hammer we find here on the workbench, not as an independent object occupying some mathematical space and possessing only physical characteristics, but as an extension of our purposes in the world of meaningful relationships and shared history. That is, the hammer is always already something ready-to-hand in its availability as a possible means of furthering our practical aims in the world. As Slife and Williams (1995) put it, "the hammer as an *objective* entity (e.g., with metal of a certain tensile strength) is simply not in our awareness. Indeed, it can be said that the hammer does not *exist* that way. The hammer has become an extension of our arm, just as our arm is an extension of us" (Slife and Williams 1995, 86).

With his identification of the ready-to-hand mode as a primordial mode of human engagement in the world, Heidegger turned phenomenology to the task of interpreting the meaning of human activity and the praxis of everyday life. By fundamentally situating all human action in the contexts of history, language, social life, moral concern, cultural tradition, and physical constraint, Heideggerian phenomenology radically redefines the project of psychological research. In place of psychology's traditional positivist project of detached observation and theoretical explanation of human behavior, psychology informed by Heidegger's hermeneutic or existential phenomenology is primarily concerned with providing interpretive understandings of the meaning of human action and relationship via a process of situated, critically reflective self-observation. However, unlike the conceptions of self-observation that informed the methodological approaches of Brentano and Husserl, self-observation as a research method in light of Heidegger is not the observation of an individual self (i.e., consciousness), and its processes of meaning-making or meaning-apprehending, by another individual self that is in some fundamental way detached from the object of its observations. Instead, the forms of psychological research inspired by Heidegger's existential (hermeneutic) phenomenology accept the inescapably intersubjective and interpretive nature of research and characterize it primarily in terms of collaboration and dialogue rather than in terms of data-gathering or data-mining (see, e.g., Crist and Tanner 2003; Halling et al. 1994; Kvale and Brinkmann 2009; Smith et al. 2009).

From the Heideggerian perspective, then, self-observation as a method of psychological research is not the observation of the self as an object of detached scientific or rational consideration. Neither is self-observation understood as a process whereby the self is somehow able to examine itself as intentional consciousness positing a world of meanings in the effort to uncover the transcendental grounds out of which the structures of consciousness as intentional first arise. Rather, inasmuch as the self (Dasein) is "in-the-world," and not an individual consciousness or private ego, self-observation is a form of engagement with the world of things and persons in the context of shared meanings and shared possibilities. Self-observation is shared observation. And, as such, it is inescapably intersubjective and necessarily hermeneutic; that is, interpretive and circular (Gadamer 2004). The hermeneutic circle refers to the notion that one's understanding of a meaningful whole is only established by reference to the various individual meaningful parts of that whole (Palmer 1969). And, likewise, one's understanding of each of those individual parts is only possible by reference to the meaning of the whole. Thus, because neither the whole nor any individual part can be adequately understood without continual reference to one another understanding is fundamentally an interpretive circle. This does not imply, however, that interpretation can never be fixed or judged regarding its faithfulness or adequacy. It means only that meaning is and must always be located within cultural, historical, social, moral, and physical contexts.

In this Heideggerian iteration of the phenomenological tradition, psychological research as self-observation is fundamentally and inescapably relational in nature. That is, psychological research in the existential-hermeneutic phenomenological tradition is grounded in recognition of the profound manner in which both the researcher and the research participant are situated together in a shared world of historical and engagement. As such, both the researcher and the research participant are informed by that shared world, its historical, cultural, moral, and physical contours, even as they themselves collaborate in the constructive interpretation of its reality and meanings. Psychological research as self-observation is, in this way, phenomenological in terms of its animating attitude but profoundly dialogical insofar as it eschews a clear linear or stepwise analysis of phenomena in favor of a more open-ended, temporally sensitive, and vibrant back-and-forth approach to the research process. Indeed, as conceived in this way, self-observation may not be so much a specific method of psychological research, in the sense that methods usually entail following a set of predefined steps or procedures, as it is a collaborative and cyclic process of inquiry, interpretation, discovery, critical reflection, revision, and inquiry again. In this sense, then, not only is self-observation fundamentally a hermeneutic enterprise, but psychology itself becomes a uniquely open and welcoming mode of bringing about even greater self-understanding.

Conclusion

The conceptual approach to self-observation in the phenomenological tradition has undergone dramatic changes and revisions. Brentano utilized methodological inner perception, which he considered to be an observation of the intentional acts of the mind. In contrast, Husserl emphasized a distinction between the empirical ego and the transcendental ego. Husserl systematized the phenomenological approach to examining the meaning of experience from the perspective of the transcendental ego. And, finally, Heidegger claimed that it is impossible to separate oneself from lived experience so as to examine that experience as an object of consciousness. He attempted to articulate a phenomenology of lived experience as we engage with it, as opposed to describing it in a detached way (as Husserl attempted to do). In other words, phenomenology's conceptual approach to self-observation has shifted from an *observation of the self* to the *self's detached observations of experience* (and the observation of the meaning of experience), and finally to the *self's engagement with the meaning of lived experience.*

The methodological techniques of each of these scholars differed widely. Brentano focused on training researchers to observe and describe their perceptions and inner acts of consciousness. Husserl's approach, however, was somewhat more reflective as it encouraged individuals to critically examine their own experiences by bracketing their biases and by imaginatively considering their experiences from as many perspectives as possible in the attempt to discern the essential structures of experienced phenomenon. Heidegger's hermeneutic perspective encourages active participation in historically situated and contextually sensitive forms of inquiry, engendering research that is more dialogical in nature and which emphasizes engagement with experience, rather than artificial separation from it. This Heideggerian iteration of self-observation emphasizes the inescapably relational and contextual nature of all observation and interpretation.

The phenomenologist wishing to engage in self-observation as an avenue of psychological inquiry should be aware of these various and evolving approaches to the technique. Specifically, it is important to be aware that contemporary phenomenologists seldom if ever use self-observation in the same way as originally described by Brentano, Wundt, or others whose early work positioned them in the more empirical tradition of psychological investigation. Rather, for contemporary phenomenologists, self-observation is less a matter of the empirical observation of one's own behavior or mental processes and impressions, and more of an engaged form of reflection on lived experience as fundamentally meaningful. One of the important lessons that the phenomenological tradition teaches is that we cannot rely on the notion of objectivity in order to secure knowledge by means of observations of the self. The observing self cannot be separated from the world of lived experience that constitutes it as an observing self and, thus, the self cannot observe itself in an "objective" or detached manner. This does not, however, make self-observation an unreliable or unscientific form of psychological inquiry. Rather, it simply means that we must acknowledge and take account of the relational and experiential context in which all self-observation necessarily takes place.

Notes

1. Those interested in more particular histories of phenomenological psychology are referred to excellent works by Ashworth (2006), Cloonan (1995), Giorgi (2010), and Spiegelberg (1972).

2. Indeed, as Giorgi (1985) has noted, "a consensual, univocal interpretation of phenomenology is hard to find" (23–24). He has more recently lamented that phenomenological psychology only exists "in a most fragmented, incomplete way" insofar as "there have been fits and starts but nothing like a sustained development by psychologists where later workers built upon the work of earlier ones" (Giorgi 2010, 147–48). This is not surprising given that phenomenology resists rigid codification into a specific method, set of universal procedural steps, or formal system of explanation. "Unlike other methodologies," Keen (1975) notes, "phenomenology cannot be reduced to a 'cookbook' set of instructions. It is more an approach, an attitude, an investigative posture with a certain set of goals" (41).

3. Stumpf was also responsible for establishing the Berlin School of Experimental Psychology, and, thereby, profoundly shaped the thinking of the cofounders of Gestalt Psychology: Max Wertheimer, Wolfgang Köhler, and Kurt Koffka.

4. Although Freud was an enthusiastic student, Brentano's impact on Freud's later thinking was of more general in nature than it was for Husserl and most of Brentano's other students. As Zentner (2002) observes, "If we consider the important role Brentano played in Freud's life, it is surprising

how little the young Freud seems to have derived from Brentano's ideas" (379). Indeed, Zentner further points out, "Brentano's rationalism and, in particular, his refutation of unconscious mental activity were later opposed and even caricaturized by Freud as typical examples of the philosopher's limited view of the mind" (379).

5.   Weierstrass was famous for his pioneering theoretical work on the functions of complex variables and is often cited as the "father of modern analysis" (McElroy 2005, 249), while Kronecker—a brilliant mathematician in his own right—is perhaps most remembered for having reportedly quipped, "God made the integers; all else is the work of man." Recently, theoretical physicist Stephen Hawking drew on Kronecker's quote for the title of his own book, *God Created the Integers: The Mathematical Breakthroughs that Changed History.*

6.   The other being, of course, Ludwig Wittgenstein.

7.   Among his students while at Marburg were Hans-Georg Gadamer, Hannah Arendt, Karl Löwith, Gerhard Krüger, Leo Strauss, Jacob Klein, and Hans Jonas. His students at Freiburg included Charles Malik, Herbert Marcuse, and Ernst Nolte. Among others who attended his lectures were the French phenomenologist Emmanuel Levinas, the theologian Rudolf Bultmann, the physicist Werner Heisenberg, and the psychologists Ludwig Binswanger and Medard Boss.

8.   Indeed, of all of the students Husserl taught over the years, Heidegger was the one in whom he felt the most promise for an intellectual heir who would carry on his work in a relatively unchanged manner. However, in the end, Heidegger radically historicized phenomenology by infusing it with principles of interpretation, hermeneutics, and an overriding concern for ontology (see Spiegelberg 1994, 190 and 205–207).

9.   Schacht (1972) notes that the "epistemological character of Husserlian phenomenology is not merely implicit in the program Husserl sets for himself; it is also explicitly acknowledged. 'Phenomenology seems rightly to be characterized,' he says, 'as transcendental theory of knowledge'" (295).

References

Ashworth, P. 2006. "Introduction to the Place of Phenomenological Thinking in the History of Psychology." In *Phenomenology and Psychological Science: Historical and Philosophical Perspective,* edited by P. Ashworth and M. C. Chung, 11–44. New York: Springer.

Bargdill, R. W. 2000. "The Study of Life Boredom." *Journal of Phenomenological Psychology* 31, no. 2: 188–219.

Barrell, J. E. 1997. "Feeling Alone." In *The Phenomenology of Everyday Life,* edited by H. R. Pollio, T. Henley, and C. B. Thompson, 157–90. Cambridge, UK: Cambridge University Press.

Brentano, F. 1995a. *Descriptive Psychology* (B. Muller, Trans.). London, UK: Routledge.

_____. 1995b. *Psychology from an Empirical Standpoint* (A. C. Rancurello, D. B. Terrell, and L. L. McAlister, Trans.). London, UK: Routledge. (Original work published in 1874.)

Churchill, S. D. and Wertz, F. J. 2001. "An Introduction to Phenomenological Research in Psychology: Historical, Conceptual, and Methodological

Foundations." In *The Handbook of Humanistic Psychology: Leading Edges in Theory, Research, and Practice*, edited by K. J. Schneider, J. F. T. Bugental, and J. F. Pierson, 247–63. Thousand Oaks, CA: Sage Publications.

Cloonan, T. 1995. "The Early History of Phenomenological Psychological Research in America." *Journal of Phenomenological Psychology* 26: 46–126.

Crist, J. D. and Tanner, C. A. 2003. "Interpretation/Analysis Methods in Hermeneutic Interpretive Phenomenology." *Nursing Research* 52, no. 3: 202–5.

Fancher, R. E. 1996. *Pioneers of Psychology*, 3rd edn. New York: W. W. Norton and Company.

Fischer, C. T. ed. 2006. *Qualitative Research Methods for Psychologists: Introduction through Empirical Studies*. Boston, MA: Academic Press.

Fuller, A. R. 1990. *Insight into Value: An Exploration of the Premises of a Phenomenological Psychology*. Albany, NY: SUNY Press.

Gadamer, H. -G. 2004. *Truth and Method* (J. Weinsheimer and D. G. Marshall, Trans., 2nd edn. revised). London, UK: Continuum Publishing.

Giorgi, A. 1985. "The Phenomenological Psychology of Learning and the Verbal Learning Tradition." In *Phenomenology and Psychological Research*, edited by A. Giorgi, 23–85. Pittsburgh, PA: Duquesne University Press.

_____. 1989. "One Type of Analysis of Descriptive Data: Procedures Involved in Following a Phenomenological Psychological Method." *Methods* 1: 39–61.

_____. 2010. "Phenomenological Psychology: A Brief History and Its Challenges." *Journal of Phenomenological Psychology* 41, no. 2: 145–79.

Giorgi, A. and Giorgi, B. 2008. "Phenomenology." In *Qualitative Psychology: A Practical Guide to Research Methods*, edited by J. A. Smith, 26–52. Thousand Oaks, CA: Sage Publications.

Gurwitsch, A. 1966. *Studies in Phenomenology and Psychology*. Evanston, IL: Northwestern University Press.

_____. 1974. *Phenomenology and the Theory of Science* (L. Embree, ed.). Evanston, IL: Northwestern University Press.

Halling, S., Kunz, G., and Rowe, J. O. 1994. "The Contributions of Dialogical Psychology to Phenomenological Research." *Journal of Humanistic Psychology* 34, no. 1: 109–31.

Halling, S., Leifer, M., and Rowe, J. O. 2006. "Emergence of the Dialogical Approach: Forgiving Another." In *Qualitative Research Methods for Psychologists: Introduction through Empirical Studies*, edited by C. T. Fischer, 247–77. Boston, MA: Academic Press.

Heidegger, M. 1962. *Being and Time* (J. Macquarrie and E. Robinson, Trans.). New York: Harper & Row. (Original work published in 1927.)

Hoeller, K. 1988. "Introduction." In *Heidegger and Psychology*, edited by K. Hoeller, 3–6. Atlantic Highlands, NJ: Humanities Press International.

Husserl, E. 1954. *The Crisis of European Sciences and Transcendental Phenomenology* (D. Carr, Trans.). Evanston, IL: Northwestern University Press. (Original work published in 1939.)

_____. 1977. *Phenomenological Psychology* (J. Scanlon, Trans.). The Hague, The Netherlands: Martinus Nijhoff Publishers. (Original work published in 1962.)

_____. 1983. *Ideas Pertaining to a Pure Phenomenology and to a Phenomenological Philosophy* (F. Kersten, Trans.). The Hague, The Netherlands: Martinus Nijhoff Publishers. (Original work published in 1913.)

_____. 1999. *The Idea of Phenomenology* (L. Hardy, Trans.). Dordrecht, The Netherlands: Kluwer Academic Publishers. (Original work published in 1950.)

Keen, E. 1975. *A Primer in Phenomenological Psychology.* Lanham, MD: University Press of America.

Keller, P. 1999. *Husserl and Heidegger on Human Experience.* Cambridge, UK: Cambridge University Press.

Kruger, D. 1988. *An Introduction to Phenomenological Psychology.* Cape Town, South Africa: Juta & Company, Ltd.

Kvale, S. and Brinkmann, S. 2009. *InterViews: Learning the Craft of Qualitative Research Interviewing,* 2nd edn. Thousand Oaks, CA: Sage Publications.

McCall, R. 1983. *Phenomenological Psychology.* Madison, WI: University of Wisconsin Press.

McCormick, P. 1981. "Husserl on Philosophy as a Rigorous Science." In *Husserl: Shorter Works,* edited by P. McCormick and F. Elliston, 161–65. Notre Dame, IN: University of Notre Dame Press.

McElroy, T. 2005. *A to Z of Mathematicians: Notable Scientists.* New York: Facts on File Science Library.

Merleau-ponty, M. 1962. *Phenomenology of Perception* (C. Smith, Trans.). London, UK: Routledge and Kegan Paul.

Moran, D. 2000. *Introduction to Phenomenology.* London, UK: Routledge.

Nelson, B. and Rawlings, D. 2007. "Its Own Reward: A Phenomenological Study of Artistic Creativity." *Journal of Phenomenological Psychology* 38, no. 2: 217–55.

Palmer, R. E. 1969. *Hermeneutics: Interpretation Theory in Schleiermacher, Dilthey, Heidegger, and Gadamer.* Evanston, IL: Northwestern University Press.

Pollio, H. R., Henley, T., and Thompson, C. B. 1997. *The Phenomenology of Everyday Life.* Cambridge, UK: Cambridge University Press.

Rao, A. and Churchill, S. D. 2004. "Experiencing Oneself as Being Beautiful: A Phenomenological Study Informed by Sartre's Ontology." *Qualitative Research in Psychology* 1, no. 1: 55–68.

Robbins, B. 2006. "An Empirical, Phenomenological Study: Being Joyful." In *Qualitative Research Methods for Psychologists: Introduction through Empirical Studies,* edited by C. T. Fisher, 173–211. Burlington, MA: Academic Press.

Schacht, R. 1972. "Husserlian and Heideggerian Phenomenology." *Philosophical Studies: An International Journal for Philosophy in the Analytic Tradition* 23, no. 5: 293–314.

Slife, B. D. and Williams, R. N. 1995. *What's Behind the Research? Discovering Hidden Assumptions in the Behavioral Sciences.* Thousand Oaks, CA: Sage Publications.

Smith, J. A., Flowers, P., and Larkin, M. 2009. *Interpretive Phenomenological Analysis: Theory, Method and Research.* Thousand Oaks, CA: Sage Publications.

Smith, J. A. and Osborn, M. 2007. "Pain as an Assault on the Self: An Interpretative Phenomenological Analysis of the Psychological Impact of Chronic Benign Low Back Pain." *Psychology and Health* 22, no. 5: 517–34.

_____. 2008. "Interpretive Phenomenological Analysis." In *Qualitative Psychology: A Practical Guide to Research Methods,* edited by J. A. Smith, 53–80. Thousand Oaks, CA: Sage Publications.

Sokolowski, R. 2000. *Introduction to Phenomenology.* Cambridge, UK: Cambridge University Press.

Spiegelberg, H. 1972. *Phenomenology in Psychology and Psychiatry.* Evanston, IL: Northwestern University Press.

_____. 1994. *The Phenomenological Movement: A Historical Introduction* (3rd edn. expanded and revised). Dordrecht, The Netherlands: Kluwer Academic Publishers.

Tymieniecka, A. -T. 2002. *Phenomenology World-wide: Foundations, Expanding Dynamisms, Life-Engagements: A Guide for Research and Study.* Dordrecht, The Netherlands: Kluwer Academic Publishers.

Viney, W. and King, D. B. 2003. *A History of Psychology: Ideas and Context,* 3rd edn. Boston, MA: Allyn and Bacon.

Wertz, F. J. 1985. "Methods and Findings in an Empirical Analysis of "Being Criminally Victimized"." In *Phenomenology and Psychological Research,* edited by A. Giorgi, 155–216. Pittsburgh, PA: Duquesne University Press.

_____. 2005. "Phenomenological Methods for Counseling Psychology." *Journal of Counseling Psychology* 25, no. 2: 167–77.

Zentner, M. R. 2002. "Nineteenth Century Precursors of Freud." In *The Freud Encyclopedia: Theory, Therapy, and Culture,* edited by E. Erwin, 370–83. New York: Routledge.

9

A Phenomenologically Informed Theory of Self-Observation: Intra-spection as Hermeneutic Reduction on the Self

Samuel D. Downs

While philosophy has struggled with Cartesian dualism, attempting to overcome it, self-observation, as discussed by Boring (1953) and this book, has remained dualistic throughout much of its history. Boring (1953) points out that self-observation, under different names such as self-report, has persisted throughout psychology. However, most types of contemporary self-observation still persist in dualism and inherit the problems of dualism. Dualistic self-observation has problems (see Clegg 2012) such that self-observation is no longer considered a viable methodology by many researchers because of the problems of dualism (Boring 1953). Briefly: dualistic self-observation is different from empirically derived knowledge, does not provide knowledge about the external world, and cannot be shown to correspond with the external world. All three problems are due to dualism. More importantly, all three problems are reasons why self-observation was abandoned (Boring 1953).

Philosophy provides insight into a solution to problems inherent in dualistic self-observation. Specifically, the main solution to dualism that philosophy offers is phenomenology. Phenomenology seeks to erase the divide between subject and object by focusing on meanings as experienced by humans. Phenomenology rejects dualism in favor of a position that connects the internal and external aspects of the world in such a fashion that internal and external are no longer valid descriptions of the world. Since philosophy has attempted to move away from dualism, and self-observation needs to, it may help to use philosophy's solution to dualism, namely phenomenology, with dualistic self-observation. A phenomenological understanding of self-observation may move toward a viable methodology for self-observation because phenomenology has attempted to move away from dualism toward a more viable, nondualistic, philosophy. This rejection of dualism means that self-observation may be a practical source of knowledge if the distinction between subject and object is eradicated. In other words, a phenomenological understanding of self-observation must follow phenomenology's erasure of dualism. This argument requires three points: first, self-observation has been discredited due to dualism, the focus of other sections of this book; second, phenomenology has succeeded in overcoming dualism, a secondary argument of the current chapter and the goal of phenomenology (see, e.g., Heidegger 1962); and, third, the success of phenomenology can be applied to self-observation, the main goal of this chapter.

In this chapter, I discuss Husserl's intentional arrow as the foundation for Heidegger's holistic concept of being-in-the-world and present an understanding of self-observation that relies on these phenomenological concepts. With these concepts defined, I move toward an understanding of self-observation that does not participate in a dualism that divides the world between subject and object just as these thinkers moved philosophy away from Cartesian dualism. Specifically, I discuss self-observation as a type of phenomenological reduction with a particular goal, or focus, for that reduction. I provide a detailed example of this reduction. Finally, I discuss how phenomenological reduction overcomes some problems of dualism.

The Phenomenological Response to Dualism

Many phenomenological thinkers have explicitly attempted to reject dualism; Heidegger is noteworthy among these thinkers in his attempts to reject dualism (see, e.g., Heidegger 1962). Yet, Heidegger's work relies on the philosophy of Husserl (Dowling 2007), who, some thinkers have argued, may not avoid dualism (see, e.g., Bernet et al. 1993). Since Heidegger's work relies on Husserl, I briefly discuss Husserl's intentional arrow even though scholars debate Husserl's trend toward dualism. The intentional arrow is the first concept needed (in this chapter) to overcome dualism because it provides the groundwork for Heidegger's notion of being-in-the-world, a nondualistic understanding of human experience. Then, I present Husserl's notion of reduction, which will be important in developing a phenomenological understanding of self-observation, so that I can show how being-in-the-world alters Husserl's notion of reduction as well. Again, Husserl's understanding of reduction is necessary to understand Heidegger's nondualistic being-in-the-world and the Heideggerian understanding of reduction that relies on being-in-the-world. Next, I show how Heidegger's notion of being-in-the-world builds on Husserl's intentional arrow in such a way that subject and object are no longer ontologically distinct categories. In this way, I hope to show the transition from Cartesian dualism to phenomenology. Furthermore, this discussion highlights the difference between two types of reduction, Husserlian and existential, in order to draw on an existential understanding of reduction to discuss a phenomenological notion of self-observation. In other words, the move from dualism to phenomenology can be mirrored for self-observation to develop a phenomenological understanding of self-observation as existential reduction.

Husserl's Intentional Arrow, the Lifeworld, and Reduction

Intentionality

For Husserl, intentionality is consciousness of something (Benson 2002; Vernon 2005; von Eckartsberg 1992). Husserl does not mean realization of a thought when he speaks of consciousness, but, instead, broadens consciousness to include actions directed at objects. We intend objects by perceiving them, thinking about them, and using them. We never have any action of consciousness—perceiving, thinking, using—without this action being directed toward something. Husserl (1970), critiquing Hume and the accepted psychological explanations of Husserl's time, says:

> But no consideration is given to the fact that in the perceptions, in the experiences of consciousness themselves, that of which we are conscious is included *as such*—that the perception is *in itself* a perception *of* something, of "this tree." (85; original italics)

This directedness is the fundamental nature of intentionality. The metaphorical depiction of Husserlian intentionality is a unidirectional arrow from consciousness to an object (von Eckartsberg 1992), often symbolized as such: Consciousness → Object. For Husserl, every act of consciousness is intentional (Sokolowski 2000; von Eckartsberg 1992).

Through intentional actions, consciousness is meaningfully directed toward objects so that intentions provide meanings in the world as experienced (von Eckartsberg 1992). Through actions, intentionality gives meaning to the world because our actions constitute what an object is. For example, when I use an object as a marker, I constitute it as a marker instead of a projectile or paperweight. I could act toward the object in various other ways, and my actions bring about other meanings for the object, such as a projectile if I threw it. Through intentionality, meaning is possible. However, some meanings are hidden from me because I cannot intend them. For example, I cannot intend subatomic particles in the same way that physicists can. These meanings are outside my current intentions because my current actions toward subatomic particles are not the same as a physicist's. Thus, meaning depends on, and is limited by, my intentions.

Since every action is intentional, every action constitutes meaning in the world, and different actions constitute different meanings. The intentional arrow indicates a meaningful connection between consciousness and the world. For Husserl, it is through intentionality that meanings are given to the world (LeVasseur 2003). Furthermore, these meanings provide knowledge about the world because the meanings constitute our understanding of the world. For Husserl, knowledge is intentional because intentions constitute the meanings of knowledge.

For self-observation, intentionality implies that thoughts about one's self are meaningfully directed toward something since every action is meaningfully directed toward something. Even knowledge about ourselves, typically considered as within our minds (due to dualism), are directed toward something other than mind, such as our actions in the world; even self-observation does not occur solely within the mind. Instead, self-observation, as will be seen more fully later, is intimately connected with our actions in the world. More importantly, intentionality implies that all knowledge, knowledge of the self, of other people, and of subatomic particles, is consciousness of something. All knowledge is not within the mind or in the external world, but is a meaningful intentional act. Already, Husserl's understanding of intentionality begins to disrupt the traditional understanding of self-observation since self-observation, just like all knowledge, is an intentional act. Furthermore, intentionality as meaningful allows for self-observation as meanings in the world. Self-observation, just like other intentions, intends a meaningful object in the world. In this way, self-observation participates in the meanings of the world as a meaningful intentional action.

The Lifeworld

For Husserl, these meaningful intentional actions never occur alone but happen in conjunction with other intentions, whether my or other people's intentions. Husserl called this world constituted by intentional actions the lifeworld. The lifeworld is constituted through intentional actions such that it is "the world of taken-for-granted everyday activities [intentions] and common sense meanings" (von Eckartsberg 1992, 88); the lifeworld is a horizon of meanings of multiple objects and intentional acts (LeVasseur 2003), including the intentions of other people as taken up in culture and history. The meaning of a particular action is always connected with meanings entailed by the context, culture, and historicity of the action; there is a unity of meanings that is the lifeworld. In one place, Husserl (1970) describes the lifeworld as "constituted throughout all its relative aspects as a unity, the universe of lifeworld objects" or intentional actions (173). For example, walking is an intentional act since it is directed toward an object—my car. Furthermore, walking entails many other common sense meanings, intending many other objects, such as a way to exercise, a form of courtship, a mode of transportation, etc., even though I am not considering the relationship of this particular act of walking with these other meanings. These other meanings are constituted through intentional actions by me and other people, and are taken up in my own intending toward walking because walking is culturally and historically connected with these other meanings. Often, these actions are taken for granted in that I do not reflect on the relationship among meanings. Thus, walking is related to a multiplicity of objects and meanings because these objects and meanings are manifest in a shared activity—walking. In other words, walking is a relationship of many meanings, all of which I intend but some of which are part of my cultural and historical context.

The lifeworld implies a relationship between meanings about the self gained through self-observation and meanings gained in other ways (e.g., sensation, science, and conversation). Since, in the lifeworld, all meanings entail some other meanings, self-observation, as intentional act, is connected to other meanings. The realization, through self-observation, that I am short-tempered when hungry requires an understanding that other people are not short-tempered, my culture disapproves of being short-tempered, and short-temperedness has happened several times when I am hungry. Thus, self-observation, apart from not being within the mind when considered as an intention, extends beyond me into the world around me: into my context, my culture, its history, and my history. Self-observation as an intentional act also intends meanings, such as the various cultures in which I participate, that are not solely, or even mostly, mine. The same can be said of other types of knowledge, such as scientific knowledge: all knowledge extends beyond the knower into the world around him or her. Since self-observation and scientific knowledge are both intentional, they are no longer different types of knowledge. Thus, with intentionality, the divide between knower and known, internal and external, begins to disappear. As the distinction between internal and external begins to disappear with Husserl's intentional arrow, the distinction between subjective self-observation and objective knowledge disappears as well. Self-observation, just as other knowledge, is in the world as meanings.

Reduction

Often these meanings and actions are unexamined since they are so common and taken-for-granted. Walking and its myriad meanings are often taken for granted until someone no longer intends in the same way. Perhaps I break my leg and require a cast. At this point, the unexamined activity of walking can now be examined because I recognize my intentions as potentially different. In short, I am focused toward—or intend—walking with a cast such that walking—with or without a cast—becomes foregrounded for me. In other words, I can focus or foreground specific intentional actions, or meanings, among the multitude of meanings of the lifeworld. So while the lifeworld allows for intentions and meanings to be taken for granted, these intentions and meanings can also be a point of focus.

Foregrounding intentions is possible without some interruption in my activity. For example, I may be able to consider walking and its meaning without breaking my leg so that I can intend toward walking differently. The interruption is not required; the only requirement for foregrounding is the ability to focus on the action in a different way. For Husserl, the action of foregrounding phenomena to focus on them is called reduction (Dowling 2007; Gearing 2004; LeVasseur 2003).

For Husserl, reduction—also called bracketing or epoché at times—is an examination of prejudgments, assumptions, and prejudices with the goal of suspending these judgments (Dowling 2007; Gearing 2004; LeVasseur 2003) and is rooted in the Greek word that means to refrain from judgment or avoid common place meanings (Dowling 2007). The prejudgments are meanings that have not been foregrounded, and Husserl calls these meanings prejudices in the sense that these meanings have not been reflected on through foregrounding, or are prejudgments. Just as contemporary prejudice influences our actions and meanings—at times without our awareness—so, too, do prejudgments influence meanings (but not necessarily with the negative connotation of contemporary prejudice). Husserlian prejudice might include contemporary racial prejudices, but it also includes any prejudgments and assumptions about the world. Until meanings are foregrounded, these meanings are prejudices, or prejudgments. For Husserl, these prejudgments do not allow the true essence, or necessary and sufficient qualities, of objects to be known (Dowling 2007; Gearing 2004; LeVasseur 2003).

Reduction involves the foregrounding of these prejudgments in order to remove them from our understanding of experience and leave the essence of the phenomenon. In other words, by removing these prejudgments, the essence of an object can be known. For Husserl, this description of essences was the goal of reduction (Dowling 2007; Gearing 2004; LeVasseur 2003). He says:

> The very epoché [reduction] itself frees our gaze not only for the intentions running their course within the purely intentional life (i.e., the 'intentional experiences') but also for that which these intentions in themselves, with their own 'what'-content, posit as valid in each case as their object; . . ." (Husserl 1970, 241)

Reduction allows the "what"-content, or essential qualities, of an object to be manifest through the intentional act. By attempting to remove the prejudgments we have, Husserl thought we could arrive at the true essence of objects (LeVasseur 2003).

Finally, after stripping away prejudgments and learning about the essence of an object, that new understanding can be integrated into the rest of our knowledge (Dowling 2007). The reduction, for Husserl, reveals an object's essence that can be reintegrated into other knowledge to increase understanding. The new knowledge becomes part of the context of intentionality so that intentionality, or action, includes this new knowledge. Actions are now influenced by this new knowledge. The meaning gained through reduction is interpreted in light of other connected meanings so that new meanings become a context for understanding other meanings. In this way, the new meaning influences the meaning of the world because the new meaning is brought about through actions. My new understanding about walking, because I performed a reduction on the meaning, can become part of the meaning of walking even after the cast is removed. For example, I will be more careful in situations similar to how I broke my leg. I most likely will appreciate differently walking without crutches as well. This appreciation will be revealed as I walk because I intend walking differently due to a new understanding of walking. The knowledge gained through reduction influences intentionality toward the particular action that was foregrounded.

For self-observation, this understanding of reduction indicates that it is possible to perform a reduction on intentional acts to learn about them. Husserl's understanding of reduction makes possible a method through which someone can strip away unessential meanings to examine specific meanings and gain new insight about those specific meanings. While intentional actions result in meanings with relation to other meanings, it is possible to purposefully understand more about a particular meaning through reduction. For self-observation, the reduction is on the self. Through reduction, knowledge can increase in a goal-directed manner. In other words, I do not simply wait until my leg is in a cast before I can understand more about walking. Instead, from a Husserlian perspective, through reduction, I can purposefully foreground my intentional act of walking, or any other meaning connected with the self, and strip away the unessential aspect of meaning. Furthermore, the process of gaining scientific knowledge can be understood in this same way: a purposeful reduction of particular meanings. Scientists emphasize particular meanings, for example, serotonin re-uptake in the brain's emotional pathways, to gain better understanding of these meanings. By removing other meanings, the scientist can better understand his or her area of study. Once someone, including scientists, gains new insight through reduction, the new meaning can influence other meanings since meanings are in relation. Once I have a better understanding of the experience of walking, I can better understand the experience of running as well.

Heidegger and Being-in-the-World

Heidegger, as a student of Husserl, extended and critiqued Husserl's ideas of intentionality and the lifeworld. Particularly, Heidegger accepted Husserl's notion of intentionality as consciousness of something but moved Husserl's understanding of the lifeworld toward an emphasis on existence (Dowling 2007). Heidegger emphasized that human beings exist in a world that is already meaningful such that meanings are not simply created through intentionality. Instead, intentionality is directed toward an already meaningful world: it is as if human beings have been thrown into a world of meanings that is not of their making. Heidegger thought that the lifeworld included a notion of thrownness, or existing in an always and already meaningful world, such that it is impossible to escape all of our prejudgments because human beings are thrown into a world in which meanings are constitutive and connected before intentionality. Heidegger (1962) says, "Whenever we encounter anything, the world has already been previously discovered, though not thematically" (114). We are thrown into an already meaningful, or discovered, world. For Heidegger, thrownness and intentionality reveal meanings that do not have essences, or are not thematic. For this reason, reduction cannot, for Heidegger, strip away all prejudgments and reveal essences. Meanings do not have essences because intentionality, for Heidegger, is constituted as actions in an already meaningfully connected world. As will be discussed more fully later, the world is always and already meaningful, beyond human intentions, because the world participates in meanings. Thus, Heidegger supplants Husserl's concept of the lifeworld with his own concept of being-in-the-world, or acting in an already meaningful world (LeVasseur 2003).

For Heidegger, being-in-the-world is a relationship between intentionality and the meanings the world reveals (Heidegger 1962). *Being* is a verb used to describe the process of meaning formation as an active process as humans perform actions in the world. My use of the door (e.g., opening it, propping it open, holding it open for someone else) is a process that constitutes the meaning of the door. This process is akin to intentionality as described by Husserl in that actions constitute meanings. *In-the-world* indicates that the process of meaning formation (as human action) takes place in a world of meanings already constituted by other people, cultures, history, and nature. For Heidegger, *world* includes the sociocultural, historical, and personal contexts as well as the physical Earth (Heidegger 1962) whereas, for Husserl, meanings are only possible through intentional actions. Thus, for Heidegger, the world is never a blank slate that humans write on through their actions, but a nexus of meanings that make intentional human actions intelligible. Importantly, being-in-the-world denotes a relationship between intentionality and the world; Heidegger (1962) says, "The compound expression 'Being-in-the-world' indicates in the very way we have coined it, that it stands for a *unitary* phenomenon" (78; original italics). For example, my action of holding the door open for someone is only intelligible as acted in the world. My cultural context *and* my actions constitute the meaning of holding a door open for someone. Furthermore, the door constrains the meaning because it reveals the possibility of being opened. If the object was without a door knob and extremely heavy, then the meaning of door would not be possible since I could not open it. In this way, human beings are thrown into a world of meanings and then continue to constitute meanings through actions.

From Heidegger's perspective, the intentional arrow is no longer unidirectional but bidirectional because the world and I reveal meaning. Being-in-the-world is bidirectional because humans are thrown into a world that involves meanings that are constantly being enacted through intentionality since some meanings exist without requiring a particular person to intend them. While, for both Husserl and Heidegger, humans can intend multiple meanings at one time, for Heidegger, but not for Husserl, the world constrains these meanings. So, for Husserl, the intentional arrow is only directed toward objects, or unidirectional. For Heidegger, the world also constrains the meanings for someone who intends, and the arrow indicating meaning formation moves from the world toward the person as well. Heidegger's (1962) example of this idea is useful. A carpenter has many tools at his disposal and some tools are better suited for certain jobs. The hammer is better suited to hit nails than wood glue. However, it is not better suited only because I intend it to be that way (or because someone else intended it). Another person intended connecting boards together and intended a tool for that purpose. Yet, the person did not, and could not, intend the constraints of the hammer that make it, in its current form, able to hammer nails better than wood glue can. The hammer is better suited to hit nails because there is something about a hammer that makes it better suited to hit nails. The hammer participates in the meaning of the action of hammering just as the carpenter does. Heidegger (1962) concludes this example by saying:

> But when we deal with them [objects] by using them and manipulating them, this activity is not a blind one; it has its own kind of sight, by which our manipulation is guided and from which it acquires its specific Thingly character. (98)

The hammer guides the carpenter's manipulation, his use of the hammer, and this guidance participates in providing the character of the hammer.

Thus, one way Heidegger extends Husserl's notion of the lifeworld is by including a meaningful world as context for intentionality such that the lifeworld of intentionality becomes a more existential and thrown being-in-the-world (LeVasseur 2003). Regardless of scholars' opinion about the dualism of Husserl, Heidegger intends being-in-the-world as a rejection of dualism such that the world cannot be divided into subject and object (Heidegger 1962). Heidegger defends this claim (see Heidegger 1962); in short, since human action constitutes meaning through intentionality, as Husserl says, but it is also always already in a meaningful world, there is no distinction between subject (human) and object (world). In other words, being-in-the-world relies on the world and human action being meaningful in such a way that the relationship between human action and the world is indivisible; human actions and the world constitute meaning. As such, the example of an arrow that separates the object from the person is no longer ideal because intentionality and the world are meanings and are connected meaningfully. The intentional arrow betrays its own dualistic heritage by dividing intentionality as a subject intending an object. Husserl distinguishes between objects with essences and meaningful intentional actions. Being-in-the-world simply states that people act meaningfully toward an always and already meaningful world such that there is no distinction between intentionality and the world because the world constrains meanings as well. Heidegger does not divide the world between subject and object because meanings are constituted through meaningful human action in an always and already meaningful world.

As being-in-the-world implies, self-observation must also occur in a world that constrains meaning. As with Husserl, other people's intentions constrain meaning; but, being-in-the-world allows the world to constrain meanings as well. When I learn that I am short-tempered when hungry, it is not simply because I intend differently when hungry; instead, my meaning depends upon what it means to be hungry, including the bodily sensations that constrain hunger and short-temperedness, as well as the cultural expectations of anger management that I am responding to. These meanings do not participate because I intend them but participate because they constitute the world in which I act, including my short-temperedness. In this way, human action is not the sole constraint on meaning, including meanings about the self. In other words, self-observation is not simply human interpretation of human existence. Instead, self-observation is constrained by the cultural, historical, and physical world. The importance of this difference with Husserl will become apparent in the next section as we discuss the different understandings of reduction for Husserl and Heidegger.

Being-in-the-World and Reduction

Reduction, as described by Husserl, is not deemed possible from a Heideggerian perspective because it is impossible to escape all our prejudgments as being-in-the-world. From the perspective of being-in-the-world, prejudgments are constituted by the relationship of action in the world and cannot be bracketed or suspended completely because, from a Heideggarian perspective, there is no essence to completely reveal. Instead, existential bracketing, influenced by Heidegger's understanding of being-in-the-world, focuses on meanings in the world as experienced by humans (Dowling 2007; Gearing 2004; LeVasseur 2003) and not on essences. Existential reduction focuses on assumptions as prejudgments that cannot be fully bracketed or set aside but can reveal meanings in the world because of their relationship to human actions and sociocultural, historical, and personal contexts (Dowling 2007; LeVasseur 2003). For Heidegger, meaning, such as the hammer, can be focused on without needing to clear away all unessential parts of the meaning because meanings do not have essence. Instead, meanings have constraints, through our actions and the world. The very way I use the hammer reveals something about the hammer and the contexts in which I use the hammer, such as the purposes and constraints of hammers; the hammer "raises the totality of equipment [objects] into our circumspection so that together with it the worldly character . . . announces itself" (Heidegger 1962, 110). Through the hammer, the character of other objects is announced.

The relationship of human action in the world established by being-in-the-world allows reduction to occur as a hermeneutic circle such that meanings in the world can reveal assumptions, or implicit meanings, and vice versa. My use of the hammer reveals my implicit meanings about hammer use as compared to the use of other tools. Further, my use of the hammer is constrained by my implicit meanings of hammer use. For the hermeneutic circle, actions and meanings are intimately connected and cannot be divorced. The meaning gained through existential reduction provides a new context, constrained by the world, for further reduction. When I understand my assumptions about hammer use, I can begin to understand assumptions about screwdriver use and carpentry. Through the hermeneutic circle, a more reflexive understanding is achieved in existential reduction (LeVasseur 2003). Thus, for Heidegger, reduction and bracketing are possible as long as revealing essences is not the purpose. For Heidegger, this process of revealing meaning through our actions, which are constrained by our assumptions, is called disclosure, and "shall signify 'to lay open' and 'the character of having been laid open'" (Heidegger 1962, 105).

For self-observation, existential reduction implies that knowledge about ourselves comes from the way we act in a meaningful world, which includes assumptions and the world as constraints. Even though hammers are not separate from my intentional actions, my use of the hammer can show me something about the hammer; it can also show me something about myself: e.g., how I think hammers are used or how good I am with tools. In other words, my use of the hammer discloses particular meanings of the hammer and myself. Is this not what we mean when we say that someone is good with his or her hands? And, we can say the same thing about ourselves because we experience our own use of tools. Furthermore, this meaning can alter other meanings: do I call a repair man or fix the washing machine myself? If I am not good with my hands, my monthly budget for home repairs must be higher because I cannot do as many home repairs myself. My use of the hammer discloses these meanings for me through a hermeneutic. Self-observation is hermeneutic just as other types of knowledge can be called hermeneutic. The difference is the focus, or reduction, of the hermeneutic. For self-observation, the focus is on the self—but the hermeneutic discloses in the same way.

Self-Observation as Hermeneutic Reduction

The hermeneutic reduction allows meanings to be disclosed such that these meanings can be better understood. For self-observation, the reduction focuses on what my own actions disclose about myself.

While disclosure often emphasizes the way the world is revealed to me, self-observation simply emphasizes the self as participatory in the hermeneutic. Self-observation can be understood as hermeneutic reduction such that the world is present but the focus is on the actions of the self in the world. In other words, a phenomenological understanding of self-observation focuses on the relationship between the world and the self that constitutes experience while foregrounding the meanings of the self. Furthermore, self-observation allows for an interpreting being (the self) to be the focus of interpretation, and hermeneutics makes it possible to understand these meanings as disclosed through self-observation.

This focus moves self-observation outside the self, from intro-spection to intra-spection, or a focus on the self's constitution *within* the world. In other words, the goal of intra-spection is reduction with the self as foreground instead of the world, which is often what other types of knowledge foreground. Typically, reduction is performed on something other than the self, such as a Biblical text. The emphasis is on gaining meaning about the text through understanding the constraints of the self, such as belief in God, and the constraints of the text, such as the words on the page. Self-observation emphasizes gaining meaning about the self through this same process. However, the constraints serve to inform a person about him- or herself instead of to inform the person about his or her meanings for something in the world. As such, intra-spection does not mean within the self; instead, intra-spection deals with the meanings within the world as these meanings are constituted by intentional actions and the world. Since being-in-the-world discloses meanings within the world, intra-spection addresses the relationship of these meanings within the world while focusing on the self.

Self-observation is one particular way to perform a reduction that discloses meanings as connected with the self. In other words, while the focus of intra-spection is the self, the meanings of other people and the world are important for understanding the self. In fact, being-in-the-world implies that meanings about the self cannot be divorced from meanings disclosed by other people's actions and given by the world. These various sources of meaning, all of which can be the focus of reduction, often reinforce each other. For intra-spection, the focus is on how the cultural, historical, and physical context influences meanings about the self. A fictitious example may help. This example is commonly used in therapy literature because of the vicious cycle of the issue that perpetuates the problem. I hope to show that the cyclical nature of the issue results from the hermeneutic relationship of meaning: the example is cyclical because it participates in the hermeneutic circle. Furthermore, self-observation, and the solution to the problem, also participates in the hermeneutic circle.

An Example

A couple enters therapy because they are having trouble with their marriage. She claims that he does not pay enough attention to her: he stays at work longer than before and spends less time with her. She even wonders if he is having an affair, which he denies. He claims that she is constantly hovering over him and checking in on him. He says she wants to spend every free moment engaged with him in something meaningful. After a few weeks of dealing with the issues, it has become clear to the therapist that the husband does not come home when he could. The wife discloses his absence in a particular way by wanting to spend more time with him when he is at home. These experiences have often led to fights and bitter feelings. Unfortunately, the bitter feelings provide a context such that the husband wants to stay longer at work. He also admitted to flirting with a coworker. At some point, the relationship of the husband and wife changed such that the fighting brought about the very things the couple was fighting about. The wife is right: the husband does not come home when he could and is thinking about another woman. The husband is right: the wife does want more attention. Furthermore, these problems are hermeneutic in nature because they inform and strengthen each other. In other words, the meanings of their marriage are constituted by the relationship of the husband's and wife's actions.

Yet, the very same issues can potentially lead to insights when intra-spection is considered. The husband's action—staying at work and flirting with his coworker—disclose the way he is feeling about his wife. This disclosure is not, and cannot be, divorced from the intentions of his wife, who wants to spend time with him, and his coworker, who flirts back. The husband's actions disclose a source of the problem: the husband's intentions. Yet, the husband's actions only disclose this meaning because they are in relation to the wife's and coworker's actions. Furthermore, his actions reveal the purpose of his wife's actions: to be closer to her husband who is distancing himself from her. The husband's actions are meanings that reveal his own desires and the desires of his wife and, perhaps, his coworker.

In this light, the husband realizes that his actions are connected to his wife's actions since their actions are mutually defined. This realization may even provide some insight into why he no longer enjoys being at home, such as how he discloses his wife's actions. Furthermore, he may also realize that changing his intentions, his actions, will disclose new meaning for his wife's and, perhaps, coworker's actions. This new knowledge can then make sense of his claims that his wife wants more attention. He has not been giving her attention because he no longer enjoys being at home. His wife is correct. The problem, which before was about a disagreement with his wife, is no longer about a disagreement but is now about his actions toward his wife as well as his wife's, and coworker's, actions. Furthermore, the issue is about how the husband and wife mutually constitute the problem. The husband may realize, through intra-spection, how his own intentions have brought about the issues in their marriage, and how these intentions are constituted by his own actions as in relation to other people's, including his wife, intentions.

The wife's actions—seeking more attention—disclose the way she feels about her husband and disclose another source of the problem—the wife's actions. Similar to the husband's actions, the wife's actions also reveal the meanings intended by her husband and, perhaps, his coworker. The wife's actions disclose her meanings and the meanings enacted by her husband as he stays late to work. If the wife looks at her own actions, in relation to her husband's action, as indicators about her thoughts and feelings about her husband, she can realize that she is earnestly seeking his attention. In fact, she can realize that she has been constantly forcing him to spend time with her when at home, and how, together, their actions have disclosed this meaning. This new knowledge can then make sense of the husband's actions to stay away from home. Home is not inviting because of her actions as taken up in a world that includes her husband's, and his coworker's, actions. Again, the relationship between the husband's and wife's actions constitute the meaning of their marriage problems. The problem is now the meanings each spouse intends in their relationship.

Through intra-spection, the husband and wife can disclose new meanings about their relationship. Each person relied on intra-spection to gain new insight into their behavior, and the relationship of meanings that constitutes the problem. The insight, in turn, made possible a new understanding of their relationship—an understanding in which each took responsibility for their actions. However, this responsibility is not because one individual decided to step up and save the marriage. Instead, the responsibility results from the disclosure of the problem as constituted by shared meanings and behaviors. In other words, the hermeneutic of self-observation provides a solution to the problem: change the shared meaning. The problem has ceased to be about the wrong-doings of the other person and has become about the perversion of their relationship, and how this perversion is mutually constituted. In other words, the problem is no longer caused by the other person—he does not come home or she is too attached; instead, the problem is about the shared meanings they have enacted in the world—a problem they are both involved in. This problem is one they are in together and is potentially solvable together. The couple is no longer at odds with each other but is together in the relationship, and may be together in a solution to the problem. The solution is to mutually constitute different meanings through intending differently.

Hopefully, this example has provided insight into how intra-spection focuses on the self but can reveal truth about the meanings in our world through the hermeneutic circle. Specifically, intra-spection reveals truths about the husband and wife's relationship even though the focus of the husband and wife was on each person's actions. Since meaning is hermeneutic and related to other meanings, the truths revealed through intra-spection about the self were not isolated; instead, these truths helped reveal truths about each spouse's actions, the response of the other spouse, and the meanings of their current relationships with each other and other people. The truth gained through intra-spection helped continue the hermeneutic circle of understanding as these truths, taken up in the spouses' lives, revealed more truths. This understanding of self-observation is different from the traditional understanding of self-observation. Particularly, intra-spection participates in the hermeneutic nature of meaning. This difference does have implications for self-observation.

Implications of Existential Reduction for Self-Observation

With a better understanding of what I mean by intra-spection, we can now take a look at theoretical implications of intra-spection for dualistic self-observation. Traditionally, self-observation, as outlined in this book, participates in dualism since self-observation distinguishes between internal and external states that provide knowledge. There are three issues that arise for dualistic self-observation: the interaction, the distinction, and the correspondence of objective and subjective forms of knowledge. A phenomenologically informed self-observation provides answers to these issues because, as hermeneutic, phenomenological self-observation will be based in existential reduction as an epistemological method (Dowling 2007). Since other authors in this book have discussed the problems of traditional self-observation, let me only briefly remind the reader about these problems to discuss how intra-spection overcomes them.

The problem of interaction and intra-spection's solution. The problem of interaction is the issue of how two distinct realities can influence each other (Slife et al., in press). How does subjective experience receive information from objective reality or how does objective reality become subjective experience? For self-observation, this problem manifests in the dismissal of insight from self-observation. How can introspective insights say anything about the external world since the external world and self-observation never interact? If the subjective and objective realities never meet, then subjective experience, or self-observation, cannot say anything about objective reality.

While dualistic self-observation is plagued by this problem, intra-spection as hermeneutic reduction is not. In fact, intra-spection rejects the primary premise of dualistic self-observation that subjective and objective knowledge are two distinct realities. Intra-spection denies this division such that the problems associated with two distinct realities are not present. For intra-spection, all knowledge is brought about by meaningful intentions, or actions, in a meaningful world. From this perspective, meanings exist throughout the world such that the world is constituted through meanings. Whether these meanings are understood through intra-spection or empirical science does not change the constitutive nature of meanings. Empirical sciences are certain kinds of intentional actions with certain goals that disclose meanings in a certain way. Intra-spection, as well, is certain kinds of intentional actions with certain goals that disclose meanings in a certain way. Both intra-spection and empirical science are meaningful intentions. Hence, there is no difference between the types of knowledge gained through intra-spection and empirical sciences. In fact, the only difference between these types of inquiry is a meaning—the different goals. Intra-spection and empirical science have different goals and, thus, disclose the world differently. But, to say they have different goals is simply to say they intend different meanings. From a phenomenological perspective, empirical sciences attempt to disclose the world in a different way, or perform a different reduction, than intra-spection, but both attempt, through reduction, to disclose meanings in the world.

This similarity between intra-spection and other types of knowledge rejects the distinction between subjective and objective knowledge. First, there is no problem of interaction. The meanings disclosed through intra-spection always already infuse the meanings of the world, even scientific meanings. Thomas Kuhn and others have explicated how scientists' beliefs and expectations influence how they see the world around them (see, e.g., Kuhn 1996), indicating the role of meaning in scientific endeavors. Intra-spective meanings must be recognized as having a different goal, or reduction, than other types of meanings, even though they are disclosed through the hermeneutic circle just as all other types of meaning. This different goal of self-observation has implications. For example, I may realize that I am short-tempered but my realization does not mean my neighbor is necessarily short-tempered, or that intra-spective insights can always be generalized. However, my insights may help my neighbor if he also realizes he is short-tempered since I can tell him how I deal with my temper. Thus, while there is no divide between subjective and objective knowledge, intra-spection cannot and should not make claims outside of the world that it discloses. Yet, the same can and should be said of other types of knowledge, including empirical knowledge.

The problem of distinction and intra-spection's solution. The problem of the distinction between the subjective and objective is the question of where we draw the line between the subjective and objective (Slife et al., in press). If knowledge about the external world is gained through the senses, which require subjective interpretation, how can we distinguish between the external world and our interpretations of the external world? For self-observation, the problem manifests in researchers' desire to eschew any and all biases that are the result of researchers' personal thoughts about experience. Informal theories can be guided by these introspective hunches, but scientific research must present empirical support. Yet, researchers must interpret results, which is influenced by the researcher's thoughts, including thoughts that result from self-observation. In other words, researchers' interpretations, influenced by self-observation, are the only way researchers know empirical data. Since knowledge is not obtained except through some interpretation of the external world, it is difficult to differentiate between subjective and objective reality, or self-observation and the external world.

For intra-spection, there is no need to distinguish between two types of knowledge because there is no distinction. If different types of knowledge are not endorsed and there is no problem of interaction, then the quest to show exactly how types of knowledge differ is irrelevant. So there is no epistemological difference between intra-spection and other types of knowledge. Yet, I seemed to claim in the previous paragraph that intra-spection and empirical knowledge did differ. This question reveals the impact of dualism on our thinking: any difference almost always means a distinction that separates into two realms. The goals of reduction do differ, but the epistemological approach does not; both empirical science and self-observation rely on hermeneutic reduction. My claim is that our actions, not the foundational nature of the world, differentiate between intra-spection and empirical knowledge. Intra-spection and empirical knowledge reveal meanings in the world and, so, are not distinct except that they have different goals. If this is the case, then there is no reason, in general, to prefer one type of knowledge over another. My argument extends beyond an inclusion of intra-spection as an acceptable method; instead, I claim that empirical knowledge is not objective—it is hermeneutic reduction as well. If the phenomenological position is correct, both intra-spection and empirical science are intentional actions in a meaningful world. It is for this reason that there is no distinction between intra-spection and empirical knowledge and no need to stipulate where the distinction happens.

The problem of correspondence and intra-spection's solution. The problem of correspondence dovetails from the previous problem: if knowledge is always interpreted, then how can we make sure our interpreted knowledge corresponds with reality (Slife et al., in press)? The problem is compounded since objective reality is never experienced by people, so people are always using a subjective experience with which to compare other subjective experiences. So any experience, including experiences of scientific data, is always subjective experience that is attempting to be compared to objective reality to which scientists have no access. For self-observation, this problem manifests in the replacement of self-observation with measures that supposedly remove the researcher's biases and experiences from the research situation. For this purpose, researchers have constructed instruments and questionnaires and validated these with the expectation of moving away from subjective interpretations of data.

The problem of correspondence disappears as well when there is nothing that needs to correspond with something else. Without two distinct types of knowledge, correspondence between one type—meaning—with itself does not make sense. Intra-spection does not need to correspond with objective reality because hermeneutics rejects the distinction between objective and subjective realities. This issue has been the main problem with dualistic self-observation: how can we be sure that introspective knowledge matches the real world.

Intra-spection does not have this problem because the real world and intra-spection are constituted by meanings. Instead, the question becomes about the goals that disclose particular meanings. In other words, the question is as follows: is it appropriate to disclose particular meanings in a certain way. For example, is it appropriate to disclose the physiological pathways of heart disease through intra-spection? If it is, intra-spection plays a very limited role in this focus of disclosure. Yet, this limited role does not mean that, in general, intra-spection is useless as a method. The same can be said of empirical methods. Are empirical methods appropriate to disclose the experience of love between newly weds? It may be to a limited extent, just as intra-spection is limited at disclosing physiology. Does that mean we do not use empirical methods ever? No, empirical methods are very appropriate for disclosing some meanings: the physiology of heart disease, for example. But, if we confuse one way of disclosing meanings as the only way to disclose a specific meaning, then we may be closing off some of the experience. Thus, for any type of disclosure, the goal must be intimately connected with the knowledge gained through disclosure so that scientists do not overstep their bounds when making claims with a limited disclosure about the world.

Conclusion

Heidegger's understanding, dependent on Husserl's work, of being-in-the-world provides a hermeneutic foundation that provides insight for self-observation. Being-in-the-world offers an understanding of meaning that allows self-observation to be in relation to other meanings as enacted in the world. In this sense, self-observation is no different than other forms of disclosure as all forms of disclosure reveal meanings in particular ways. Specifically, self-observation foregrounds the self and how the self is in relation to other intentions and meanings. Intra-spection, as a phenomenologically informed understanding of self-observation, does not deny this relationship of intentions and meanings; instead, intra-spection takes up these relationships to disclose meanings about the self without denying the hermeneutic nature of meaning. Since intra-spection does not deny hermeneutics, it provides a solid foundation for self-observation because intra-spection recognizes the contextual nature of disclosure, connects intra-spective disclosure to meanings disclosed through other methods, and provides a context for determining what meaning should be foregrounded given the hermeneutic situation. As such, intra-spection can be a useful method for gaining insight through self-observation.

References

Benson, B. E. 2002. *Graven Ideologies: Nietzsche, Derrida, and Marion on Modern Idolatry*. Downers Grove, IL: InterVarsity Press.

Bernet, R., Kern, I., and Marbach, E. 1993. *An Introduction to Husserlian Phenomenology*. Evanston, IL: Northwestern University Press.

Boring, E. G. 1953. "A History of Introspection." *Psychological Bulletin* 50, no. 3: 169–86. doi: 10.1037/h0090793.

Clegg. J. W. 2012. "Developing an Adequate Theory of Self-Observation." In *Self-Observation in the Social Sciences*, edited by J. W. Clegg, 3–21. New Brunswick, NJ: Transaction Publishers.

Dowling, M. 2007. "From Husserl to van Manen. A Review of Different Phenomenological Approaches." *International Journal of Nursing Studies* 44, no. 1: 131–42. doi: 10.1016/j.ijnurstu.2005.11.026.

Gearing, R. E. 2004. "Bracketing in Research: A Typology." *Qualitative Health Research* 14, no. 10: 1429–52. doi: 10.1177/1049732304270394.

Heidegger, M. 1962. *Being and Time* (J. Macquarrie and E. Robinson, Trans. 7th edn.). New York: Harper and Row.

Husserl, E. 1970. *The Crisis of European Sciences and Transcendental Phenomenology* (D. Carr, Trans.). Evanston, IL: Northwestern University Press.

Kuhn, T. S. 1996. *The Structure of Scientific Revolutions*, 3 edn. Chicago, IL: University of Chicago Press.

LeVasseur, J. J. 2003. "The Problem of Bracketing in Phenomenology." *Qualitative Health Research* 13, no. 3: 408–20. doi: 10.1177/1049732302250337.

Slife, B. D., Reber, J. S., and Faulconer, J. in press. "Implicit Ontological Reasoning: Problems of Dualism in Psychological Science." In *Psychology of Science: Implicit and Explicit Reasoning*, edited by R. Procter and J. Capaldi. New York: Oxford University Press.

Sokolowski, R. 2000. *Introduction to Phenomenology*. Washington, DC: Cambridge University.

Vernon, R. F. 2005. "Peering into the Foundations of Inquiry: An Ontology of Conscious Experience along Husserlian Lines." *Journal of Theoretical and Philosophical Psychology* 25, no. 2: 280–300. doi: 10.1037/h0091263.

von Eckartsberg, R. 1992. "Plurality in Social Psychology." *Theoretical & Philosophical Psychology* 12, no. 2: 79–102. doi: 10.1037/h0091116.

10

The Practice of Self-Observation in the Phenomenological Traditions

Svend Brinkmann

As living human beings, we all have the capacities for self-observation. As language users, we also have the capacity to conceptualize and reflect upon the ways we observe ourselves, and we can communicate our self-observations to others. Artists and human and social scientists alike make use of these capacities. Great novelists have provided us with detailed accounts based on self-observation, and a rigorous and systematic use of the capacities for self-observation is central to many disciplines in the human and social sciences. This chapter addresses the practice of self-observation within a broad phenomenological context.

The chapter tackles issues about the *what*, the *who*, and the *how* of self-observation. Concerning the *what*, it is crucial for an understanding of self-observation to make clear what one wants to observe. Obviously, self-observation involves an observation of the self. All empirical sciences from astronomy to sociology involve observing selves, i.e., scientists who observe processes and properties of the world. Essential to self-observation, however, is the fact that the self is both subject and object in the process of observation. Thus, the self that observes is also the self that is observed. This, evidently, has generated a lot of discussion and critique of self-observational methods in the history of psychology and other social sciences, mainly under the heading of introspection. Can reports based on self-observation be reliable and valid? The main methodological problems in introspection are twofold: First there is the problem of intersubjectivity (how can other people know and check that the introspective person reports correctly?), and second there

195

is what we may call the problem of mediation (does not the activity of introspection itself unavoidably mediate and thereby change the psychological reality that is observed?).

The discussion of these questions, however relevant they are, has led to a neglect of a more fundamental issue, which may, incidentally, lead us to a clearer view of these other problems. This is the question of the self as such. What is the self that observes and is observed in self-observation? This is the first and most fundamental question to be addressed below. The other questions that I shall address concern *who* observes in self-observation, where a relevant distinction emerges between direct and indirect self-observation, and finally *how* one proceeds in practice to conduct research based on self-observations. Before moving on to these sets of questions, however, I shall begin by explaining how this chapter relates to the phenomenological traditions.

The Phenomenological Traditions

According to Amedeo Giorgi, a leading phenomenological psychologist, phenomenology is "the study of the structure, and the variations of structure, of the consciousness to which any thing, event, or person appears" (Giorgi 1975, 83). Phenomenology was founded as a philosophy by Edmund Husserl around 1900 and further developed as an existential philosophy by Martin Heidegger, and then in an existential and dialectical direction by Jean-Paul Sartre and Maurice Merleau-Ponty.

The subject matter of phenomenology began with consciousness and experience—the most intimate and immediate reality available to human observers. It was later expanded by Husserl and also Heidegger to include the human lifeworld, and to take account of the body and human action in historical contexts by Merleau-Ponty and Sartre (Kvale and Brinkmann 2008, 26). The goal in Husserlian phenomenology was to arrive at an investigation of essences, i.e., to describe the essential structures of human experience from a first-person perspective. Phenomenology was then a strict descriptive philosophy, employing the technique of *reduction*, which means to suspend one's judgment as to the existence or nonexistence of the content of an experience. The reduction is often pictured as a "bracketing" (also called the *epoche*), an attempt to place the common sense and scientific foreknowledge about the phenomena within parentheses in order to arrive at an unprejudiced description of the essence of the phenomena (27).

The concept of the lifeworld eventually became central to Husserl. He introduced the concept in 1936 in *The Crisis of the European Sciences* (Husserl 1954) to refer to the shared and intersubjective meaningful world in which humans conduct their lives and experience significant phenomena. It is a pre-reflective and pretheorized world in which shame, for example (I shall use shame as a recurrent example in this text), is a way of being-in-the-world, a meaningful response to certain events, *before* it (shame) may be explained with reference to its neurochemical correlates or by other objectifying means. If shame did not appear to human beings as an *experienced phenomenon*, a meaningful, yet painful, phenomenon in their lifeworld, there would be no reason to investigate it scientifically, for there would in a sense be nothing to investigate. There is thus a primacy of the lifeworld as experienced, since this is prior to the scientific theories we may formulate about it, which was well expressed by Merleau-Ponty:

> All my knowledge of the world, even my scientific knowledge, is gained from my own particular point of view, or from some experience of the world without which the symbols of science would be meaningless. The whole universe of science is built upon the world as directly experienced, and if we want to subject science itself to rigorous scrutiny and arrive at a precise assessment of its meaning and scope, we must begin by re-awakening the basic experiences of the world of which science is the second order expression. (Merleau-Ponty 1945, ix)

Using a metaphor, we can say that when we are concerned with human life, the sciences may give us maps, but the lifeworld is the territory or the geography of our lives. Maps make sense only on the background of the territory, where human beings act and live, and should not be confused with it. Phenomenologists are not against scientific abstractions or "maps," but they insist on the primacy of concrete descriptions of that which is prior to maps and analytic abstractions. This means that self-observation comes to matter not simply as some additional peripheral methodology, but rather as one of the central means of accessing the lived territory of the lifeworld. The only instrument that is sensitive enough to grasp the intersubjective and meaningful realm of the lifeworld is an observing self that must itself be understood as a part of what is observed and described.

What initially looks like a paradox—that the self that observes is the self that is observed—turns out to be a precondition for knowledge of the lifeworld, since the lifeworld can only be known "from within," by a participating and observing self. How can one understand the experience of shame, to stay with this example, without understanding the existential situations in which the self is painfully revealed to the gazes of others—e.g., when one is caught looking through a keyhole? The answer is that no scientific perspective that transcends the lifeworld and the first-person perspectives within it (e.g., from the neurosciences) can ever grasp the *experience* of shame. Surely, we can study the level of stress in situations of shame by measuring hormone levels in the blood, for example, but this does not tell us what shame is as a meaningful, experienced phenomenon in the lifeworld. Shame and other such human phenomena can only be understood from an immanent position within "the whole hurly-burly of human actions," as Wittgenstein once put it (1981, no. 567), and this is where self-observation turns out to be not only legitimate, but likely the only adequate method of inquiry.

When Husserl turned his phenomenology into a philosophy of the lifeworld in the 1930s, it marked a turning point away from Cartesian and Kantian philosophies of consciousness and toward a much more social and intersubjective philosophy. This also paved the way for phenomenology's influence on the social sciences. In sociology, for example, Alfred Schutz' phenomenology of the social world deserves to be mentioned, which was further "socialized" and historicized by Berger and Luckmann in *The Social Construction of Reality* (1966), and also (in a different way) in Harold Garfinkel's (1967) ethnomethodological studies of the practical production of social order. Today, the term "phenomenology" is often used quite loosely in the social sciences, signifying an interest in understanding social phenomena from the actors' own perspectives, describing the world as experienced by the subjects, with the assumption that the important reality is what people perceive it to be (Kvale and Brinkmann 2008, 26).

In psychology, however, some researchers have stayed with a more rigorous and strictly Husserlian phenomenological psychology, in particular Amedeo Giorgi and other phenomenologists with relations to Duquesne University. In a recent exposition of the phenomenological method, Giorgi and Giorgi have outlined the following steps (Giorgi and Giorgi 2008, 170): (1) Obtain a concrete description of a phenomenon as lived through by a person. This can be directly described, e.g., by the researcher herself, or the description can be obtained by interview. Then, assuming the phenomenological attitude of reduction and *epoche*, the researcher should read the description as a whole. (2) After grasping the whole, the researcher should go back and read again more slowly with the aim of establishing meaning units in the description. (3) The next step involves leaving the participant's perspective in order to convey the psychological sense of the description. This may involve using theoretical concepts that the participant may not employ herself. (4) Ultimately, based on the analysis of meaning units, the general structure of the experience of the phenomenon can be articulated. This represents one well worked-out phenomenological method, which we may designate as self-observation, but for the phenomenologists, it is a basic and very general method to understand any phenomenon as experienced. Below, I shall present three more concrete methods of self-observation.

All in all, it is clear that phenomenology has branched and now lives in different theoretical traditions. These are united, however, in their shared ambition to be descriptive, to use the first-person perspective as a point of departure for social and psychological analyses, and also in an insistence on the lifeworld as the primary human reality. It should be said that by conceiving of phenomenology in this broad sense, we are also able to include other traditions as phenomenological, e.g., the linguistic phenomenology articulated by Ludwig Wittgenstein, culminating in his *Philosophical Investigations* (Wittgenstein 1953). According to Gier's (1981) comparative study of the later Wittgenstein, Husserl, Heidegger, and Merleau-Ponty, Wittgenstein should be read as part of the phenomenological canon, concentrating on descriptions of our linguistic practices with the aim of dissolving the philosophical problems that arise from misguided dualist metaphysics. Centrally, Wittgenstein's linguistic phenomenology demonstrated that "language is living proof of intersubjectivity" (218), something that was also central to Merleau-Ponty and Heidegger.

Also pragmatism must be seen as a close ally with phenomenology, if not simply an Americanized version of it. Kestenbaum (1977) has demonstrated the huge common ground between Dewey and Merleau-Ponty, and Herzog (1995) has developed a similar argument with respect to James and Husserl, arguing that Husserl was greatly inspired by James' philosophy (and psychology) of experience. James' later "radical empiricism" can be read as a powerful articulation of a phenomenological stance: "To be radical," James famously wrote, "an empiricism must neither admit into its constructions any element that is not directly experienced, nor exclude from them any element that is directly experienced" (James 1912, 22). Thus, James would say, we not only experience particulars like cups, cutlery, food, and wine directly, but also the relations between them, e.g., the ways that such particulars together constitute a dinner party. The radical empiricism of James, the immediate empiricism of Dewey, stressing what he called "the ordinary qualitative world" (Dewey 1929, 103), and the linguistic phenomenology of Wittgenstein can all be seen as deeply related to traditional continental phenomenology and therefore relevant to practices of self-observation, in particular those practices that are concerned with self-observation in social situations.

The Self That Is Observed

I shall now address the what of phenomenological self-observation. The self observes and is observed in self-observation, but what is the self? When one observes oneself in introspective studies, the self is often implicitly seen as something "inner," as an inner experiential realm or a "Cartesian theater" in which mental objects appear. Costall (2007) has criticized this conception as a "windowless room," which is part of a more comprehensive epistemology according to which we cannot be in direct contact with our surroundings. Phenomenology aims to overcome this conception by focusing on consciousness as always already intentional, i.e., directed at something (and, in this sense, "outside of itself"). We—including our "selves"—are indeed both in and of the world, and self-observation is just as much a matter of observing ourselves acting, living, and interacting, as it is a matter of inward introspection. The idea of the lifeworld as a world of social practices that take place, or—we should perhaps say—are performed, in the world and change it should also point in this direction, i.e., beyond the Cartesian idea of inner, mental objects to be observed as the locus of self-observation. Drawing on a number of sources, Gillespie and Zittoun (2010) have recently distinguished between a Cartesian and a Hegelian approach to the study of psychological processes, which can also be called the product and process paradigm, respectively, and the ideas of self-observation to be unfolded below are primarily set within the Hegelian, process-oriented paradigm, where the self involves a stream of thoughts and actions mediated by cultural signs (74). In this sense, the self and its "movement of thought" are in large part external and open to observation.

Rom Harré's (1998) distinction between three uses of the concept of self is helpful in outlining the *what* of self-observation: First, we can think of the self as a phenomenological standpoint from which one observes. Harré calls this Self 1. Second, we can conceive of the self as the totality of attributes of a person, which includes ideas about what sort of person one is, and this—Self 2—can also be radicalized to a Jamesian perspective on the self as *"the sum total of all that* [someone] *CAN call his"* (James 1890, 279), which, for James, includes clothes, family, friends, reputation, and material objects. From this perspective, self-observation includes a careful study of the symbolic *and* material resources that make up the self. Third, we can approach the self in more Meadian terms as an interactional self or a Self 3. Here, self-observation is primarily concerned with observing the self in social interaction, and recording one's own reactions (this method has been used, for example, by Milgram and Garfinkel, as we shall see below). I shall say a few words about each self-conception in turn.

Self 1

Harré's notion of Self 1 is close to the phenomenologists' understanding of the consciousness of the first-person perspective. Harré writes that to have a sense of self "is to have a sense of one's location, as a person, in each of the several arrays of other beings, relevant to personhood" (1998, 4). This sense of location relates fundamentally to occupying a location in space from which one perceives and acts in the material environment, but I believe that it can also refer more broadly to one's sense of being someone in a social environment. When someone describes what it feels like to be ashamed (e.g., that it feels like shrinking and being naked in the presence of others), then she is articulating that description from a Self 1 perspective, i.e., from the perspective of someone who experiences the world from this specific standpoint. Harré argues that the sense of occupying a standpoint—and only *one* standpoint—is a cultural universal, and that there is just one Self 1 for each person, even for those who seem to suffer from Multiple Personality Disorder, for even these people experience the world from the spatial location of a single body (9). Self 1 is also close to the pragmatists' (James, Mead) idea of the I, the self as subject, i.e., the impulsive, agentive side of the self.

Self 2

Self 2 is close to James' and Mead's notion of the Me, i.e., that phase of the individual's life process that occurs when the self appears as an object with certain properties. Self 2 is the totality of attributes of a person, including that person's beliefs about herself. This is often conceptualized as the self-concept in psychology. Mead was clear that the self, as that which can be an object to itself, is a social entity arising in social experience (Mead 1962, 140). A person can only have beliefs about herself because she has acquired the capacity to look at herself from the outside, which is a capacity that develops in social situations. We learn to objectify ourselves by taking the attitudes of others toward ourselves. And we need a language, itself a social tool, in order for us to entertain beliefs about ourselves, so also in this sense is Self 2 a social product. Self 2, as the beliefs one has about oneself, will often be articulated in narrative form, for the kind of self-understanding that this sense of self implies manifests itself in the stories we tell about ourselves. Thus, someone does not think of herself as having done something shameful out of the blue, but there will almost always be a story to tell that frames a certain shameful incidence within a narrative structure with a plot. When such stories become particularly salient for an individual's self-understanding, they may even constitute what narrative psychologists like McAdams call a personal myth that make up a person's identity (McAdams 1997). As part of Self 2, I would also include the material resources that are available to a person in her life and enable her life processes. As I said with reference to James, this includes the sum total of all that someone can call his (or her). We literally study ourselves when we begin to analyze the material objects that we possess, for example. These are often extensions of the self's capabilities (glasses, computers, notebooks, etc.) or social identity (clothes, car, house) and are in that sense co-constitutive of the person's attributes. A truly relational view of the self would also include other people as aspects of a person's self.

Self 3

The third use of the concept of self that is relevant for self-observation refers to the sort of person that we are taken to be by others (Harré 1998, 177). Although all self-concepts have social aspects, this is therefore the most directly social side of the self. There may be discrepancies between the self that I intend to make manifest in what I say and do, and the self that others see in my actions and speech. "I am not crazy!" is a classic example of a sentence that may sound quite different to the person who utters it, and the psychiatrists who hear it, perhaps after having decided that the speaker is a psychotic patient. On a less dramatic note, people may interpret a person's reaction in a given situation as one of shame, whereas the person herself is unable to see anything shameful in the situation, but simply acts timidly—or vice versa. Obviously, there is also sometimes consistency between how a person understands herself and how she is taken up by others. The point is here that the self—as Self 3—is a conversational process. Like utterances, the self makes personal impressions on others, who then use these impressions to interpret the person and act in return. This process is dialogical in that each interpretation and act must be seen as a *response* to what went before in the process. There is a flow in human social life that cannot be understood if we cut the episodes up into separate units. This notion of dialogical flow has methodological implications for self-observation, since it underlines the importance of attending to the socio-temporal context within which something occurs or is done. It is not enough to observe something here and now without including the temporal background that enables something to appear in a certain way in the foreground. Again, shame not simply *happens*, but is *done* in dialogical encounters between persons in certain unfolding social situations.

The three concepts of the self are included here to remind us that self-observation can be many different things depending on which aspects of the self that researchers intend to capture. If we want to study how people experience shame as a lifeworld phenomenon, we can try to describe as closely as possible what it feels like to experience this emotion from the first-person perspective as it happens (Self 1) (e.g., through the Experience Sampling Method to be addressed below). We can also ask people to look at themselves and inform us of situations in which they felt shame, i.e., we can get them to talk about their "shameful selves" (Self 2), which is what we often do in research interviewing. Alternatively, we can observe the social-discursive negotiations of emotions like shame in everyday life (Self 3) by studying how others ascribe this emotion to people (e.g., to ourselves as researchers) or how people refuse to accept some incidence as shameful. Traditionally, phenomenologists have focused on Self 1, narratologists (but also many others) on Self 2, and symbolic interactionists and discourse analysts on Self 3. But I believe that it is perfectly possible and legitimate to combine these theoretical traditions in creative research projects, and I even think that an argument can be made that the most comprehensive understanding of some lifeworld phenomenon (such as shame) would include perspectives from all three angles on the self. In relation to shame, three guiding questions would then be:

- How does shame *feel*, how is it experienced? (Self 1)
- How is shame *understood*, e.g., how do people tell stories of shame? (Self 2)
- How are people *taken up by others* as shameful, how is shame negotiated discursively? (Self 3)

I shall describe three specific methods of self-observation below, but in a brief theoretical intermezzo, I will introduce one important issue that confronts self-observation researchers, although it is often bypassed in silence. This issue concerns the nature of self-talk, and it is particularly relevant for phenomenological research projects that focus on Self 1 observations, i.e., observations stemming from one's consciousness (such as "I feel sad now").

The Nature of Self-Talk

Self-talk generally works in one of two ways: It can be descriptive or expressive. It is important for researchers to understand the differences between these modes when considering the nature of one's data—are they descriptions or expressions? This distinction, which goes back to Wittgenstein's (1953) argument against the possibility of a logically private language, is often overlooked in self-observation methodologies. The basic distinction between these modes of self-talk hinges on whether the speaker can be corrected. When one describes something, the description can be more or less correct, and others can often inform the speaker that she is incorrect (if this is the case). If I talk about how certain other people understand me, I may say that "they think I'm shy," and in that sense I am describing their perception of myself (as it occurs to me). But I may be wrong (for perhaps they believe that I am arrogant rather than shy), and I may come to learn that I was wrong by obtaining the relevant evidence. The situation is different, however, if I sincerely say that "I am in pain" or that "I am happy." In these cases, and if I am not pretending, there is a way in which I cannot be wrong. These latter sentences do not describe my pain or happiness, but express them. Wittgenstein famously analyzed linguistic expressions of pain ("ouch!", "that hurts!" etc.) as natural expressions of pain (groans and cries) that have been transformed into verbal avowals. It would be just as false to say that "I am in pain" describes an inner object (pain) that one has observed, as it would be to say that the dog that cries out in pain after having been hit by a car is describing its pain. In both cases we witness expressions (that cannot as such be wrong, although they may be inappropriate) rather than descriptions.

This is not to deny that self-talk sometimes works descriptively. Concerning Self 2 and 3 we should often consider verbal reports of the self as descriptions. If intelligence is an attribute of the self (Self 2), then a sentence like "I am intelligent" is surely not as such an expression of intelligence (often quite the opposite!), but should be treated as a description (that may be false). But with regard to talk of sensations, intentions, emotions, beliefs, and states of mind, we should normally think of these as expressive. The methodological lesson for psychology of this has been spelled out by Harré:

> [T]he ontological distinction between thought (ineffable and mean-ingful) and language (audible, visible, tangible and meaningful) does not matter in certain key cases, because in the expressive mode there is a holistic unity. Part of the art of psychological method is to be right in distinguishing those psychological phenomena for which the holistic principle holds and those for which it does not. There is no epistemological gap between a feeling and the expressions of a feeling. (Harré 1998, 43–44).

In many ways, this is a great advantage in self-observation. For when someone expresses pains, moods, intentions or whatever in self-observation studies (e.g., "I feel ashamed"), there is no methodological (or ontological) question whether this expression adequately describes the "true" psychological state (as long as respondents are sincere). For the expression does not function descriptively at all. The expression is part of the holistic unity of the psychological phenomenon (e.g., shame). This, we should bear in mind, does not hold for third-person utterances. There is an asymmetry between first- and third-person self-talk. If I say about someone else that she felt shame, then it is legitimate to treat my utterance as a description, which it is not when I express my own shame.

I believe that Wittgenstein's analysis of these modes of self-talk answers some of the criticism one can direct at self-observational studies. For it actually annuls the question about how we can know that self-reports (in relation to Self 1) are correct descriptions (for the simple reason that most of them are not descriptions at all). People may certainly pretend to be in pain or feel ashamed, and in this sense there is a risk of error in self-observational data, but in these cases we should not say that people are speaking falsely or give incorrect descriptions of their states of mind, but that they are acting insincerely (Harré 1998, 42). This is a moral fault that can never be ruled out entirely, but it does not constitute an epistemic problem about self-observation. For there is not in such cases an "epistemological gap" between the feeling and its expression, as Harré pointed out with reference to Wittgenstein (again, this is different for properties like intelligence, where the holistic principle does not hold).

Who Observes in Self-Observation?

I have now introduced one distinction between self-observation data as either descriptions or expressions, and another one between different ways of answering the "what" question in self-observation studies. The "what" that is observed (oneself) may be conceived as one's consciousness, location or point of view (Self 1), one's sense of having a set of attributes, including self-conceptions (Self 2), or one's participation in conversations and practices where the self is equated with the impressions that one person makes on another (Self 3). The data in self-observation studies can come from all three sources.

The next question to address is the "who" in self-observation. Who should observe? Here, we can distinguish between direct and indirect self-observation. Direct self-observation is when the researcher takes her own self and experiences as subject matter. Indirect self-observation is when informants (e.g., assistants, students, or others) are recruited as self-observers. Observers may be trained or not, depending on the kind of reports that the researcher is interested in. An example of a significant historical instance of a large self-observation study with nontrained participants is the Mass-Observation Archive established in Britain in 1937, intended to create a "people's anthropology," where several hundred ordinary people from Britain volunteered to keep daily diaries about their lives (see Zittoun and Gillespie 2010, for a description of this archive and an analysis based on a close reading of one diarist).

Indirect self-observation is advocated in a number of methodologies, where the idea is to get data from a representative sample (Hektner et al. 2007; Rodriguez and Ryave 2002). If we want to know how young people, in general, feel during a day at school, how their moods and motivations fluctuate, or when they feel shame, and if we are interested in charting possible common patterns in these fluctuations, then it is obviously necessary to recruit a number of participants that are representative of this part of the population. When one uses participants, it may be important to teach them how to observe. If they have been told to observe specific events or processes in their everyday lives, then they should try as much as possible to go about their daily life without acting differently because of the assignment (Rodriguez and Ryave 2002, 16). It is also a good idea to instruct participants not to judge (e.g., morally) the phenomenon that one is interested in as it occurs. Needless to say, this may be artificial and cannot always be maintained without destroying the phenomenon itself (it is hard not to judge oneself when feeling shame, since a certain form of judgmental relation to oneself seems to be central to this emotion). Still, Ryave and Rodriguez recommend that participants are told something like the following: "Once you notice it [the topic] is happening: do not judge it, do not slow down, do not speed up, do not change it, do not question it – just observe it" (16–17). Hence, participants should try to be as descriptive (rather than analytical) as possible when reporting their self-observations (e.g., on a report sheet), and the idea is to make them write the report immediately after a relevant event. Researchers can favorably prepare participants with training exercises.

Direct or researcher-based self-observation has a long history in psychology and the social sciences ranging from early introspective studies to more recent studies of driving to work (Anthony Wallace), daydreams (Jerome Singer), playing jazz piano (David Sudnow), and other forms of systematic sociological introspection, as Carolyn Ellis calls them (Ellis 1991) (see Rodriguez and Ryave 2002, for these and more references to self-observation studies). The studies cited here are relatively unobtrusive in people's everyday lives, but some researchers have also developed ways of intervening quasi-experimentally in social life. The most famous of these is Harold Garfinkel, who developed the so-called "breaching experiments" as part of his ethnomethodological investigations. In one variety of these, Garfinkel asked his students (here acting as researchers) to engage in ordinary conversations and insist that the person clarify the sense of commonplace remarks:

> (S) Hi, Ray. How is your girl friend feeling?
>
> (E) What do you mean, "How is she feeling?" Do you mean physical or mental?
>
> (S) I mean how is she feeling? What's the matter with you? (He looked peeved.)

(E) Nothing. Just explain a little clearer what do you mean?

(S) Skip it. How are your Med School applications coming?

(E) What do you mean, "How are they?"

(S) You know what I mean.

(E) I really don't.

(S) What's the matter with you? Are you sick? (Garfinkel 1967, 42–43).

"S" is the subject and "E" is the "experimenter," deliberately breaching the ordinary production of social order with the aim of understanding the normativities that are tacitly taken for granted (until they are broken). Such conversational experiments highlight the background expectancies that are rarely thematized in everyday life, and a typical result of Garfinkel's breaches was bewilderment, unease, anxiety, and even anger on behalf of the conversationalists, including the researcher.

It is perhaps less known that Stanley Milgram (famous for his obedience experiments) conducted similar experiments in the 1970s, e.g., in a New York subway car, where he would ask another passenger for his seat in order to study the maintenance of social norms. Milgram recorded the number of passengers who gave him their seats (for no reason other than being asked), but his phenomenological self-observations are equally important data, which is seen in the following account by Milgram:

> I approached a seated passenger and was about to utter the magical phrase. But the words seemed lodged in my trachea and would simply not emerge. I stood there frozen, then retreated, the mission unfulfilled. My student observer urged me to try again, but I was overwhelmed by paralyzing inhibition. I argued to myself: "What kind of craven coward are you? You told your class to do it. How can you go back to them without carrying out your own assignment?" Finally, after several unsuccessful tries, I went up to a passenger and choked out the request, "Excuse me sir, may I have your seat?" A moment of stark anomic panic overcame me. But the man got right up and gave me the seat. A second blow was yet to come. Taking the man's seat, I was overwhelmed by the need to behave in a way that would justify my request. My head sank between my knees, and I could feel my face blanching. I was not role-playing, I actually felt as if I were going to perish. Then the third discovery: as soon as I got off the train, at the next station, all the tension disappeared. (Milgram 1992, xxiv)

This wonderful phenomenologically accurate and evocative passage has also been analyzed by Valsiner (2006), and it is a good example of a self-observation report that captures many aspects of the self. Few people would find a reason to argue against the trustworthiness, validity, and scientific merit of such an account. Just as it is relevant to recruit and train participants for specific purposes (to do with representativeness) in some projects, it is equally relevant for other purposes to develop one's own skills of self-observation and reporting as a researcher in order to attain a level of clarity and precision like Milgram's. This is particularly the case when it is analytic depth (rather than representative breadth) that one is after as researcher. It is difficult to imagine that participants, who are not researchers, could approach the level of precision and theoretical relevance that Milgram demonstrates in the quote above.

How Does One Practice Self-Observation?

I will now introduce three general ways of answering the "how" question in broadly phenomenological approaches to self-observation. These are:

- Creative Analytical Practices—or CAP: An impressionistic and artful approach to self-observation with a focus on autoethnography and writing as a method of inquiry.
- Experience Sampling Method—or ESM: A systematic phenomenology of the stream of consciousness in everyday life, which is often suitable for quantification.
- Systematic Self-Observation—or SSO: Useful for depicting the self in hidden and elusive social situations, primarily based on narrative reports.

These are all varieties of the phenomenological approach, focusing on lived experience from a first-person perspective. The first one covers a variety of different creative analyses of experience, while the others are much more standardized methodologies, which nonetheless build upon the phenomenological groundwork that was laid out at the beginning of this chapter.

Creative Analytical Practices (CAP)

From a certain perspective, we are all engaged in self-observation as we go about living our daily lives. Most of us notice from time to time how we experience and act in the world. As language users, we not only live in the present, but we have the capacity to distance ourselves from the immediate impressions the world makes on us and the immediate impulses we have to act. This distancing involves self-observation in a minimal sense. Humans have developed different cultural tools and practices that aid in the process of distancing one from oneself, ranging from simple note taking to psychotherapy. One helpful tool in self-observation is the diary or journal, which has been advocated as a qualitative research instrument by Janesick (1999). Of course, diaries are used rather unreflectively in people's lives, but a focused use of journal writing can refine the researcher's understanding of her role as research instrument and also of the responses of participants (506). Janesick describes how the making of lists, portraits, maps of consciousness, guided imagery, altered points of view, unsent letters, and dialogues may facilitate the journal writer's phenomenological awareness (519). Often, there is a short route from journal writing to actual self-observation analyses.

Using personal journals in the way advocated by Janesick is related to the current interest in autoethnography (Ellis et al. 2011) as the most visible of the Creative Analytical Practices (CAP) in qualitative inquiry to have emerged in recent years (some of the others are investigative poetry and performance ethnographies). Autoethnography seeks to describe and analyze (this is the "graphy" aspect) personal experience (this is the "auto" aspect) in order to understand cultural processes (this is the "ethno" aspect) (1). The goal is to craft aesthetic and evocative thick descriptions of experience with inspiration from the arts. Autoethnographers put emphasis on writing as a method of inquiry (Richardson and St. Pierre 2005) and are generally skeptical of more standard methodological guidelines for analysis. Some favor the use of theoretical concepts to analyze experience—Ellis and colleagues thus refer to theoretical tools as that which makes autoethnography potentially more valid than Oprah Winfrey's talk show, for example (Ellis et al. 2011, 8)—while others prefer to write more descriptively, e.g., in the tradition of intimate journalism (Harrington 1997).

In any case, it is difficult to present guiding principles for how to work with self-observation in these traditions that Richardson has referred to as CAP (Richardson and St. Pierre 2005). She does, however, encourage researchers to (1) join a writing group, (2) work through a creative writing guidebook, (3) enroll in a creative writing workshop, (4) use "writing up" fieldnotes to expand one's writing vocabulary, (5) write an autobiography (e.g., about how one learned to write),

(6) transform field notes into drama, (7) experiment with transforming an interview or an observation into a poem—and there are several other pieces of advice concerning the craft of writing. Regardless of one's understanding of CAP inquiries, it is useful to regard writing as a mode of inquiry throughout a self-observation study. Like Richardson, who reports having been taught "not to write until I knew what I wanted to say" (Richardson and St. Pierre 2005, 960), I believe that writing is a central way for qualitative researchers not just to report some findings, in the final instance, but also to experiment with analyses, different perspectives on the textual material, and ways of presenting, as a method of inquiry in its own right. Writing should thus be treated as an intrinsic part of the methodology of research—and not as a final "postscript" added on.

CAP methods comprise a motley bouquet of impressionistic approaches to self-observation. I shall now present two much more standardized ways of working with self-observation. The first (ESM) is useful primarily in relation to Self 1 studies, while the second (SSO) is most useful concerning Self 2 and 3.

The Experience Sampling Method (ESM)

The Experience Sampling Method (ESM) has been developed and practiced since the 1970s by Mihalyi Csikszentmihalyi and coworkers. In a recent comprehensive book on the method, they describe it as "systematic phenomenology" (Hektner et al. 2007, 4). Building on Husserl's "pure phenomenology," they use the tools of mainstream psychological investigations, including technologies (such as signaling devices), research designs, and statistics, to develop ESM. This systematic phenomenology is meant to capture the events occurring in the stream of consciousness over time, and with its focus on Self 1—the contents of consciousness—it departs from the focus on the self in social situations (Self 2 and 3) that we find in Systematic Self-Observation (to be addressed below). The idea is to achieve the highest degree of immediacy possible by asking people (normally recruited participants who are nonresearchers) to provide written responses to a set of questions at several random points throughout each day of a week (6). The self-observer is prompted to provide the response by a signaling device (e.g., a pager), and experience is thus ideally sampled the moment it occurs. Thereby, the proponents of the method argue that the distortions of experience associated with the use of retrospective accounts (e.g., the diaries used by CAP researchers) are avoided.

ESM studies are particularly well suited to investigate daily fluctuations in motivations, moods, or subjective well-being, and can thus be used to identify the typologies of experience that arise during the day. One can say that the Husserlian lifeworld is captured in bits and pieces throughout a number of days in a person's life. ESM scholars argue that the rather time-consuming work that is needed to build a good database will quickly pay off, as one can continually go back to the data and find new and surprising structures in them for years. And even small studies with five or ten participants may prove sufficient to be used reliably in simple statistical analyses.

How is an ESM study carried out in practice? Obviously, one should begin by considering whether one's research problem fits this methodology. ESM is designed to capture individuals' representations of experience as it occurs (Hektner et al. 2007, 32). It can favorably be used "to measure dimensions of experience that are likely to be context-dependent" (32) and that fluctuate over a day or a week. Questions such as "How do you feel about yourself right now?" are relevant in ESM studies whereas questions like "How do you generally feel about yourself?" are better suited to qualitative research interviewing, for example. It is also important to consider the signaling schedule. Most ESM studies use signal-contingent sampling, where participants respond to a signal (often randomized). But it is also possible to use interval-contingent (responses are expected at the same time every day) or event-contingent (a self-report is completed following certain specified events) forms of sampling. It should normally not take participants more than one or two minutes to complete the form (49).

When the data are in, they should be coded, and the authors recommend developing a codebook that targets both the external coordinates of experience (e.g., date, time, location) and the internal ones (here Likert scales are often used). Then, the data should be analyzed, and the analytic options are legion. Pure qualitative approaches can be used that focus, for example, on the life of a single respondent (or a single kind of situation found in the material), or statistical analyses can be used to calculate correlations between a number of variables. This, however, is hardly in line with the original phenomenological ambition to go to "the things themselves" (one of Husserl's famous credos) rather than scientific abstractions. I will confer the reader to the ESM method book for details about different forms of analysis and end this section on this methodology by giving a few examples of studies that have employed ESM before presenting some problems associated with this method.

ESM studies have given us a look at the landscape of everyday life. What do people do? How do they spend their time? And what do they feel about being engaged in certain forms of activity as they occur? ESM researchers have found, for example, that watching television is the single-most time-consuming activity that people engage in at home (in the United States), taking up 25 percent of all home time and 40 percent of all leisure time (Hektner et al. 2007, 130). While watching TV, however, people engage in other activities (like eating, chatting, etc.) 70 percent of the time. In terms of subjective experience, it seems to be a rather robust finding that watching television does not make people happy, nor particularly unhappy. People generally report rather flat affect, and "TV appears to have the function of draining people of negative emotions, stress, and tension" (131), but does not as such lift people up. Other studies have focused on the experience of work, cross-cultural variations, educational, and also clinical experiences.

Kahneman and colleagues refer to ESM as the "gold standard" in the field (Kahneman et al. 2004, 1777), and it is true that the use of ESM has resulted in interesting research reports. That said, however, I believe that ESM has drifted away from its phenomenological background and its ambition to study "the flow in everyday life" (Hektner et al. 2007, 286). First, there is often (although not necessarily) a quantification of people's experiences built into the forms that are given to participants, which may not be true to the qualitative world of human experience. Consequently, most ESM studies proceed by studying statistical averages, which may give us fascinating demographical facts, but says little of human experience in the lifeworld. The rather mechanical and quantitative approach of ESM may, however, have the advantage of persuading some people to study experience in at least a quasi-phenomenological way who would otherwise not have been attracted to such a research method from fear that it would become too subjectivist.

Other problems of ESM include what could be called a "fetishization of the present," as if human experience must be captured the moment it occurs in order to be valid, as purely and unmediated as possible, with the risk of overlooking the temporal and mediated nature of much, if not most of our experience. ESM researchers are skeptical of the diary method, for example, but they do not tell us why the mediated externalization of thought processes in diaries is less true to human experience than the "inner experience" reported in ESM forms (on the use of diaries, see Zittoun and Gillespie 2010). Finally, the implicit philosophical position in ESM seems to be rather mentalistic, and its proponents typically address self-observational data as "contents of mind (Hektner et al. 2007, 6). The human mind is seen as a storehouse of mental phenomena, a Cartesian theater or a "windowless room" (Costall 2007). ESM is thus designed to observe the mental entities that reside in the storehouse, theater, or room, but this spatial understanding of mental phenomena is far from the sophisticated approaches developed by Husserl, Heidegger, and Merleau-Ponty, who stressed the inherent intentionality and world-directedness of the mind, and also from Wittgenstein's philosophical psychology. To have a mind for a human being is not to have an inner stage where mental "contents" appear, but rather "to have a distinctive range of capacities of intellect and will, in particular the conceptual capacities of a language-user which make self-awareness and self-reflection possible." (Bennett and Hacker 2003, 105). ESM researchers seem to subscribe to the idea that self-observational accounts are necessarily descriptive and atomistic (and that the descriptions can be captured in codeable forms) and tend to overlook the expressivist and holistic aspects of human experience that were stressed by Wittgenstein and the phenomenologists. Nevertheless, it is a suitable research methodology for a number of purposes related to large-scale sampling of people's everyday lives.

Systematic Self-Observation (SSO)

Systematic Self-Observation (SSO) has been developed as a rigorous qualitative research methodology by Rodriguez and Ryave, mainly from a sociological perspective (Rodriguez and Ryave 2002). SSO is particularly well suited to study hidden and elusive aspects of social life such as lies, withholding of compliments, how individuals compare themselves to others and the experience of envy (3). A SSO topic should preferably address a single, focused phenomenon that is natural to a culture, and which is noticeable, intermittent, bounded in time, and of relatively short duration (5). As the examples testify, SSO has primarily been used to study the dimensions of the self that Harré called Self 2 and 3, perhaps due to the sociological background to this methodology (Goffman, Garfinkel, and the symbolic interactionists are mentioned as sources of inspiration). The goal of SSO is to generate field notes that are accurate descriptions of the participants' experience in social situations. Unlike ESM, SSO encourages participants to write narrative reports of their experiences after they have occurred.

An SSO study normally proceeds according to the following sequence of tasks: (1) Choose a subject matter appropriate to the methodology, (2) formulate the topic, (3) recruit informants, (4) guide the informants to understand the logic of social science, (5) teach informants to observe in a sensitive way, (6) teach them to report observations in a detailed and accurate manner, and (7) prepare the informants with training exercises (Rodriguez and Ryave 2002, 10). Emphasis is put on training participants/informants from the conviction that good data are here completely dependent on the participants' skills. After these steps, however, comes the process of reading the data analytically, ordering them, making typologies and choosing typical, critical, or extreme cases to report, depending on one's research interest.

In many of the reported studies that use SSO, the data are in the form of short conversational sequences. In the study of lies, an observed sequence was reported as follows:

> First Instance
>
> Place: In a parking lot outside a high school.
>
> Who: Basketball friend and myself.
>
> Situation: Standing by our cars talking about nothing.
>
> Friend: We play tomorrow in Pacific Palisades. Why don't you come see us play?
>
> Me: Oh really? What time do you play?
>
> Friend: We play at 7:30 on Friday. You should come down if you get a chance.
>
> Me: Okay, I'll be there [Lie]. (Rodriguez and Ryave 2002, 30)

This is not the place to unfold the authors' findings concerning lies, but they argue rather convincingly that lying emerges primarily from the general features of social interaction. All informants lied and most lies occurred spontaneously, and although it goes against our common sense understanding of lies as immoral, lying often seemed to be a preferred action according to the normative conventions of social interaction. In short, lying is a pervasive feature of our lives that often, and perhaps paradoxically, serves a moral function.

There is nothing in SSO studies that prevents researchers from counting and quantifying data (see the example in Rodriguez and

Ryave 2002, 47), but the methodology has its strength in the immediate qualitative descriptions, often in narrative form, that participants are encouraged to construct. Unlike ESM, which often charts people's doings and sufferings, in general, during a day, week, month or so, SSO is rather more focused on specific issues such as telling lies, name dropping, gossiping, and other similar aspects of our conversational reality. With SSO we have a manageable method for social phenomenological studies of self-observation, which is flexible enough to suit a number of different research purposes, but which is at the same time rigorous enough for researchers to communicate their findings in efficient ways to others who are familiar with the method.

The main conclusion that emerges from these considerations is that different approaches are suitable for different research questions. We should engage systematically *and* creatively in self-observation and judge the different methodological perspectives pragmatically in light of the scientific results that ensue. CAP approaches, when done well, may give readers a deep understanding of possible human experiences, in most cases the researcher's, whereas ESM and SSO approaches are better suited to studies on a larger scale that can throw light on different aspects of the self.

Ethical Considerations

Regardless of one's specific method, it is important to consider the ethical implications of a self-observation study. Such studies frequently deal with private and intimate aspects of people's lives that are subsequently placed in a public arena. The following list of ethical questions to address by researchers was originally developed for qualitative research interviewers, but it has here been modified to fit self-observation purposes (the original list is found in Kvale and Brinkmann 2008, 68–69):

- What are the *beneficial* consequences of the study?

How can the study contribute to enhancing the situation of the participating subjects? Of the group they represent? Of the human condition? Ideally, one should not engage in research projects if there is no likely way that human beings can gain from the study being done. This is not to say that all studies should have immediate beneficial effects in practice; a gain in understanding something important is often worthwhile in itself.

- How can the *informed consent* of the participating subjects be obtained?

How much information and training should be given in advance, and what can wait until a debriefing after the study? (this question is relevant when one intends to analyze the materials from the participants in a specific way, and when it would likely tamper with the self-observation reports, if the participants were aware of his beforehand)

Who should give the consent—the subjects or their superiors?

- How can the *confidentiality* of the participants be protected?

How important is it that the subjects remain anonymous?

How can the identity of the subjects be disguised?

Who will have access to the self-observation reports?

Can legal problems concerning protection of the subjects' anonymity be expected?

- What are the *consequences* of the study for the participating subjects?

Will any potential harm to the subjects be outweighed by potential benefits? One possible source of harm is the awareness of certain aspects of oneself that results from self-observation—and which the participant may not wish or have asked for.

When publishing the study, what consequences may be anticipated for the subjects and for the groups they represent?

- How will the *researcher's role* affect the study?

How can a researcher avoid co-option from the funding of a project or over-identification with his or her subjects, thereby losing critical perspective on the knowledge produced?

How will the researcher's expectations influence the way that informants report and express their experiences?

These ethical questions can be used as a framework when preparing a self-observation study, and they can be used as reminders of what to look for in practice when one is doing the actual research.

Conclusions

The goal of this chapter was to give an introduction to self-observation from a phenomenological perspective and present a number of methods for working concretely in self-observation studies. Phenomenology is the study of the structure of the consciousness to which something appears, and, in addition to a general phenomenological method (represented by Giorgi), we have seen three more specific methods that are suitable for different research purposes.

Furthermore, I have introduced some distinctions that together comprise something like a conceptual toolbox, which may inspire others to do self-observation research. Relevant distinctions emerged between direct and indirect self-observation, and also between data as either descriptions or expressions. Moreover, we looked at three different senses of the self that are relevant in self-observation. It is clear that phenomenological self-observation can be many things, and that the self that observes and is observed is a heterogeneous notion. These complexities should not discourage us, however, but rather persuade us that self-observation covers many rich and interesting methods that enable us to understand the intricacies of the human lifeworld.

References

Bennett, M. R. and Hacker, P. M. S. 2003. *Philosophical Foundations of Neuroscience*. Oxford: Blackwell.

Berger, P. and Luckmann, T. 1966. *The Social Construction of Reality*. Garden City, NY: Doubleday.

Costall, A. 2007. "The Windowless Room: Mediationism and How to Get Over It." In *Cambridge Handbook of Sociocultural Psychology*, edited by J. Valsiner and A. Rosa, 109–23. Cambridge: Cambridge University Press.

Dewey, J. 1929. *The Quest for Certainty*. (This edition 1960). New York: Capricorn Books.

Ellis, C. 1991. "Sociological Introspection and Emotional Experience." *Symbolic Interaction* 14: 23–50.

Ellis, C., Adams, T. E., and Bochner, A. P. 2011. "Autoethography: An Overview." *Forum: Qualitative Social Research* 12: Article 10, http://www.qualitative-research.net/index.php/fqs/article/viewArticle/1589/3095.

Garfinkel, H. 1967. *Studies in Ethnomethodology*. (This edition 1984). Cambridge: Polity Press.

Gier, N. F. 1981. *Wittgenstein and Phenomenology: A Comparative Study of the Later Wittgenstein, Husserl, Heidegger and Merleau-Ponty*. Albany, NY: State University of New York Press.

Gillespie, A. and Zittoun, T. 2010. "Studying the Movement of Thought." In *Methodological Thinking in Psychology: 60 Years Gone Astray?* Edited by J. Valsiner, A. Toomela, and Val, 69–88. Charlotte, NC: Information Age Publishing.

Giorgi, A. 1975. "An Application of Phenomenological Method in Psychology." In *Duquesne Studies in Phenomenological Psychology II*, edited by A. Giorgi, C. Fischer, and E. Murray, 82–103. Pittsburgh, PA: Duquesne University Press.

Giorgi, A. and Giorgi, B. 2008. "Phenomenological Psychology." In *The SAGE Handbook of Qualitative Research in Psychology*, edited by C. Willig and W. Stainton-Rogers, 165–78. London: Sage.

Harré, R. 1998. *The Singular Self: An Introduction to the Psychology of Personhood*. London: Sage.

Harrington, W. 1997. "A Writer's Essay: Seeking the Extraordinary in the Ordinary." In *Intimate Journalism: The Art and Craft of Reporting Everyday Life*, edited by W. Harrington, xvii–xlv). Thousand Oaks, CA: Sage.

Hektner, J. M., Schmidt, J., and Csikszentmihalyi, M. 2007. *Experience Sampling Method: Measuring the Quality of Everyday Life*. Thousand Oaks, CA: Sage.

Herzog, M. 1995. "William James and the Development of Phenomenological Psychology in Europe." *History of the Human Sciences* 8: 29–46.

Husserl, E. 1954. *Die Krisis der europäischen Wissenschaften und die tranzendentale Phänomenologie*. Haag: Martinus Nijhoff.

James, W. 1890. *The Principles of Psychology*. (This edition published 1983). Cambridge, MA: Harvard University Press.

———. 1912. *Essays in Radical Empiricism*. New York: Longman Green & Co.

Janesick, V. 1999. "A Journal about Journal Writing as a Qualitative Research Technique: History, Issues, and Reflections." *Qualitative Inquiry* 5: 505–24.

Kahneman, D., Krueger, A. B., Schkade, D. A., Schwartz, N., and Stone, A. A. 2004. "A Survey Method for Characterizing Daily Life Experience: The Day Reconstruction Method." *Science* 306: 1776–80.

Kestenbaum, V. 1977. *The Phenomenological Sense of John Dewey: Habit and Meaning*. Atlantic Highlands, NJ: Humanities Press.

Kvale, S. and Brinkmann, S. 2008. *InterViews: Learning the Craft of Qualitative Research Interviewing*, 2nd edn. Thousand Oaks, CA: Sage.

McAdams, D. P. 1997. *The Stories We Live By*. (Først udgivet 1993). New York: The Guilford Press.

Mead, G. H. 1962. *Mind, Self, and Society: From the Standpoint of a Social Behaviorist*. (First published 1934). Chicago, IL: University of Chicago Press.

Merleau-Ponty, M. 1945. *Phenomenology of Perception*. (This edition published 2002). London: Routledge.

Milgram, S. 1992. *The Individual in a Social World: Essays and Experiments*. New York: McGraw-Hill.

Richardson, L. and St. Pierre, E. A. 2005. "Writing: A Method of Inquiry." In *Handbook of Qualitative Research*, 3rd edn, edited by N. K. Denzin and Y. S. Lincoln, 959–78. Thousand Oaks, CA: Sage.

Rodriguez, N. and Ryave, A. 2002. *Systematic Self Observation*. Thousand Oaks, CA: Sage.

Valsiner, J. 2006. "Dangerous Curves in Knowledge Construction within Psychology." *Theory & Psychology* 16: 597–612.

Wittgenstein, L. 1953. *Philosophical Investigations*. Oxford: Basil Blackwell.

———. 1981. *Zettel*, 2nd edn. Oxford: Blackwell.

Zittoun, T. and Gillespie, A. 2010. "Using Diaries and Self-Writings as Data in Psychological Research." In *Developing Methods in Psychology*, edited by E. Abbey and S. Surgan. New Brunswick, NJ: Transaction Publishers.

Part V

Self-Observation in the Narrative Traditions

11

A Practice of
Self-Observation in
Narrative Psychology

Andrew McCarron

Introduction

In this chapter I explore how self-observation has informed research I have done on the lives of several older poets affiliated with the New York School of Poetry. In addition to a lifelong interest in poetry, my research was inspired by a claim Freud made in a letter of Jung: "Before the problem of the creative artist analysis must, alas, lay down its arms" (SE XXI, 177). Although proud of his monograph on Leonardo da Vinci (1910), Freud was doubtful that psychoanalysis could penetrate to the sources of creativity. Elsewhere, he wrote that "all genuinely creative writings are the products of more than a single motive and more than a single impulse in the poet's mind, and are open to more than a single interpretation" (Freud 1900, 266). Unfortunately, psychological analyses of artists all too often reduce their motivations to a single cause. My research involved searching the life stories and creative works of subjects for clues to help determine the specific psychological reasons why they felt impelled to write. Because my subjects were understandably wary of speculating on *why* they wrote, I found myself searching their more narrative poems for clues.

Phenomenological self-observation was central to my methodological approach. Artists are often natural self-observers, actively conceptualizing and reflecting upon the ways that they observe themselves in the world. Those who write lyrical and narrative poetry are often *especially* engaged in acts of self-observation. This chapter shows what indirect self-observation helped me to determine about one of my subjects, a seventy-two-year-old poet named Tony. Although he was forthcoming about his life during our many conversations, he was not interested in speculating on *why* he wrote. Writing, he explained, was just something that he did. After composing his first poem in May 1960, the experience began working on him "below the surface," as he put it. When interpreted alongside his life story, analyses of the self-observing language in Tony's poems helped to reveal a specific cluster of psychological motivations underlying his compulsion to write.

Self-Observation in the Narrative Tradition

Many of the concepts behind self-observation presented in this volume are hardly new to narrative psychology. Life narratives, after all, would cease to function without a good deal of self-observation. We convey identity to ourselves and others by continually reorganizing self-defining memories and scenes based upon ongoing observations in which we are both subject and object, or what William James (1890) referred to as the self as subject, or the "I," and the self as object, or the "Me."

Along these lines, the French postmodern philosopher Paul Ricoeur conceptualized life as an activity and passion in search of a narrative (Ricoeur 1992). Ricoeur imagined a personal narrative as a *discordant concordance* between the manifold of events in life and the temporal unity of the story recounted, thus "integrat*ing* with permanence in time what seems to be its contrary in the domain of sameness-identity, namely diversity, variability, discontinuity, and instability" (Ricoeur 1992, 140). As speaking beings, we create *discordant concordances* through an action he called emplottment, which involves composing ourselves as protagonists into a storyline flexible enough to strike a balance between consistency and change. In addition to changing biologically, shifting sociopolitical realities require that we update our personal stories or else suffer fragmentation or loss of identity altogether.

Similar ideas can be found in the work of Dan McAdams (1993), who also conceptualizes identity as a life story—an internalized narrative integration of past, present, and anticipated future that seeks to maintain a personal myth over time (McAdams 1997). Life stories are *myths* insofar as they possess a tenuous relationship to so-called objective reality (hence the tenuous place of narrative psychology within the increasingly scientific halls of academic psychology). Individuals, according to McAdams, begin to organize their lives through unified and purposeful stories during late adolescence and early adulthood. What Erikson called "ego identity" is synonymous with a stable personal narrative in which a person situates himself/herself in a particular psychosocial niche. Life stories are created from a menu of cultural scripts, and can be analyzed for plots, settings, scenes, characters, and themes.

Another leading narrative theorist, Gary Gregg, divides personality into two categories: *core-level personality*, defined as the affective states and tensions at the genotypic level, and *social personality*, which is an ongoing reconfiguration of core-level personality in congruence with cultural prototypes and moral sentiments (Gregg 2007). Life stories seek to encompass and represent these sub-selves to oneself and others. Gregg argues that in narrative self-representations persons use some of the same structures that are present in tonal music in that key symbols and metaphors bring about a system of relations resembling those of a musical scale within which individuals move emotionally and ideologically, though within a prescribed range (Gregg 2010, 15). From Gregg's perspective, the narrative realm is an excellent place to excavate the sediments that constitute personality and identity.

Phenomenological self-observation improves upon narrative psychology in that it encourages researchers to think more deeply about the nature of the self doing the observing, whether it is the subject's self, the researcher's, or both. There are multiple layers of self-observation in narrative work: (a) the subject reflecting upon the ways that he/she observes himself/herself and (b) the researcher reflecting upon himself/herself reflecting upon the subject's self-reflections. And in Tony's case, there were additional layers of self-observation; at times I was observing myself observing a man making sense of experiences written about by an earlier self—not to mention the fact that some of these experiences were apocryphal while others were closer to his actual experience in the world. For the purposes of this chapter, though, I will forgo a detailed analysis of these interpenetrating layers to focus on self-observing language in his poetry. Because much of his poetry was narrative in nature, I found myself using it as an important source of knowledge. My argument is that Tony's poetic "emplottments" (Ricoeur 1992) reveal clues that help to reveal *why* he felt—and continues to feel—a need to write poetry. Even though the content of his poems was far from objective, the positioning of the self within his poems revealed a great deal when considered alongside the extensive biographical information he provided during our conversations.

Svend Brinkmann [in the present collection] writes about the *who*, *how*, and *what* behind self-observation work. In terms of *who*, he distinguishes between direct and indirect self-observation—the former pertaining to when the researcher takes his/her own self and experiences as subject matter, and the latter pertaining to when others (e.g., assistants, students, subjects, etc.) are doing the observing. *How* one goes about conducting self-observation research is open to an array of methodological approaches, three of which are outlined by Brinkmann in his chapter. Of particular interest to me is the *what* of phenomenological self-observation. Rom Harré (1998) distinguishes between three uses of the concept of self—summarized by Brinkmann in the following way: "The 'what' that is observed (oneself) may be conceived as one's consciousness, location or point of view (Self 1), one's sense of having a set of attributes, including self conceptions (Self 2), and one's participation in conversations and practices where the self is equated with the impressions that one person makes on another (Self 3)" (Brinkmann 2012, xx).

The jag of my research presented in this chapter involves locating Harré's three self-concepts in Tony's narrative poetry. I should say upfront that my approach was novel in that I included artistic artifacts as a central part of my analysis. Narrative researchers have generally been chary of looking outside the realm of traditional life stories, which implies that the aesthetic realm is little more than a depository of dead ends and distorted projections that invariably cloud scientific–empirical understandings of human persons. I disagree, emphatically. In addition to life stories, I believe paintings, music, and creative writing of all stripes—*in fact, any expressive genre that employs the symbolic* (Lacan 2007)—may constitute psychologically significant modes of self-observation that lend themselves to psychological interpretation.

I will now present a brief introduction to Tony's life, followed by a literary-critical overview of his poetic oeuvre. The final third of the chapter will explore Tony's self-observations via Harré's three types. I will show how each of the three reveals a separate motivation behind Tony's compulsion to write. These analyses underscore Freud's claim that all genuinely creative writings are the products of more than a single motive, but take a step further by providing a theoretical approach for locating them.

Tony: A New York Poet

I first met Tony in the spring of 2003 at the Fish Bar in Manhattan. For a time we were part of a small, quasi-regular group of writers who gathered to discuss literature and life. I learned that Tony was once a close friend and protégé of first-generation New York School poet Frank O'Hara. I was also told that he was handsome when younger, something of a lady's man, and had once been a heavy drinker. He continued to drink, but moderately, rarely exceeding two drinks. My first impression was of an opinionated man in his mid-to-upper sixties who walked with a cane and enjoyed sardonic conversation. (He has had to use a cane since 1997, as a result of slipping on a patch of ice in front of his building on Warren Street in 1991, in addition to a neurological condition called cerebella degeneration.) Slightly over six feet, he carried himself with a combination of vigor and fragility. He was verbally sharp, but required extra time making his way to and fro and had a slight tremor in his hands.

Five years later, in 2008, I began working on a book-length psycho-biography on the second generation of the New York School. Tony was initially wary about my research and explained that the psychological treatments of poets he had read tended to "ransack" the life to explain the poems, whereas poetry, for him, was, if not *outside* of life exactly, not autobiographical, per se. He did not decide to write poetry, he was impelled to. However, he was intrigued by the idea of a book being written on his cohort, which he feels has been routinely ignored by the poetry establishment. We met every few months over the course of a year for anywhere between two and six hours, usually over dinner at a restaurant in lower Manhattan. I recorded the conversations, produced transcripts, and wrote a sixty-page life narrative. I also drew from a short memoir called *Memoir: 1960–1963* that Tony wrote and published about his early years on the poetry scene in New York City.

Tony was born into a middle-class family in 1939 at Lenox Hill Hospital in Manhattan. The Towles lived in Inwood before moving to Rego Park, Queens, when he was two, so his father, who did (nonaviation) interior design work for American Airlines, could be close to the airport that would be named LaGuardia. After a relatively happy childhood and early adolescence, life took an unexpected turn when Tony impregnated his teenage girlfriend, Monica, at the end of high school, shortly after being accepted by Georgetown University's School

227

of Foreign Service. A year younger, Monica dropped out of school and followed him to Washington, DC.

Not surprisingly, the pressures of supporting a pregnant girlfriend necessitated that Tony drop out of Georgetown and find a job halfway through his first semester. Monica gave birth at Georgetown Hospital to a girl they named Melissa Ann, but there were serious complications. She developed hydrocephalus a few days after they brought her home from the hospital. Requiring special care, Tony did research and located a "D.C. home" and arranged for Melissa Ann to be taken away permanently.

Within months Monica was again pregnant. A second baby, Malcolm Scott, was born. Despite having a healthy son, Tony's mood deteriorated and he experienced episodes of suicidal ideation. At one of his many jobs during 1958, he had purchased a pistol from a coworker with five bullets. He would load the gun and place it in the dresser drawer and Monica would find it and take the bullets out. By the spring of 1960, things were unbearable. He recalls a terrible argument during which he took out the gun, which just so happened to be unloaded, pressed it to his temple and squeezed the trigger six times in front of his horrified wife. He then tossed the gun on the bed and went out for a walk, strolling into a "beat" coffee house, a type that had started becoming fashionable everywhere. Two important things happened at the café: first, he wrote some lines that could be considered his first poem; and second, he began to seriously consider leaving his domestic situation. Here is how the dramatic sequence is described in *Memoir*:

> I had begun, surreptitiously, writing poems in 1960, in Washington, in reaction to and escape from a two-and-a-half-year-long teenage marriage that had become unendurable. Sometime that May, I found myself sitting alone in a Beat-style coffee house, writing down a few lines I felt were a poem. With that experience working on me below the surface, in mid-July, on what seemed at the time an impulse from nowhere, I called in sick to my job of two years at a furniture store, walked over to a park on Wisconsin Avenue near our apartment, and wrote my second and third poems. This was exhilarating and at the same time instantly made my current life seem even more unbearable. That evening I had yet one more horrible argument with my wife, Monica, and a day or two later I moved out and got a room by myself, leaving her with Scott, our infant son. I left the job, too, a week or so later, and by mid-August, with a scant forty dollars to my name, I was on the train to New York. I would stay at

my parents' house in Rye, their final move in Westchester, until I reestablished myself somehow. I was impelled to leave the situation I was in. Suicide had often struck me as one alternative, poetry had unexpectedly provided another.

Tony left his young family and moved to New York City (after a short sojourn in Rye) where he has lived and worked ever since. Taken under the wing by Frank O'Hara, who died tragically in 1966, Tony eventually experienced a reasonable amount of success as a young poet, culminating in his being awarded the Frank O'Hara prize by Columbia University Press in 1970. The prestigious prize involved a monetary award and the publication of his first major collection, *North*, by Columbia University Press. Looking back, Tony sees the publication of *North* as the climax of his career in terms of recognition. He remembers having an optimistic feeling that he was at the beginning of a long, potentially distinguished career as a writer. "Things took a downturn," he explained wryly, "and by '75 or '76 I felt passed by altogether." Although many artists feel underappreciated during their lives, there was something particular about Tony's feelings. Overall, his narrative was saturated with real and perceived slights from members of the poetry community intent on excluding him from the public recognition he deserved.

Knowledge of Tony's personal life helps shed light on this. His life has been marked by instability and disruption. His mother died in 1965 from recurring cancer and he was estranged from his father, who had a host of legal and psychological problems that Tony did not care to discuss. Tony chose not to attend his father's funeral when he died in 1983 in Florida. After his mother's death, Tony's younger siblings were placed into foster families. In addition to Monica, Tony had a second marriage that ended in divorce and a subsequent long-term relationship that fell apart in the mid-1990s. O'Hara's death, understandably, was a devastating event for Tony. On several occasions in *Memoir* and in many poems, Tony describes O'Hara in fatherly terms, praising him for helping to encourage his burgeoning identity as an artist. Tony has had a host of jobs from which he was either fired or quit. His alcoholism was so severe through the 1970s and 1980s that his friends thought he was going to die. Luckily, his life turned around after entering into a relationship with a recently divorced actress named Diane in 1997 with whom he still lives. He maintains a close relationship with his daughter, Rachel, from his second marriage, but rarely sees his son. Other than Diane, his most constant companions are his poet friends, a contingent of which he gets together with once or twice a month for dinner.

My analyses of Tony's life led me to conjecture a few things about the motivations underlying his writing practice: (1) Poetry entered into his life and helped him to navigate the waters of an acute developmental crisis. For Tony, the life-disrupting event of Monica's unwanted pregnancy and the subsequent sickness of their baby, compounded by a need to quit Georgetown University's School of Foreign Service (which had been a longstanding dream to attend), caused a confusion of roles so severe that it led to suicidal ideation. Poetry came into his life accidentally—an unintended consequence of strolling in a "beat" coffee house in May 1960—and stuck as a personal and social identity. Wheaton and Gotlib (1997) write about how life-disrupting events that are not buffered by psychosocial resources often result in identity changes that endure over time. Galvanized by a sudden desire *to be a poet*, Tony decided to cut his losses and start over—a decision he characterized as both the most precipitate and necessary of his life, as well as the least defensible from a conventional point of view. (2) I conjectured that poetic father figures, principally O'Hara, played a surrogate role in Tony's life, hence his emulation of O'Hara's style. (3) From a narrative perspective, I argued that Tony's autobiographical poems helped him to organize the fragments and disruptions of his life into a meaningful whole.

My ability to see these motivations hinged upon my use of Rom Harré's (1998) three concepts of self. I discovered that each self-concept was influenced by distinct developmental, psychodynamic, and socio-cultural variables. Although I surmised the presence of these motivations during my analysis of the transcript, the self-representations that populated his poems helped confirm my hypotheses. Before I flesh out these observations, though, let me share a few reflections on Tony's poetry by drawing from a small body of critical literature that has been generated in response to it.

Tony's Poetry

Tony divides his work into four periods: poems written between 1963 and 1965; poems written between 1965 and 1969; poems written between 1970 and 1979; and poems written from 1980 until the present. His 250-page new and selected poems *The History of the Invitation* (2001) is divided accordingly, with short critical essays introducing each section written by a cadre of fellow poets, all of whom are personal friends.

On Tony's early poems (1963–1965), Ron Padgett writes, "The reader owes a debt of gratitude to the young author: he does not allow us to distinguish between the real and the imagined. When the "I" in a poem ponders, say, his health or his feelings, we have no way of knowing if that speaker is Tony Towle, or even partly Tony Towle" (Padgett in Towle 2001, 15). Poems from this period might begin autobiographically but quickly veer off into lyrical abstraction. The "here" and "now" exist, though primarily as points of departure toward a world of imaginative possibility. Similar to the work of John Ashbery, the poems convey feeling without possessing a single thematic center or tone.

Of the poems written between 1965 and 1969, Charles North has written that "their cohesive look masks a pervasive and frequently enigmatic disjunction featuring surreal and cinematic jumps, dramatic shifts in voice, narrative that doesn't add up, strings of participial phrases that don't clearly refer, false parallels, and the like. Yet the poems have an extraordinary depth of feeling" (North in Towle 2001, 49). The work is not easy to grasp. Lines, for instance, from *Today*, read: "Today the phantoms pass through rock. / The phantoms move higher in the rock, the smoke, / the fumes, and the powdered ash. / Instinctively I scale a tree, I vanish. / The clouds are torn apart to show the moon; / he drops to a bench; the telephone rings, / a hypnotic background for the words." There is an abundance of movement upward: e.g., the scaling of a tree, phantoms moving up through rock, a quickening of instincts, etc. The poet-speaker vanishes, and then returns two lines later in the third-person singular, as if the "scaling" culminated in a momentary escape from subjectivity.

Compared to his abstract beginnings, the work he was writing by the early seventies was increasingly autobiographical. Tony supposes that he was probably trying to write poems in a style and voice influenced by his mentor. Like O'Hara's "I do this, I do that" poems, he was finding materials in personal experience, whether real, or fictional, or both—and writing in a voice that swerved from the satirical to the comic, tragic, or celebratory in the space of a single poem. Tony sees the seventies as the decade in which he did his best work. And he is not alone in thinking this. Paul Violi, for example, has written: ". . . Towle's style evolved and culminated in his finest achievements. To what a degree a poet can be conscious of his own development is hard to tell, but Towle seems to have known what he was after all along" (Violi in Towle 2001, 85). And also: "The 'Towle poem' is often an exploratory account of its own making, a search for meaning or, when none turns up, dealing with the inconsequential. The tone shifts, a blend at times remote and passionate, colloquial and eloquent, self-deprecatory and inspirited. His freewheeling narrative line encompasses the metaphysical and the immediate, and is open to any possibility between . . ." (Violi in Towle 2001, 86).

As the seventies came to a close, Tony continued to change poetically. "His work became more audience friendly," one critic explained. "And it darkened too." In his introduction to the work from the 1980s until the present (then 2001), Jack Kimball emphasizes the increasing presence of satire. Kimball suggests four keys that define the work: (a) fulfilled premises; (b) narration flowing forward and back in time; (c) a slapstick engagement with tradition; and (d) what he calls "deep punning." And as Kenneth Koch pointed out (2001), the later poems are as incisively witty as they are dark and brooding. Although many are playful and breezy, many are marked by an elegiac tone and a preoccupation with self-defeat, transience, and mortality.

Poetic Self-Observations

The self-observations strewn through Tony's poems reveal a great deal about why he felt and continues to feel compelled to write, especially when they are looked at through the lens of Harré's (1998) three concepts of self.

The first self, or Self 1, is thought of, in basic terms, as a phenomenological standpoint from which one observes (Harré 1998). This standpoint involves a location in space from which one perceives and acts in the world. There is a basic or thin consciousness here devoid of metanarratives and interpersonal dynamics. Researchers on the hunt for Self 1 should look for expressive (as opposed to descriptive) first-person utterances. For instance, a mood-state like anger is not *understood*, per se, but experienced directly. A Self 1 voice does not espouse self properties or narrate histories. It perceives and experiences the world from a location. "Self-observations" of a Self 1 type pervade Tony's early work. Take, for example, *Poem*:

Poem
Awake, I move in a doubtful margin.
New York is a cloud. I awaken

and pictures move on the wall.

There is nothing to say;

I am alone with the changing weather

and I made sure I was going to be here.

The self-observing speaker is rooted in a specific place (New York City) observing his material environment with minimal appeal to metanarratives or interpersonal discourses. The intriguing images of "a doubtful margin" and of New York as "a cloud" suggest a pre-theorized, pre-reflective consciousness indicative of a Self 1 position.

Similar can be said about the final stanza of the early poem *Prologue*:

The pilgrims are cautious and exact

and only a trickle comes to the edge.

I stir slightly.

The residue, white, is hung

without sound.

There are no metaphors or similes in this stanza, which conveys strong emotion without revealing or interpreting the conditions that prompted it.

Tony's life story helps explain the self-observations that populate poems from his early period. The developmental project of moving to New York City and starting over influenced the nature of these self-observations. Recall, again, Ron Padgett's statement that ". . . he does not allow us to distinguish between the real and the imagined. When the "I" in a poem ponders, say, his health or his feelings, we have no way of knowing if that speaker is Tony Towle, or even partly Tony Towle" (Padgett in Towle 2001, 15). Although this style of self-representation was an aesthetic choice, and drew from a host of precedents from the French surrealist poet André Breton to John Ashbery, it can also be explained psychologically. In this work the reader encounters a young, bewildered man trying to begin a new life free of old narratives about what and who he is—hence the radically open, unfinished quality of both the poems and then speaker in them. Not surprisingly, Self 1 reappears in later poems that Tony composed during periods of acute crisis and developmental transition. Poetry offered him a space to be unfinished, to experience feelings without having to narrate them into a conventional story of self. Accordingly, he referred to his early work and the work he was writing during the breakdown of his second marriage in the mid to late 1970s as an escape from life. The nature of the self-observations in these poems confirm this characterization.

**

As he became more established in New York City, and more comfortable with his public identity as a poet, Tony's poetry became increasingly autobiographical. In Harré's (1998) system, Self 2 appears as an object with particular properties. Self 2 constitutes the personal narratives that more explicitly fulfill Ricoeur's (1992) requirement of emplottment. Ricoeur (1992), once again, conceived of a personal narrative as a *discordant concordance* "between the manifold of events and the temporal unity of the story recounted" (Ricoeur 1992, 141). The psychological goal of a personal narrative was to craft a story that "integrate(s) with permanence in time what seems to be its contrary in the domain of sameness-identity, namely diversity, variability, discontinuity, and instability" (Ricoeur 1992, 140). Ricoeur demonstrated how a *discordant concordance* strove to achieve a flexible dialectical balance between diversity and consistency without breaking down into rigidity, silence, or chaos.

Many of Tony's narrative poems—specifically autobiographical ones like *The Morgan Library* and *Nearing Christmas*—present the reader with *discordant concordances* in miniature. The selves presented in these poems are flexible without losing personal consistency. A reader will encounter both finite and expansive swaths of Tony's life in a single poem, although the events included and the significance assigned to each event varies. The poems are constructed around significant and banal episodes alike, in addition to incorporating sequences from dreams and fantasies. There are poems built around the act of eating a hamburger (*New York*), walking to the Morgan Library (*The Morgan Library*), Christmas shopping drunk at Macy's (*Nearing Christmas*), or visiting a new Korean laundry in the neighborhood (*Ethnicity*). Every autobiographical poem presents a slightly different autobiography of Tony, culling together a discordant constellation of scenes, sequences, thoughts, feelings, and associations into the concordance of a single poem.

Despite this diversity, the poet-speaker maintains a consistent personal chronology. The poems are meticulously dated—as are many of the events described in them. The long poem *Autobiography*, for instance, is peppered with temporal material—e.g., wheeling his daughter Rachel through Washington Square Park in 1970, a moment in 1950 standing "in the playground next to my school," and several memories of Queens Boulevard and Rego Park from the "late forties." Here are two other examples from the poem:

> Long before 1950 I knew that one of the numerous years
>
> would bring death, as 1939 brought life,
>
> in the way that two poems on universal themes
>
> open and close an important collection . . .
>
> [. . .]
>
> I walk into the wind, continually,
>
> have lunch on velvet burgundy tablecloths with friends,
>
> dress for dinner in elegant striped jackets,
>
> or fabulous gray suits,
>
> a pestilent green hat or short furry slippers,
>
> fashion with charm like the perennial sea
>
> in that it is always pulling at your leg,
>
> or concocting a simple soup.
>
> I enter another year, 1973 . . .

The formal and thematic flexibility of poetry provided Tony a space within which to narrate the story of his "self," no matter how disrupted and/or distributed that self was, and to contextualize his experiences within a temporal totality found in poems like *In the Coffee House* (2001):

> I told Diane I'd be here 'til six. Waiting
>
> for a girlfriend literally is a great improvement
>
> over the afternoons at the Figaro;
>
> and in fact it's cool to have a girlfriend at my age
>
> I think amusedly to myself
>
> behind the overpriced coffee,
>
> 2.95 to contemplate the traffic
>
> fleeing down the avenue and into the past
>
> which has brought me up to the present,
>
> where I put down my pen, figuratively.

A Self 2 conceptualization helped Tony piece together a narrative that without such a center might have met the requirement for a "broken" and/or "contaminated" narrative (McAdams 2006), especially considering the regrets and life-disrupting struggles he talked about during our conversations.

***

Harré's (1998) third concept of self, Self 3, is also present among Tony's poetic self-observations. This concept of self is tied up with the ways that social interactions and intersubjectivity influence self-perceptions and actions. The social nature of many of Tony's poems—in the form of direct addresses, elegies, dedications, and social reportage—helped him forge a social network that granted him a poetic identity of a public nature.

Many of the self-conceptualizations found in his poems are tied in with poets and artists active in and around New York City. Reading Tony's middle and later work, it is hard not to be struck by the sheer number of names, including but not limited to Charles North, Paul Violi, Larry Rivers, Robert Motherwell, Frank Lima, Ted Berrigan, David Shapiro, Frank O'Hara, John Ashbery, Kenneth Koch, and James Schuyler. The vast majority of these relationships were fostered through his affiliation with the downtown poetry scene. To this day, and despite precarious health, he attends the readings, dinners, and book openings of his friends (and vice versa).

Many of the social poems contain conversations that he probably could not have had in his actual life. Either the material is too personal—such as in *A Note to Charles North*—or else the person in question is no longer living—such as in *Nearing Christmas* or *Thoughts at Frank O'Hara's City Poet Party, 6/9/93*. In the absence of a traditional nuclear family (at least not a consistent one), poetry helped Tony to cultivate a different kind of family—a homo-social gaggle of men. Poetically honoring and elegizing poet friends and mentors allowed Tony to infuse these self-defining bonds with new imaginative possibilities—e.g., continuing a conversation with Frank decades after his death, in addition to expressing affections and sentiments that are traditionally anathema for American heterosexual men of his generation to express. Take the first lines of the second stanza from *A Note To Charles North:*

> It's approaching death of course, if you want to know,
>
> and I don't think you want to know,
>
> which makes two of us, at least . . .

Or, the final lines of *Nearing Christmas:*

> You call that lyric you big bag of shit?
>
> I am not talking to myself,
>
> or in that manner to a great poet of the past,
>
> that must be Frank, talking to me;
>
> I am at last fully awake in this mortal life,
>
> for the few years in the middle,
>
> and I keep myself opaque and I don't regret it,
>
> on the promontory.
>
> Frank you've got to help me
>
> and there is an answer but not at this moment.

Conclusion

Freud was absolutely correct. A narrow question like— *Why does a poet write?* —has no single answer because creative writings are the product of more than a single motive. Psycho-biographical work on artists (e.g., see Todd Schultz's *Handbook of Psychobiography* [2005]) often fails because it insists upon locating a single motive or epicenter behind why artists feel impelled to create. On the contrary, Rom Harré's (1998) three concepts of self offer researchers a method for thinking deeply about artistic motivations that is consummately open to multiplicity. Alongside the data of a personal narrative, the self-observations present within the creative work of an artist can help reveal the complex and ever-changing role that the art plays in his/her life.

The self-observations present in Tony's poems reveal a man for whom poetry has had important psychological utilities. Poetry helped him to escape from life, to maintain a coherent personal and social identity, and to foster a surrogate family of fellow artists. Tony is all too aware of the central place that poetry has had in his life since writing his first poems in 1960. As he put it movingly during our last interview, at a time when he was lamenting a disconcertingly long fallow period: ". . . through the relationships, the bad relationships, jobs, losing jobs, and not having money, or very little. That is the only thread and I've had a very difficult time in the last year writing. I stopped writing when I got the proofs for my last book. I took a vacation and when it was time to get back on the horse I'd forgotten how to ride." What Tony was perhaps less aware of was how the modes of self-observation present in his work reveal clues about the psychological motivations behind his need to write. My work on Tony's life and creative output presents several implications for self-observation work in narrative studies:

1. Harré's (1998) three modes of self-observation are an effective means of achieving a comprehensive view of specific and general phenomena within a life.
2. Self-observing language can provide clues about latent psychological motivations that drive behaviors and self-perceptions.
3. Narrative psychology can greatly benefit from creative usages of self-observation work preset in this volume.

References

Freud, S. 1964. *Leonardo da Vinci and a Memory of His Childhood*. New York: W.W. Norton.

Gay, P. ed. 1989. *The Freud Reader*. New York: W. W. Norton.

Gregg, G. 2007. *Culture and Identity in a Muslim Society*. New York: Oxford University Press.

Harré, R. 1998. *The Singular Self: An Introduction to the Psychology of Personhood*. London: Sage.

James, W. 1890. *The Principles of Psychology*. (This edition published in 1983). Cambridge, MA: Harvard University Press.

Lacan, J. 2007. *Écrits*. New York: W.W. Norton.

McAdams, D. P. 1993. *The Stories We Live by*. New York: Morrow.

_____. 2006. *The Redemptive Self: Stories Americans Live By*. New York: Oxford University Press.

Ricoeur, P. 1992. *Oneself as Another*. Chicago, IL: University of Chicago Press.

Schultz, W. T. ed. 2005. *Handbook of Psychobiography*. New York: Oxford University Press.

Towle, T. 1970. *North*. New York: Columbia University Press.

_____. 2000. *Memoir: 1960–1963*. Cambridge, MA: Faux Press.

_____. 2001. *History of the Invitation: New and Selected Poems*. New York: Hanging Loose Press.

_____. 2003. *Nine Immaterial Nocturnes*. New York: Hanging Loose Press.

_____. 2008. *Winter Journey*. New York: Hanging Loose Press.

Wheaton, B. and Gotlib, I. 1997. "Trajectories and Turning Points Over the Life Course: Concepts and Themes." In *Stress and Adversity Over the Life Course: Trajectories and Turning Points*, edited by I. Gotlib and B. Wheaton. Cambridge: Cambridge University Press.

12

Self-Observation Theory in the Narrative Tradition: Rescuing the Possibility of Self-Understanding

Mark Freeman

Preliminaries

There are so many reasons to question the validity and value of "self-observation" in the social sciences. Indeed, I just put "self-observation" in scare quotes because the very idea of self-observation may be deemed problematic at its core. For one, there is not much agreement about what exactly we mean by "self." For another, whatever we might mean by this difficult, ambiguous term, it is not at all clear what it can possibly mean to "observe" it. Generally speaking, I "observe" things outside myself: my computer, the books lining my shelf, the clouds in the sky. I can also observe physical dimensions of my self—my hands, for instance, as they (I?) type away, and I might even make some contact with psychological dimensions of my self through encountering my own image, in the mirror or via video. (The latter process is almost invariably weird, which is telling in its own right [though what exactly it tells is less clear].) But strictly speaking, I surely do not observe myself. Do I? Can I? As Roland Barthes has put the matter in his cleverly titled book *Roland Barthes* (1989), "You are the only one who can never see yourself except as an image" (36). And even if I could (who knows what technology will bring?), it would be difficult to call such "seeing" "self-observation."

There is a further, deeper problem with the idea of self-observation as well. As Heidegger points out in an important essay entitled

"Knowledge and reflection" (1977), the term "theory" —*theōria* in (ancient) Greek—had been considered a process of "[looking] attentively on the outward appearance wherein what presences becomes visible and through such sight – seeing – to linger with it" (163). Put another way, it was understood as entailing "the reverent paying heed to the unconcealment of what presences" (164). We might think here of the mindful, attentive beholding that is sometimes associated with insight or illumination. This meaning, however, would eventually change with the Romans, such that there would emerge the idea of "a looking-at that sunders and compartmentalizes. A type of encroaching advance by successive interrelated steps toward that which is to be grasped by the eye makes itself normative in knowing" (166). Rather than insight or illumination, therefore, we come to have *observation*, which is to say, a form of knowing—in this case, self-knowing—predicated on the possibility of somehow catching oneself in the act and thereby encountering oneself as *object*, able to be compartmentalized, encapsulated. Along these lines, it might be suggested that the process of self-observation, strictly understood, cannot help but deform and distort the very phenomenon it seeks to understand, precisely by its reliance on an objectified and objectifying form of seeing. Is there another way to think about the process?

We cannot, and ought not, forget the problem of the *unconscious* either. Even assuming the possibility of returning to the somewhat blurrier, more open and attentive conception of understanding found in Greek thought, there still remains the glaring fact (or at least what I take to be a glaring fact) that what one observes in oneself is frequently quite puzzling, even opaque, indecipherable. One can observe one's behaviors to some extent, and even one's thoughts. But what do these tell us? What *can* they tell us? If Freud revealed anything about us humans, it was that we were often quite clueless about our innermost motives and truths. Self-observation, therefore, was at best a starting point for the project of self-understanding, and a rather tenuous one at that. What exactly was to be done? Following Freud, "Reflection," Paul Ricoeur writes, "must become interpretation because I cannot grasp the act of existing except in signs scattered in the world" (1970, 46). Phenomenology thus gives way to hermeneutics, the "prerogative" of reflection thus being dismantled and displaced by the demand for interpretation. So it is that Ricoeur would reject the "short-cut" of self-understanding through conscious reason. "There is no direct apprehension of the self by the self, no internal apperception or appropriation of the self's desire to exist through the short-cut of consciousness but only through the long road of the interpretation of signs" (1974, 170). The Cartesian *cogito*, vain in its aspirations, was more appropriately seen as a "wounded *cogito*, which posits but does not possess itself, which understands its originary truth only in and by the confession of the inadequation, the illusion, and the lie of existing consciousness" (173). So much for self-observation!

Another idea that Ricoeur was pursuing around the time of his encounter with Freud is that consciousness is a movement that continually "annihilates" its own starting point, such that the meaning of a given incident or event is *deferred* until later on, after the passage of time. Freud himself had been alerted to this idea of "deferred action" early in his psychoanalytic musings when he discovered that one may undergo experiences that, while not traumatic at the time of occurrence, may become so at some subsequent point, as further experience and development make possible new understandings of what had transpired (e.g., 1962, 1966). Alongside the subterranean workings of the unconscious, therefore, was the fact that, in a distinct sense, one frequently does not *know* what is going when it is going on and can only gain a sense of things later, looking backward over the terrain of the past. This simple fact has important implications for thinking about both the limits and possibilities of self-understanding, and I shall explore these in due time. For now, and bearing these two realities in mind, we have in hand a rationale for the process of self-understanding being not only *interpretive* through and through but also *retrospective*—that is, relying on the process of looking backward. Psychoanalysis, in turn, thus becomes not only a *hermeneutical* science but a *narrative* science, one that sees deciphering and telling the self's story, in all of its profound depth and obscurity, as the only viable path to self-understanding.

The "narrative psychology" that would eventually emerge in the 1980s was an extension of these ideas—albeit largely shorn in most quarters of the psychodynamic dimension (see, e.g., Bruner 1986; Freeman 1984; McAdams 1985; Polkinghorne 1988; Sarbin 1986). In certain respects, the idea was a relatively simple one: given the irrevocable limits of self-observation, one could turn to self-narration as a suitable replacement. For, what better way to gain access to the inner realities of the self than through the vicissitudes of its history? And what better way to gain access to this history than through story? As psychoanalytic critics might well have complained, the stories that

241

were eventually gathered by narrative psychologists and others would too often remain at the surface—at the manifest level of meaning rather than the latent. (There was just so much meaning to be had on the basis of a single life history interview or some other social science method for charting the trajectory of a life.) Nevertheless, this "narrative turn," as it has been called—this movement, in the direction of history via story—proved to be a vitally important vehicle for clearing a space, anew, for something at least akin to self-observation.[1]

But of course there are two, quite distinct meanings of "history." The first refers to the discrete events of the past, moving forward, into the future, via the well-known arrow of time. Tagging along behind me (so to speak) is just such a history, beginning with my birth and culminating in now, the present moment.[2] The second meaning of the term refers to what historians *do*, that is, *write stories* of the past from the perspective of the present—hopefully, of course, without allowing this present-day perspective to intrude too much on the resultant account. This is where the problems begin, for history and for narrative psychology. Actually, let me put that differently. The problems begin before that, much earlier in fact; what they do is come to a head in this process of writing, of "emplotting" the movement of the past in some serviceable form (see especially White 1978, 1990; also Ricoeur 1981, 1991). Let me therefore take some time to identify these problems, in the hope that we might gain a clearer sense of how the narrative tradition might contribute to the project of self-observation.

History, Memory, Narrative

In my first book-length foray into these issues, *Rewriting the Self: History, Memory, Narrative* (1993), my primary focus was methodological: armed with the insights of Ricoeur and numerous others, I sought to provide a comprehensive rationale for undertaking a narrative psychology. In my recent book *Hindsight: The Promise and Peril of Looking Backward* (2010), I tried to sharpen and extend these ideas by focusing more explicitly on the actual process of narrative, particularly in regard to the "problem"—should we consider it to be one—of looking backward over the terrain of the past from the vantage point of the present. In both, the history/memory/narrative triad figures prominently in my thinking. In the term "history," we have the aforementioned duality of "the past" and the *story* of the past. It has of course become commonplace to assume that there is no recovering and re-presenting "the past" as it was; that would mean returning to the past present in all of its openness and indeterminacy, which we cannot do. The reason is simply that it is *past* and that, consequently, we can only examine it from some present. What this also means is that there can be no "observation" of the past per se. Again, strictly speaking, I can only observe what is right there in front of me, sensuously present, at and in the moment. Here, then, is both a problem and a paradox: the very historical perspective that is ostensibly required for there to be any understanding at all militates against the possibility of observation. Simply put, history entails *interpretation* and *imagination*—the making-present of what is now irrevocably gone—not observation. On the face of it, therefore, narrative psychology, despite its best intentions, would seem to run counter to the project of self-observation. Indeed, it might be said that the impossibility of self-observation is the very takeoff point for narrative psychology: because there is no meeting oneself face to face, one can only look backward, interpreting and imagining as best one can.

None of what has been said thus far about history should be taken to mean that it is a relativistic free-for-all. As Ricoeur (1981a) has argued, the "plurivocity"—many-voicedness—at hand is a *specific* plurivocity, circumscribed and delimited by virtue of the semantic particularity inherent in texts and human actions alike. Nevertheless, the hermeneutical situation, as considered in the context of historical interpretation and in the interpretation of texts more generally, remains "unsurpassable." For one, what a literary text or sequence of actions means is always relative to time, place, interpreter, context. Moreover, and again, meaning—in history and elsewhere—is not something that is just "there," like some inert thing, but has to be fashioned, created, through interpretation and imagination.

Now, when it comes to life history, especially as told by oneself, as in autobiography and memoir, there is the added challenge of *memory*. It is indeed a manifold challenge, and I shall only scratch the (proverbial) surface in identifying its facets. First, and perhaps most basically, there is the fact that memory, like history, cannot pretend to re-present the past (i.e., the past present) as it was; it too issues from some present moment, some act of remembering. This is challenging in its own right and, once more, militates against the possibility of observation, strictly understood. But there is more, much more. As Ernest Schachtel pointed out long ago in his seminal essay "On memory and childhood amnesia" (1959), what we remember is inevitably a function of the fundamental categories we bring to the act of remembering.

Along these lines, the well-known phenomenon of childhood amnesia generally has less to do with repression of some specific incident or experience than with the fact that "the biologically, culturally, and socially influenced processes of memory organization results in the formation of categories (schemata) of memory which are not suitable receptacles to receive and reproduce experiences of the quality and intensity typical of early childhood" (284). For this reason, "The adult is usually not capable of experiencing what the child experiences; more often than not he is not even capable of imagining what the child experiences. It should not be surprising, then, that he should be incapable of recalling his own childhood experiences since his whole mode of experiencing has changed" (285). There is no going back.

Schachtel also calls attention to the seemingly inevitably "conventionalization" that takes place in the act of remembering. He writes:

> If one looks closely at the average adult's memory of the periods of his life after childhood, such memory, it is true, usually shows no great temporal gaps. It is fairly continuous. But its formal continuity in time is offset by barrenness in content, by an incapacity to reproduce anything that resembles a really rich, full, rounded, and alive experience. Even the most 'exciting' events are remembered as milestones rather than as moments filled with the concrete abundance of life. . . . The signpost is remembered, not the place, the thing, the situation to which it points. And even these signposts themselves do not usually indicate the really significant moments in a person's life; rather they point to the events that are conventionally supposed to be significant, to the clichés which society has come to consider as the main stations of life. Thus the memories of the majority of people come to resemble increasingly the stereotyped answers to a questionnaire, in which life consists of time and place of birth, religious denomination, residence, educational degrees, job, marriage, number and birthdates of children, income, sickness, and death. (287)

Schachtel's tale of the developmental process is a kind of paradise lost, such that "perception and experience themselves develop increasingly into the rubber stamps of conventional clichés. The capacity to see and feel what is there gives way to the tendency to see and feel what one expects to see and feel, which, in turn, is what one is expected to see and feel because everybody else does" (288). As for memory, it "is even more governed by conventional patterns than are perception and experience" (291). What one "observes" in one's past, therefore, may ultimately be little more than one's own schematized designs.

Then, of course, there is the *motivated* dimension of memory, the fact that "memory as a function of the living personality can be understood only as a capacity for the organization and reconstruction of past experiences and impressions in the service of present needs, fears, and interests" (284). Not only is there no direct encounter with the substance of the past, there is no *neutral* encounter. How I remember, what I remember, and of course what I *forget*, whether consciously or unconsciously, depends on numerous factors, ranging from my state of psychological health all the way to the self-image I need to maintain in order to reassure myself that I am a good and worthy person. Michael Gazzaniga speaks explicitly to this issue in his rather more upbeat (if extreme and philosophically questionable) rendition of things. On his account,

> Reconstruction of events starts with perception and goes all the way up to human reasoning. The mind is the last to know things. After the brain computes an event, the illusory 'we' (that is, the mind) becomes aware of it. The brain, particularly the left hemisphere, is built to interpret data the brain has already processed. Yes, there is a special device in the brain, which I call the *interpreter*, that carries out one more activity upon completion of zillions of automatic brain processes. The interpreter, the last device in the information chain in the brain, reconstructs the brain events and in doing so makes telling errors of perception, memory, and judgment. The clue to how we are built is buried not just in our marvelously robust capacity for these functions, but also in the errors that are frequently made during reconstruction. Biography is fiction. Autobiography is hopelessly inventive. (1998, 2).

More to the point still, what "the interpreter" tries to do is "keep our personal story together." And, "To do that, we have to learn to lie to ourselves" (26). Actually, though, there is not much that has to be learned, for the process at hand, Gazzaniga indicates, is quite automatic. The bottom line, in any case, is that "We need something that expands the actual facts of our experience into an ongoing narrative, the self-image we have been building in our mind for years. The spin doctoring that goes on keeps us believing that we are good people, that we are in control and mean to do good. It is probably the most amazing mechanism the human being possesses" (26–27). Simply put: "The interpreter tells us the lies we need to believe in order to remain in control" (138). Gazzaniga's tale is thus one of paradise gained: "Sure, life is a fiction, but it's our fiction and it feels good and we are in charge of it. That is the sentiment we all feel as we listen to tales of the automatic brain. We don't feel like zombies; we feel like in-charge, conscious entities" (172)—and, for the most part, good ones too. Shelley Taylor's (1991) work on "positive illusions" is relevant here as well.

Gazzaniga, it should be noted, is not speaking so much of actual narratives, whether spoken or written, but the process of *narrativization* that attends the process of remembering the personal past. When it comes to actual narratives—especially those crafted for some specific audience—the issues at hand become that much more pronounced. Beginning once more with the most basic of these, there is the simple fact that the story being told issues from the present moment of narration—which, of course, means that the story has already *ended*, at least for the time being. "The difficulty," Georges Gusdorf (1980) has written, "is insurmountable. No trick of presentation even when assisted by genius can prevent the narrator from always knowing the outcome of the story he tells—he commences, in a manner of speaking, with the problem already solved. . . . (T)he illusion begins from the moment the narrative confers a meaning on the event which, when it actually occurred, no doubt had several meanings or perhaps none" (42). This is not really a problem for Gusdorf. Indeed, he presents this idea in order that we might "give up the pretence of objectivity, abandoning a sort of false scientific attitude that would judge a work by the precision of its detail" (42). Nevertheless, there is no mistaking the fact that such works inevitably partake of "illusion," thereby rendering them at least partially *false*, yet another step removed from the actualities of the past, as they might be observed by some dispassionate onlooker.

There is more. Consider what Emily Fox Gordon says about the process of writing a memoir. Nearly every one, she maintains—including her own—"can be reduced to the following formula:

> The protagonist (1) suffers and/or is damaged, often at the hands of parents, but sometimes as the result of an illness or repressive thought system, (2) seeks out or encounters a person or institution or vocation or influence that offers escape, healing, relief from, and/or transcendence of the original suffering and/or damage. These persons or vocations or influences turn out to be false, unreliable, or inefficacious (think of drugs, gurus, false religions, sexual obsessions, bad marriages). (2) is repeated. Each time the protagonist's wish for relief is frustrated, the stakes grow higher: the reader's sympathetic identification grows and the narrative tension increases. Just at the point when the reader's pleasure threatens to become pain, the

protagonist (3) stumbles across the finish line. Through the agency of yet another vocation or influence or person or institution, the protagonist at last achieves the relief, escape, or transcendence he has been seeking all along. (In my memoir, therapy was the oppressive force, writing the agent of liberation.) The drive toward narrative closure, which seems to be encrypted in human DNA, is realized in an emotionally satisfying conclusion. (2003, 24–25)

Add to this whatever literary flourish as might strengthen the story and, it would seem, we are even farther removed from what, colloquially at any rate, is called "the truth." As Mary McCarthy has indicated, this is particularly so for fiction writers who turn to autobiography or memoir. "There are some semi-fictional touches here," she admits of her *Memories of a Catholic Girlhood* (1963). "I arranged actual events to make a good story out of them. It is hard to overcome this temptation if you are in the habit of writing fiction," she notes: "one does it almost automatically" (153). From other cultural and religious quarters entirely, Philip Roth, in *The Facts: A Novelist's Autobiography* (1988), says much the same thing. Armed with the tools and tricks of the novelist, he had had to "resist the impulse to dramatize untruthfully the insufficiently dramatic, to complicate the essentially simple, to charge with implication what implied very little" (7). Did he succeed? We will never know.

Where, then, does all this leave us vis-à-vis the idea of self-observation? The history/memory/narrative triad has brought a wealth of issues and problems to the fore. On the face of it, these issues and problems have only rendered this idea more suspect. Is there a way to rethink them so as to preserve a workable notion of self-observation?

Hindsight, Insight, and the (Possible) Truth of Story

As I have suggested in much of my recent work, there is indeed another way to think about the set of issues and problems before us. And perhaps the simplest and most direct point of entry in doing so is to turn to the history/memory/narrative triad once more. As you may recall, in his encounter with Freud, Ricoeur had begun to explore the idea that consciousness annihilates its starting point, such that the meaning of a given incident or event is deferred until some subsequent point in time. This was especially evident in what Freud had called "deferred action," a process wherein earlier experiences came to acquire new meaning and significance in light of subsequent experience. More recently, Ian Hacking (1995) has discussed the idea of single actions under multiple descriptions: "we rewrite the past, not because we find out more about it,"—though that sometimes is so—"but because we present actions under new descriptions" (243). As for the result, "What matters to us may not have been quite so definite as it now seems. When we remember what we did, or what other people did, we may also rethink, redescribe, and refeel the past. These redescriptions may be perfectly true of the past; that is, they are truths that we now assert about the past. And yet, paradoxically, they may not have been true in the past, that is, not truths about intentional actions that made sense when the actions were performed" (249). Notice here that Hacking is perfectly willing to speak about truth, of a sort, emerging in and through historical interpretation itself. Indeed, what Hacking is suggesting here is the idea of a truth being *made available* in retrospect—a truth, that is, *not* of the moment, of the initial action, but an *historical* truth, issuing from a later, more distanced view.

This notion of "distance" is an important one. Indeed, Gadamer (1982) speaks of the productive power of temporal distance, even flirting with the idea that such distance can yield "superior understanding" (263). Perhaps, however, "It is enough to say that [through temporal distance] we understand in a different way, if we understand at all" (264). I would not be so quick to rule out the possibility of arriving at a genuinely superior understanding. Nor, ultimately, would Gadamer. From his perspective,

> Time is no longer primarily a gulf to be bridged, because it separates, but is actually the supportive ground of a process in which the present is rooted. Hence temporal distance is not something that must be overcome. This was, rather, the naïve assumption of historicism, namely that we must set ourselves within the spirit of the age, and think with its ideas and its thoughts, not with our own, and thus advance towards historical objectivity. In fact the important thing is to recognize the distance in time as a positive and productive possibility of understanding. (264)

As Gadamer goes on to explain, "Everyone knows that curious impotence of our judgment where the distance in time has not given us sure criteria. Thus," for instance,

> the judgment of contemporary works of art is desperately uncertain for the scientific consciousness. Obviously we approach such creations with the prejudices we are not in control of, presuppositions that have too great an influence over us for us to know about them;

these can give to contemporary creations an extra resonance that does not correspond to their true content and their true significance. Only when all their relations to the present time have faded away can their real nature appear, so that the understanding of what is said in them can claim to be authoritative and universal. (265)

Whether one should speak in this context of what is "authoritative and universal" is an open—and difficult—question. "It is this experience," in any case, "that has led to the idea in historical studies that objective knowledge can be arrived at only when there has been a certain historical distance." For, "what a thing has to say, its intrinsic content, first appears only after it is divorced from the fleeting circumstances of its actuality." In this sense, temporal distance "lets the true meaning of the object emerge fully" (265).

Gadamer recognizes that "the discovery of the true meaning of a text or work of art is never finished," that "it is in fact an infinite process." There are several reasons for why this is so. First, as Gadamer well knows, there is no wholly separating out the "true meaning" of the object from the process of interpretation and in turn the prejudices of particular interpreters. Second, "fresh sources of error" are frequently identified, such that what was once taken to be the true meaning is superseded once more. Finally, and perhaps most importantly for present purposes, "there emerge continually new sources of understanding, which reveal unsuspected elements of meaning"—and, I would add, elements of meaning that are potentiated and acquire new significance as a function of what happens subsequently. One way or the other,

> The temporal distance which performs the filtering process is not a closed dimension, but is itself undergoing constant movement and extension. And with the negative side of the filtering process brought about by temporal distance there is also the positive side, namely the value it has for understanding. It not only lets those prejudices that are of a particular and limited nature die away, but causes those that bring about genuine understanding to emerge clearly as such. (265–66)

Gadamer's main focus in conceptualizing temporal distance is the idea of (hermeneutical) prejudice. Indeed, "It is only this temporal distance that can solve the really critical question of hermeneutics, namely of distinguishing the true prejudices, by which we understand, from the false ones by which we misunderstand. Hence the historically trained mind will also include historical consciousness" and "will make conscious the prejudices governing our own understanding, so that the text, as another's meaning, can be isolated and valued on its own" (266). Ricoeur, similarly, speaks of "the positive and productive function of distanciation at the heart of the historicity of human experience" (1981a, 131–32), seeing it as a key feature of historical interpretation. In addition, Ricoeur underscores the explicitly *narrative* dimension of the process, for in his view "the historicity of human experience can be brought to language only as narrativity," that is, it "comes to language only so far as we tell stories or tell history. . . . We are members of the field of historicity as storytellers, as novelists, as historians"—and, we can add, as psychologists. "The game of telling is included in the reality told. This is undoubtedly why . . . the word 'history' preserves in many languages the rich ambiguity of designating both the course of recounted events and the narrative that we construct. For they belong together" (294).

As Ricoeur was to show more fully in later work (e.g., 1988, 1991), a further rationale for turning to narrative concerns the aforementioned idea that the meaning and significance of events and experiences frequently becomes transformed as a function of what comes after. Along these lines, there is a kind of two-way temporal traffic in narrative. On the one hand, what comes before leads to what comes later. These are the "recounted events" Ricoeur refers to above. On the other hand, what comes later refigures the meaning and significance of what comes before. Hence his reference to "the narrative we construct." Ricoeur (e.g., 1991b) thus speaks in this context of the *episodic* and *configurational* dimensions of narrative, the parts that comprise the elements of the story and the poetic process by which these elements are synthesized into a whole. Now, for some, again, this very dimension of narrativity, which Ricoeur sees to be part and parcel of the human condition, would seem to preclude the possibility of self-observation. If there is any "seeing" at all, it is a *narrative* seeing, a "seeing-together," as he puts it, which renders inextricable the object seen from this synthesizing, configurational aspect of seeing. This "problem," of course, is present in any and all historical knowing, which is precisely what has led thinkers such as Hayden White (e.g., 1978, 1990) to call attention to the inescapably *literary* dimension of history. But let us move ahead. For one, most historians and philosophers would likely agree that, even while there cannot be absolute historical truths owing the storied nature of historical knowing and writing, there can surely be "truer" and "falser" ones. For another, the problem at hand—should we decide it is one—is, arguably, but the least of those faced in crafting a narrative psychology.

Narrative Psychology, Self-Observation, and the Possibility of Self-Understanding

We have already begun to address a number of these problems. Foremost among them, according to many, is the simple fact that narrative, in the context of *life* history, involves memory; and memory, as we all know, is replete not only with conventionalized schematizations of the sort Schachtel and others have identified but also distortions, corruptions, even self-aggrandizing lies. Once explicit telling enters the picture, whether in the form of speaking or writing, things become even thornier. To make things more troubling still, there is another, very basic fact that distinguishes self-interpretation from virtually all other forms of historical interpretation. Recall for a moment what Gadamer (1982) had said regarding the hope that we can and "will make conscious the prejudices governing our own understanding, so that the text, as another's meaning, can be isolated and valued on its own" (266). What is this fact to which I am referring here? It is the fact that in self-interpretation there really *is* no "text," only the quasi-text of our own past experience. What this means is that whatever image of the past we might have as we go about the process of interpretation is one that *we ourselves have fashioned in imagination*. In some ways, this brings us all the way back to the problem with which we began—namely, that we can never see ourselves except as an image. So too with the personal past. "The past," Merleau-Ponty (1962) has written, "exists only when a subjectivity is there to disrupt the plenitude of being in itself, to adumbrate a perspective" (421). "'Oneself,'" in turn, Bataille (1988) adds, "is not the subject isolating itself from the world, but a place of communication, of fusion of the subject and the object" (9). Positive and productive though the process of distanciation may be, therefore, there is simply no getting around the fact that, strictly speaking, there is no separating "me" from "I." These are but "discriminated aspects," as William James (1950) put it long ago (1890), of a single, undivided process. Does it even make sense, then, to speak of "self-observation theory in the narrative tradition"?

I hate to keep using this phrase, but strictly speaking, *no*; it really does not, for the there is nothing—no thing—to observe. I can look in the mirror, of course, but generally speaking I only do so in a given moment. I suppose I could carry one around for a lengthier period of time, but that would get very cumbersome, no? I could also go the video route, but that would not be particularly handy either. Plus, even if I had a running video of my entire life (which would, of course, be as long as my life and could get very tedious for me to watch [would that I had the time]), I still would not have a *narrative*, for that requires meaning-making, interpreting, *telling*. The bottom line: we are a long, long way from self-observation here. Strictly speaking. What about *non*strictly speaking?

Retrogressive though it may seem to those of a more postmodern/ poststructural bent, I would like to hold out the possibility of something akin enough to self-observation as to allow for the possibility of self-understanding. Here, I am referring mainly to the kind of positive and productive distanciation made possible by hindsight. More to the point still, what I have argued in my recent reflections on the idea is that self-understanding *requires* hindsight—which is to say that it is the very condition of possibility for such understanding to emerge. One reason for why this is so has already been adduced. Following Freud in broad outline, there is enough evidence confirming our own self-alienation and opacity to warrant what Ricoeur had called the "long road of the interpretation of signs" along with the corollary idea that this road must be an after-the-fact, backward-looking one. Indeed, there is a distinct sense in which the very notion of the unconscious is backward-looking at its core: we can only identify its workings after the fact, after extricating ourselves from the realities in question and gaining the requisite distance to see them more clearly. Hindsight is therefore required because there are things that we either cannot see or would not see in the moment. It thus serves as a much-needed corrective lens for viewing ourselves.

The second reason for seeing hindsight as a requirement for self-understanding is the narrative dimension we have been considering. What we experience in the moment is, in effect, an episode in an evolving story. I sit at my computer typing these words, doing my best to ensure that they say what I mean. As above, there are perhaps things I cannot see or would not see; I might therefore look back at these words at some future time with a serious dose of humility, even embarrassment. How could I have written that? What was I *thinking*? But it might also be the case that something could happen in the future—the question of self-observation becomes all the rage in psychology, and this volume, especially this chapter, comes to be seen as a truly pivotal event in the history of the discipline (doubtful!)—which in turn lends new meaning and significance to the very act in which I am currently engaged. In clock time, beginning leads to end. Recollection, Ricoeur (1981b) has noted, inverts this seemingly "natural" ordering: "by reading the end in the beginning and the beginning in the end, we learn also to read time itself backward, as the recapitulating of the initial conditions of a course of action in its terminal consequences" (176). Now, clock time, for some, may be seen not only as the natural order of time but the *true* one. This, however, is "unacceptable," Ricoeur argues. It is but one concept of time, and while it surely has its value, it cannot and does not do justice to the complex, multidimensional temporality of human experience. Yes; we are moving forward, inexorably, into the future; a virtual trail of events and experiences exists behind me. But these same events and experiences come to acquire new meaning and significance as a function of what comes later. We glean this new meaning and significance through hindsight, wherein we can begin to extract patterns and plots from the movement of experience. Hindsight therefore allows for what Ricoeur (1991) calls the "synthesis of the heterogeneous." This in turn permits a kind of knowing—*narrative* knowing—that is simply unavailable in the flux of the moment.

I might note in this context that there is an aspect of narrative knowing that is itself tied to the unconscious but in a different sense than is posited in psychoanalysis. Alongside the life experiences I myself have had, my past consists of stories that others have told me, that are themselves the products of stories others have told them (and so forth and so on). In addition, my past is comprised of the books I have read and the movies I have seen and many other "second-hand" realities. As I have suggested elsewhere, however (e.g., Freeman 2002), these second-hand features of my history often go unacknowledged, remaining essentially behind the scenes, not because they have been repressed but because they go beyond discrete events and experiences, opening into the "tradition," as Gadamer (1982) puts it, in which we are immersed. So it is that I have come to speak of the *narrative unconscious*, which refers to those aspects of my history that have yet to become part of my story owing to their being beyond the scope of what I consciously know about my own formation. On one level, this idea of the narrative unconscious brings us even farther away from the possibility of self-observation, for what it suggests is that there are aspects of my history that go beyond "my life," the discrete particulars occupying the span of time between my birth and death, into the entire, de facto *unobserved*, constellation of factors and forces that are constitutive of my existence as an historical subject. On another, deeper level, however, deciphering the narrative unconscious via hindsight is, again, nothing short of a requirement for self-understanding; and in this respect, it may plausibly be seen as a form of self-observation (nonstrictly speaking) in its own right.

There is a third, rather more "existential" reason for turning to hindsight as well. Here, I am referring to the fact that, in the moral realm especially, we human beings have a special tendency to act first and think later. This occurs routinely in everyday life when we come to see our behavior anew. But it also occurs on a much larger scale. Consider the fact that actions that once appeared to have a solid rationale—slaughtering millions in the name of racial purity, for instance—now appear (to many) to be utterly horrific and shameful. I have called this sort of tragic delay "moral lateness" (e.g., 2003, 2010), arguing that hindsight frequently provides a kind of "rescue function," a vitally important vehicle for redressing our moral shortsightedness. Does this process of seeing more clearly, and perhaps avowing more readily, what one has done warrant being called "self-observation"? More generally, does the kind of self-understanding occasioned by hindsight and instantiated in narrative warrant this designation? Acknowledging all of the aforementioned difficulties in proclaiming it so, I am prepared to answer in the affirmative. My main reason for doing so is a pragmatic one: whatever allows one to see oneself more clearly and in turn to understand oneself better—that is, better than one had before—entails self-observation, broadly conceived.

Needless to say, it is no easy task to identify the "better." Moreover, what sometimes appears to be better turns out to be worse. And, if one wants to be utterly relativistic about the whole matter, one might claim that there simply *is* no better or worse when it comes to inter-pretive processes like these, only different. But this last claim flies in the face of what most of us patently know to be the case: first, that we are sometimes quite "off" in our self-understanding (owing to our misconstruals, defenses, hermeneutical quirks, and so on); and second, that we occasionally make a bit of headway in this arduous process. But how exactly do you *know* when you are knowing? I posed this very question to a good friend of mine sometime ago. It is easy, he said: I feel bad! So, that is one possibility. But there are others as well. Put in the simplest of terms, I can sometimes see myself—virtually always from a distance; in the moment, there are only the most fleeting intimations, which are generally left behind quickly so I can resume whatever (faulty) track I am on—for what I am in a way that corrects and supersedes earlier versions, which I can now identify to have been partial, incomplete, defended, whatever. Again, I could be wrong about this new interpretation, and it too may be superseded at some point in the future as further "evidence" comes along and incites me to look, and learn, again. But it seems to me that this idea of "better," cautiously framed, is a valid one. In the present context, I see it as the pragmatic correlate of the idea of self-observation.

What is it, finally, that allows for the emergence of this betterness? Put another way, what is it that allows for self-observation rather than self-deception or self-obfuscation? Well, strictly speaking, nothing: there are no guarantees. The question is what can up the chances. And what can up the chances, I would suggest, is a kind of hermeneutical *mindfulness*—more specifically, both a willingness and a capacity to see oneself as *Other*. To do so requires a good measure of what Iris Murdoch (1970) has called "unselfing," divesting oneself of ego-driven preoccupations, anxieties, and defenses in such a way as to allow the otherness of the Other to come into view. Also required is attention, an ability to really *look* at what is there. This itself entails unselfing, breaking down and dismantling those ego needs that obscure, rather than reveal, reality. This process is easier said than done, and, like mindfulness and meditation practices, needs to be *cultivated*. Therapy—at least those forms of it oriented toward self-understanding—is one vehicle for doing so. But there is also that more garden variety form of it that sometimes emerges when one pauses and takes the time to truly look at oneself. This entails looking backward and finding out "what's the story." It is not a surefire means to self-understanding; nothing is. By all indications, though, it is the best we have.

Notes

1. Rather than speaking of a single narrative turn, Matti Hyvärinen (2010) has spoken of multiple narrative turns, extending from the 1960s through the present. In the context of academic psychology, however, the singular turn in the 1980s remains a fitting description of the movement at hand.

2. Things actually are not quite this simple. As I have suggested on several occasions (e.g., 2002, 2010), there is a very real sense in which in order to understand "my life," there is the need to move beyond the delimited swath of time between birth and death. The reason, (too) simply put, is that we belong to a history and tradition that precedes our entry into the world; and even though we do not have firsthand knowledge of this dimension of the past, it remains operative in constituting and shaping our own identities.

255

References

Barthes, R. 1989. *Roland Barthes*. New York: The Noonday Press.

Bataille, G. 1988. *Inner Experience*. Albany, NY: SUNY Press.

Bruner, J. 1986. *Actual Minds, Possible Worlds*. Cambridge, MA: Harvard University Press.

Freeman, M. 1984. "History, Narrative, and Life-Span Developmental Knowledge." *Human Development* 27: 1–19.

_____. 1993. *Rewriting the Self: History, Memory, Narrative*. London: Routledge.

_____. 2002. "Charting the Narrative Unconscious: Cultural Memory and the Challenge of Autobiography." *Narrative Inquiry* 12: 193–211. Reprinted in M. Bamberg and M. Andrews eds. 2004. *Considering Counter-Narratives: Narrating, Resisting, Making Sense*, 289–306. Amsterdam: John Benjamins.

_____. 2003. "Too Late: The Temporality of Memory and the Challenge of Moral Life." *Journal für Psychologie* 11: 54–74.

_____. 2010. *Hindsight: The Promise and Peril of Looking Backward*. New York: Oxford University Press.

Freud, S. 1962. "Further Remarks on the Neuro-psychoses of Defense." *Standard Edition III*. London: Hogarth. (originally 1896).

_____. 1966. "Project for a Scientific Psychology." *Standard Edition 1*. London: Hogarth. (originally 1895).

Gadamer, H. -G. 1982. *Truth and Method*. New York: The Crossroad Publishing Company.

Gazzaniga, M. 1998. *The Mind's Past*. Berkeley, CA: University of California Press.

Gordon, E. F. 2003. "Book of Days." *American Scholar* 72: 17–32.

Gusdorf, G. 1980. "Conditions and Limits of Autobiography." In *Autobiography: Essays Theoretical and Critical*, edited by J. Olney, 28–48. Princeton, NJ: Princeton University Press.

Hacking, I. 1995. *Rewriting the Soul: Multiple Personality and the Sciences of Memory*. Princeton, NJ: Princeton University Press.

Heidegger, M. 1977. *The Question Concerning Technology and Other Essays*. New York: Harper Torchbooks.

Hyvärinen, M. 2010. "Revisiting the Narrative Turns." *Life Writing* 7: 69–82.

McAdams, D. P. 1985. *Power, Intimacy, and the Life Story: Personological Inquiries into Identity*. New York: Guilford.

McCarthy, M. 1963. *Memories of a Catholic Girlhood*. New York: Berkley Publishing Co.

Merleau-Ponty, M. 1962. *The Phenomenology of Perception*. Pittsburgh, PA: Duquesne University Press.

Murdoch, I. 1970. *The Sovereignty of Good*. London: Routledge.

Polkinghorne, D. 1988. *Narrative Knowing and the Human Sciences*. Albany, NY: SUNY Press.

Ricoeur, P. 1970. *Freud and Philosophy: An Essay on Interpretation*. New Haven, CT: Yale University Press.

_____. 1974. *The Conflict of Interpretations*. Evanston, IL: Northwestern University Press.

_____. 1981a. *Hermeneutics and the Human Sciences*. Cambridge: Cambridge University Press.

_____. 1981b. "Narrative Time." In *On Narrative*, edited by W. J. T. Mitchell, 165–86. Chicago, IL: University of Chicago Press.

_____. 1988. *Time and Narrative*, vol. 3. Chicago, IL: University of Chicago Press.

_____. 1991. "Life in Quest of Narrative." In *On Paul Ricoeur: Narrative and Interpretation*, edited by D. Wood, 20–33. London: Routledge.

Roth, P. 1988. *The Facts: A Novelist's Autobiography*. New York: Farrar, Straus, & Giroux.

Sarbin, T. R. ed. 1986. *Narrative Psychology: The Storied Nature of Human Conduct*. New York: Praeger.

Schachtel, E. 1959. *Metamorphosis: On the Conflict of Human Development and the Psychology of Creativity*. New York: Basic Books.

Taylor, S. 1991. *Positive Illusions: Creative Self-Deception and the Healthy Mind*. New York: Basic Books.

White, H. 1978. *Tropics of Discourse*. Baltimore, MD: Johns Hopkins University Press.

_____. 1990. *The Content of the Form: Narrative Discourse and Historical Representation*. Baltimore, MD: Johns Hopkins University Press.

13

Self-Observation in Ethnographic Writing

Alessandra Fasulo

Reflexivity is still about them

—Raymond Madden (2010)

In 2008, theater scholar William Davies King published *Collections of Nothing*, a book that, as the cover explains, is "part memoir, part reflection on the mania of acquisition":

> At thirteen, I had to collect. Collecting collected me. It was 1968, and the Vietnam war was rattling, protests loud and long, hair growing everywhere, and legal and illegal, moral and immoral, smoke in the air. (2008, 35)

The text's main literary key is poetic, but in fact the work blends the sociological essay, the psychological investigation, and a more straightforward autobiographical story-telling. It is not so much a case of genres blurring (Geertz 1983), as a case of genres melting to give shape to an idiosyncratic and iconic form of writing. In the following passage, for example, a sociological description of US middle class takes the form of a list—an iconic genre in a book about collecting that in Davies' work is stretched to its extreme literary possibilities:

> Middle class life is itself a collection: a spouse, a house, a brace of children, a suitable car, a respectable career, cuddly pets, photos of grinning relatives, toys for all ages and hours, coffee and coffeepots, coffee cups and spoons, coffee table books about coffee and about coffee tables. I had the set and then I had another set—boxes and binders and closets full of stuff no one needs:
>
> *Fifty-three Cheez-It boxes, empty [list continues]. . . . (2008, 2–3)*

The book is cited in the anthropological literature as a case study in collecting; using the jargon of today, one might call it an auto-ethnography. Whichever the name, it exemplifies an approach to the understanding of human experience and conduct that has recently established itself as valid knowledge, not despite, but because of, its being grounded in personal experience and doing nothing to hide it. This chapter is an attempt to reconstruct the vicissitudes that made this form of writing possible in the human and social sciences, with a focus on the development of ethnographic sensibility in anthropology and beyond. Whereas anthropology is by no means the only protagonist in this story, it is fair to say that it is the discipline that has moved beyond objectivism first and in the most radical way, and that has done so with the most thorough examination of its epistemological bases and of the place of the self in them. In the following, we will thus be concerned with the nature of the involvement of the self in ethnographic work and with the growth of the authorial presence in ethnographic texts.

Ethnography is understood today as an epistemological attitude that can be applied to any domain; as Reed-Danahai (1997) notes citing Geertz, it has to do with investigating "informing contexts" to make sense of observable cultural practices or their outcomes. So, for example, one can do an ethnography of written texts—as Reed-Danahai (1997) does—analyzing the context in which the books were written as well as the associated practices of production, such as translation, illustration, marketing strategies and so on, together with the book contents. At its inception, though, ethnography meant more strictly a way of doing anthropological research in which the ethnographers immersed themselves for a sustained period of time in the life of an exotic cultural group, with the aim of understanding the culture by experiencing it in the first person, as it was assumed it would happen by joining the group's daily activities and social exchanges. Ethnography as a method has thus always had the self at its center as an instrument of knowing. I will start this overview, therefore, with an examination of the seminal text of ethnographic methodology, Bronislaw Malinowski's introductory chapter of *The Argonauts of the Western Pacific*. Ethnographic methods and their product—ethnographic writing—will be analyzed together, as they are so deeply connected that ethnography can also be defined as "the textual rendering of social worlds" (Abu-Lughod 2000).

The Principles of the Ethnographic Method

It is indicative of the nature of ethnography that Malinoswki, the founding father of the approach, lays out the principles of the ethnographic method by reconstructing the particularity of his own experience:

> A brief outline of an Ethnographer's tribulations, as lived through by myself, may throw more light on the question, than any long abstract discussion will do.

III

> Imagine yourself suddenly set down surrounded by all your gear, alone on a tropical beach close to a native village, while the launch or dinghy which has brought you sails away out of sight. (1922, 3)

This dramatic scene, presented as the best alternative to an "abstract discussion" of the method, presents to the anthropological trainee a form of knowledge which can only be accessed through an existential condition, that of displacement, and perhaps also through overcoming the "hopelessness and despair" (1922, 4) that often accompany it.

A strong autobiographical foundation, vivid and detailed descriptions instead of codified and formal accounts, narrative devices that transport the reader within the exotic worlds ("imagine yourself suddenly set down . . ." 3): these are forms of scientific writing commonly accepted until the nineteenth century but that anthropology solely is able to carry forward in the positivism-dominated following century.

A crucial practice in ethnography vis-à-vis self-observation is that of field notes, i.e., the diary that constitutes the ethnographer's data. Once back from the field, the notes will be the bases for writing the anthropological report. Again, we find extensive instructions about field notes in *The Argonauts'* first chapter. The ethnographer must record "carefully and precisely, one after another, the actions of the actors and of the spectators" (1922, 21) and capture quotes from the natives' conversation, recurrent phrases, and local taxonomies. Field notes should also include the natives' own accounts of their history and folklore and their explanations, elicited by the ethnographer, about specific practices or events. Field notes are there to ensure that the anthropologist will be able "to bring all this home to his readers in a clear, convincing manner" (1922, 21).

Malinowski goes on to detail the method of observation: often, he says, the ethnographer has to "put aside camera, notebook and pencil and join in" with the village life, capture the village mood by letting himself be swept along by and with it. In short, he has to gain knowledge of the "intimate side" of both ordinary and extraordinary activities in order to grasp what those mean for the natives and what is their "degree of vitality" in the culture. Such a practice of immersion was given the name of "participant observation," a trademark of ethnography and the crux of all anthropological troubles, as we shall see.

At the core of the approach just described, and validating it, was the notion of experience, as Weber and Dilthey had theorized it, namely the empathic understanding that comes from "coexistence in a shared world" (Clifford 1986). By adding "participation" to the ethnographic equation, it was postulated that the ethnographers would be able to experience and later reconstruct the world as seen by the native. The outcome of participant observation, frozen in field notes, was to be re-enlivened at a later stage to inform the analysis of the culture and the subsequent anthropological monographs and articles.

Two main problems arise, however, in relation to grounding anthropological knowledge in experience: one is the assumption that experience presents itself in a coherent fashion, offering neat and straightforward material for a "convincing" posthoc reconstruction. The second is the entitlement of the anthropologists to speak for the natives, when the only experience they can have is by definition their own. In the following, I will be concerned with the development of the first of these problems, as it relates more directly to the topic of self-observation.

The Anthropologist's Troubled Self

The assumption of experience as a coherent source of knowledge rested, in Malinowski, in the idea of a "unified personality" as the warrant of a steady point of view upon the population the anthropologist lives with. Ironically, the most powerful blow to this idea was given by Malinowski himself, if only posthumously, with the publication of his personal journal in 1967, *A Diary in the Strict Sense of the Term*. The journal revealed that a unified personality was what the author was struggling to achieve, against incontrollable emotions and thoughts. The journal reports strong negative feelings toward the villagers, frequent escapes into the Western novels he had brought with him, acute feelings of longing for friends and family, and guilt for his attraction toward Trobriand women. Itself a dramatic illustration of this lack of unification, the journal is highly discontinuous, hosting different types of texts written in different languages: Malinowski's original Polish, the English of his academic identity, and the Kiriwini he used to speak with the Trobrianders. As Geertz efficaciously summarizes:

> The problem that the *Diary* forefronts (. . .) is that there is a lot more than native life to plunge into if one is to attempt this total immersion approach to ethnography. There is the landscape. There is the isolation. There is the local European population. There is the memory of home and of what one has left. There is the sense of vocation and of where one is going. And, most shakingly, there is the capriciousness of one's passions, the weakness of one's constitution, and the vagrancies of one's thoughts: that nigrescent thing, the self. (1988, 77)

The Diary cannot be taken as the "true" report from the Trobriand islands, but it certainly unveils the nature of fabrication of the much more harmonious accounts Malinowski offers in his monographs, most notably *Argonauts.* Clifford (1988) reconstructs this process by an analysis of both the writing and the life of the author; he identifies the influences of Conrad's novels in the *Diary*—both Polish men who wrote in English about their journey through exotic lands—and highlights the simultaneous "pulling together" of both Malinowski's persona and the Trobriand culture during the liminal time spent writing *Argonauts* in the Canary Islands. "One is tempted to propose—Clifford concludes—that ethnographic comprehension (a coherent position of sympathy and hermeneutic engagement) is better seen as a creation of ethnographic *writing* that a consistent quality of ethnographic *experience*" (1988, 110).

The shift from "experience" to "writing" as the locus where the knowledge of the visited culture is created contributes to characterize the 1980s as probably the most reflexive decade that anthropology will ever know. We will discuss those developments later in the chapter, but before moving on, we shall pause to meet another anthropologist, a contemporary of Malinowski, whom the new reflexive sensibilities helped to rediscover.

Michel Leiris was hired as archivist and secretary in the massive Dakar-Djebuti expedition, funded by the French government and aimed at acquiring African art for Parisian museums. Leiris was not concerned with anthropology per se; he was an intellectual close to the Surrealists with whom he shared the interest in primitivism and African art. His principal duty in the expedition was to take notes, which he did in a very personal form; these notes were later published – still in the form of notes -under the revealing title *Afrique Fantôme* (1934). In this text Leiris is constantly addressing the problem of the simultaneous construction of "self" and "other" in intercultural encounters. Far from even attempting a unified description of the African populations he came in contact with, Leiris wrote from a strictly autobiographical standpoint and, rather than minimizing contradictions and mixed feelings, theorized that they are at the core of the encounter with cultural alterity.

Leiris had set off with the view, largely shared in his time, that the most interesting groups to study were the most isolated and untouched, and the most interesting individuals the least educated among them (Price 2004). However, after encountering individuals who engaged in strategies of self-presentation and reticence, who reflexively told the ethnographers the stories that they figured they wanted to hear, Leiris stopped being interested in the unspoiled and proposed instead that the more fertile cultural analyses were likely to develop in the sites of hybridization and cultural clash, thus favoring cultural dynamism over the allegory of authenticity. As Clifford will emphasize much later, the quest for the authentic and unspoiled that permeated the rhetoric of anthropological writing at the time betrayed Westerners' own desire to retrieve and fix their own past forms of life, endangered by a rapidly changing society (Clifford 1988).

Furthermore, in reflecting on the dual process of inscribing observations as field notes and later using them to retrieve the experience, Leiris demonstrates its intrinsic perils and vulnerabilities. He remarks that often his notes do not speak to him anymore: some of them are sheer enigmas, other more simply dead, "cut off from the significance which might have been able to animate them" (1955, 15, cited in Blanchard 1990). In the second stage of writing, Leiris notes, literary styles and genres from Western texts constantly overtook his efforts to rely "just" on his notes and memory to produce a loyal representation of what was once seen and lived through. Moreover, he acknowledged that his cultural build-up informed his experience from the very beginning; experiences are "textual" in nature, i.e., produced and isolated from the flux by the ethnographer predisposed gaze. If Malinowski's beloved novelists were only present as distant echoes in his writings, Leiris' notes openly incorporate citations and figures from disparate literary traditions, and adopt poetic devices, such as free associations, metaphors, and dream-like imagery, to stress the idiosyncrasies of his field experience and the composite nature of experience in general.

Leiris' revolutionary idea, yet to be fully digested, is that what ethnographic work reveals first and foremost is the cultural subjectivity of the observer refracted in the experience with the cultural other; in Blanchard's words, dislocation and the encounter with the other lead in Leiris to "reappropriating the parts of a subjectivity drowned in the culture" (1990, 272).

Leiris' work illustrates reflexivity at work in ethnography, not as a focus on the self per se but as an attentive and critical monitoring on one's investigative attitudes and on the cultural sources informing them. The most radical aspects of his theories will be only taken up again with the reflexive turn in anthropology half a century later, but significant changes in how to conceive of the role of experience in cultural interpretation will occur earlier in anthropology, under the influence of the strong currents in humanities questioning authorship in the creation of texts. This development is briefly illustrated in the next section.

Reading Cultures

The role of subjectivity and experience in ethnography is rediscussed in an anthropological approach which emerged at the end of the 1960s, chiefly through the work of Clifford Geertz. Geertz was influenced by the new emphasis in literary theory on readership as constitutive of textual meaning (Barthes 1970; Iser 1974) and by Wittgenstein's concept of language games as structuring meaning-making processes (Wittgenstein 1957). Geertz looked at cultural practices as texts, namely as organized forms of local knowledge towards which the ethnographer acts as the reader.

> It is with expressions—representations, objectifications, discourses, performances, whatever—that we traffic: a carnival, a mural, a curing rite, a revitalization movement, a clay figurine, an account of a stay in the woods. Whatever sense we have of how things stand with someone's inner life, we gain it through their expressions, not through some magical intrusion into their consciousness. (Geertz 1986, 373)

Exemplary of this approach is Victor Turners' work about theatrical representation in the Denbu Zambian population, in which he reads performances and other less-structured "social dramas" as the community's own interpretation—the collective enactment—of the society's internal conflicts and its attempts at their resolution. On the one hand, this approach gives more credit to the natives as authors of complex—and already interpretive—meaning systems; on the other, it diminishes the ethnographer omnipotence by implying that what she or he offers is just *a* reading, which cannot but be situated and partial in the rendition of the observed other. In fact, the "interpretive" or "hermeneutic" anthropology, as this approach is also called, acknowledges that the production of cultural descriptions is always also a form of cultural comparison, as ethnographers cannot help being guided by differences and contrasts with their expectations.

The validity of anthropological knowledge is still anchored in participant observation, but with more emphasis on the observation component—the ethnographer as spectator, at the receiver end of the natives' performances and representations. "Being there," the key requirement and rhetorical figure of the ethnographic enterprise (Geertz 1983), no longer implies a fusion of perspectives but rather the securing of a standpoint close enough to the action to provide the ethnographers with a meaningful experience. Though not coinciding with that of the natives, this experience will be at the core of that secondary process of interpretation finally enabling to "entextualize" the culture in the ethnographic report.

Interpretive anthropology represented a breakdown in the authority of the anthropologist to represent a culture as a whole and in definitive terms, but maintained the ethnographer's privileged position of powerful observer, whose sensitive instruments enable well-rounded explanations of the observed culture. Coherently, reflexivity lives in the margins of the report, typically in recollections of first impressions at the arrival in the field and of the initial mishaps revealing the ethnographer's novice status vis-à-vis the foreign culture. In Rabinow's lapidary summary of a critique to Geertz, "the anthropologist establishes he was there and then disappears from the text" (1986, 244).

A group of anthropologists from the following generation, though separated from their teachers by only a few years, will further challenge the authority of the ethnographer and dissolve ethnographic knowledge in the vagaries of particular—and to some extent serendipitous—encounters and events in the field. Reflexivity is made to leave its marginal, almost paratextual location in ethnographic reports and is given instead a center stage position.

Ethnographic Intersubjectivity

The representatives of the reflexive and dialogic approach share the stylistic choice of autobiographical and narrative writing and emphasize the role of individual informants in the production of anthropological knowledge. They will never constitute a mass movement in anthropology but their work will pose basic questions about the possibility of making science of another culture as such. Books such as those of Crapanzano (1985), Dumont (1978), Dwyer (1982), Meyerhoff (1978), Rabinow (1977), and Shostak (1981) are at pains to bring to light the particularity of field experience, and the impact that the relationship with key participants as well as their own biographical circumstances had on their understanding of a certain community. In fixating such contents onto the page, these authors struggle against the canons of anthropological writing, and come up with different solutions, each embodying a different version of dialogism. We will focus on one of these works, Paul Rabinow's *Reflections on Fieldwork in Morocco*, as it is perhaps both the most theoretically deep and the happiest textual realization.

Rabinow wrote this reflexive book after having produced a more canonical PhD dissertation. Firmly rooted in the first person, the new text is structured so as to reflect the fragmentary nature of the experience gained through different encounters in the field: each chapter is devoted to a different figure among those encountered by the author in Morocco, while at the same time illustrating a different aspect of reflexivity. For example, one chapter is dedicated to his main informant, Ali, and is rich in observations about how ethnography changes the observed together with the observer:

> This highlighting, identification, and analysis also disturbed Ali's usual pattern of experience. [. . .] Under my systematic questioning, Ali was taking realms of his own world and interpreting them for an outsider. This means that he, too, was spending more time in this liminal, self-conscious world between cultures. (1977, 39)

Observing how informants developed their own "practical art of response and presentation" (1997, 38), Rabinow steps in on Geertz' idea that ethnography can only be an interpretation of interpretations, but subverts it to the point of finding in the exchanges more fraught with misunderstandings the locus of cultural revelation. (Leiris' intuitions resonate here as well.) Exemplary in this respect is the chapter that reconstructs Rabinow's relationship (and its end) with his first Arabic teacher. After several weeks of frequent meetings, during which the teacher, Ibrahim, had been "hospitable and generous," he asked Rabinow to take him on a trip to Casablanca (the need for which turned out to be a false pretext) and provide for all his expenses. By such a move, Rabinow's definition of their relationship as 'friendship' was undermined (betrayed, according to his emotional reaction); he realized that he had incorrectly typified a utilitarian relationship following his 'home' standards and conceptions, whereas Ibrahim had been consistent and treated the ethnographer as an economic resource all along. This was a baffling experience to the young Rabinow, but a fundamental one to grasp in one shot the paradox inherent to his mission:

> I had gone into anthropology in search of Otherness. Meeting it on an experiential level was a shock which caused me to begin fundamental reconceptualization about social and cultural categories. Presumably this was the sort of thing I had come to Morocco to find, yet every time these breaks occurred they were upsetting. (1977, 29)

If Rabinow's reflexive endeavor gives a further shock to the illusion of objectivity in cultural research, it is not directed to undermine ethnographic work as such. Its main objective is to assert that the knowledge of the other progresses together with the knowledge of the self; this program is encapsulated by the quote from Ricoeur that Rabinow puts in the opening of his book, in which interpretation is conceived as "the comprehension of the self by the detour of the comprehension of the other." As in Leiris, the self Rabinow is interested in is the cultural self, the "perfectly public [. . .] culturally mediated and historically situated self which finds itself in a continuously changing world of meaning" (6). This self is not *strictu sensu* psychological, but it is constituted phenomenologically through the experience of cultural disorientation and the reflections on its effects. At the same time, the myth of a unified personality is dissolved, as the subjectivity of the anthropologists is shown here as plural, contradictory, and mutating as he erratically proceeds through the "field."

Rabinow's text is, finally, illustrative of the experimentation with different forms of ethnographic writing that flourished around those years. Despite the novelty in both style and structure, the choice of dedicating a separate book to the issue of reflexivity testify of the difficulty of integrating it within the canonical genre of ethnographic description. Other authors will choose different textual solutions, ranging from the juxtaposition of autobiographical recollection, dialogic fragments, and general explanations, as Shostak does in *Nisa* (1981), to the alternation of the voice of the informant and of theoretical discussion, chosen by Crapanzano for his *Tuhami* (1985). These texts keep within a single book-cover the reflexive and the explanatory mode, but there is a marked shift in the quality of voice of the different sections. According to Clifford's analysis, such different registers enact within the text the "impossible attempt to fuse objective and subjective practices" (1986, 109); yet, they constitute a crucial inventive phase in setting out the new conventions for cultural tales.

Insiders Trading

Self-observation will feature more prominently in ethnographical writing in the last two decades of the century, with anthropological research "going home." Anthropologists shift their gaze inward, studying either subcultures in their own country or communities they are part of. Ethnography has spread in the meantime across the social sciences, notably in sociology, history, communication studies, interactional linguistics, and geography, and most ethnographic studies within those disciplines will be also directed at groups and activities in the ethnographer's home country.

Ethnographic work "at home" can be directed at professional organizations, residential areas, interest groups, online communities, families or other circumscribed settings; research participants are less numerous than in exotic ethnographies and make a more identifiable contribution to the research. As a consequence, the relationship of the ethnographer with individual participants yields more visibility in the write-up, while the ethnographer, qualifying as an apprentice or an equal member of the community, becomes herself or himself a legitimate source of ethnographic data.

A phenomenon that is also relevant in the growth of self-observation in ethnographic works is that of "ethnic autobiographies". These can be either written by members of cultural minorities living in a Western country, such as those analyzed by Fisher (1986), or the product of someone who abandoned their social milieu of origin and later returned to visit and write about it, as in the French autobiographies discussed by Reed-Danahay (1997). These works are not ethnographies; they are memoirs which attracted the interest of anthropologists for their powerful insights into the phenomenology of divided cultural membership. Coming from individuals who have crossed borders, literally or metaphorically, they illustrate cultural origins as a point of arrival rather than a point of departure. "Ethnicity—Fisher notes—has become a puzzling quest for those afflicted by it" (1986, 230). Ethnic autobiographies reveal that cultural membership needs to be recreated with each new generation, rather than being inherited, and that this is done by combining and mixing elements which are subjectively ascribed cultural significance.

The knock-on effect on anthropology, in general, has been to further promote the study of cultural transformations and exchanges—*routes* and not *roots* (Clifford 2000)—in its research programmes. As concerns the self in anthropological research, these works and the analysis anthropologists made of them have posited the multiplicity of identities as a natural condition; not something to disguise in the production of homogeneous cultural descriptions but something that needs to find adequate means of representation. The autobiographical posture still seems insuperable in this regard.

By virtue of such interbreeding of different writing traditions and research agendas, ethnography itself has seen its boundaries dramatically widened to include, on the one hand, any sort of cultural critique based on observation, and, on the other, detailed illustrations of practices or communities based on the author's personal engagement with them. The text about collections cited in the opening of this chapter—and its notoriety in scientific circles—testifies of this broader understanding of ethnographic work.

Autoethnography

The term "autoethnography" refers, within this fuzzy area, to both kinds of research introduced in the previous section, namely "either to the ethnography of one's own group or to autobiographical writing that has ethnographic interest" (Reed-Danahai 1997, 2). Investigative methods and writing formats multiply within this broader framework. In Carolyn Ellis' (2004) experimental textbook—written as a fiction about teaching a group of university students about autoethnography—the methods and genres introduced include writing ethnographically about one's own life experiences (Ellis herself has written about her experience of looking after her ill mother and her bereavement at the loss of her brother), co-constructing ethnographies with a person with whom the ethnographer shares some experience or condition, interviewing a participant and then build the ethnographic text as the reported dialogue interpolated with general comments, or creating poetry or other artistic representations of the object of ethnographic interest.

Autoethnographies fight against the "othering" of any individual, group, or ethnicity, stressing instead the continuity of experience between authors, informants, and readers; as "othering" is embedded in inherited ways of representing culture, resisting it coincides with a shift toward innovative styles of representation aimed to reduce the distance between those parties.

Autoethnographic works also incorporate the ethnographers' motives to choose a certain area of study, even though sometimes these are arrived at as post hoc realizations. Motives may be bridging a gap in the knowledge about one's cultural descent, or the need to give voice to a marginalized group, or the urge to go through the process of self-understanding and self-reconstituting inherent to autobiographical writing. It is understood that such driving motivations would contribute to shape the research in multiple ways, and that their reconstruction would help the reader to position the author and understand the larger social processes constituting the context of her or his anthropological work. For example, commenting about her research on Arab Jews in Israel, Motzafi-Haller, an Israeli Arab Jew herself, reports:

> The issue, I argue, is not that all "native writers" are conditioned by virtue of their birth to write about oppression and exclusion in insightful ways and clearly not that we have some "moral right" or a monopoly over such work. The point here is not one's indigenous qualifications but rather the connection that is always there between the researcher's positioning in society and history and the kind of research agenda and understanding such personal background shapes. (1997, 217)

Including the anthropologist's personal history in the analysis it is not done to enhance the ethnographer's authority, as Haller clarifies; it has instead become a parameter of methodological correctness, part of the reflexive development in the discipline that sees the voice of the ethnographer become progressively more embodied, historically and geographically situated.

Names of women become more frequent in the territory of autobiographical anthropology. Interestingly, it turns out, there is a tradition of field autobiographies from women dating far back before any first-person revolution in anthropology. In the 1950s and 1960s, women accompanying expeditions as students or wives produced autobiographical reports showing "the impurities of experience . . . while the men were exclusively doing the 'real thing'" (Dumont 1978, 8, cited in Callaway 1992). The contribution of feminism in anthropology has contributed to the affirmation of the dialogical program but also constantly denounced subtle and less subtle forms of domination in ethnographic work. Feminist anthropology, at least in some of its determinations, consciously cultivates a distance from established forms of knowledge production in anthropology and theorizes the value of difference and conflict (Strathern 1984; see also Rabinow 1986), established from an autobiographical standpoint (Callaway 1997).

Conclusions

This chapter has shown how the self has been part of the instrumentation of ethnography since its inception, and that what has changed through the history of the discipline has been the degree to which self-observation has been topicalized and brought into the open. But, perhaps more interestingly, also the cultural inflections that the "self" of ethnographic self-observation has assumed across the last century have kept mutating. Leiris' lesson proves right here once again: reconstructing the history of ethnography gave us back the history of Western subjectivity over the past century, from Malinowski's heroic struggles in the Trobriands, through the ironic twist of Rabinow's confused persona in Morocco, all the way to autoethnographies, in which the ethnographers, skeptical of the possibility of comprehending distant others, interrogate their past or their own multifarious self. Yet, a common underlying trait of the ethnographic self can perhaps be identified in the "bifocality" (Fisher 1986), or the feeling of being "off-center" (Clifford 1988) at the origin of the quest to bridge gaps in understanding, to open paths for a commerce of meaning between different worlds out there which are also different parts of the self. The practice of participant observation, oxymoronic as it is, represents the disciplinary mandate to make science of the schism, whether one that is present from the beginning, as it is with people with a complex cultural background, or as the outcome of a method that sends the researchers out of their habitual paths. From that position, cultural forces shaping both the research and the researcher can be more readily identified and exposed, self-observation shedding light on the wider context while revealing the work that simultaneously constructs the other and transforms the self.

References

Abu Lughod, L. 2000. "Locating Ethography." *Ethnography* 1: 261–67.

Barthes, R. 1970. *S/Z*. Paris: Seuil.

Blanchard, M. 1990. "Visions of the Archipelago: Michel Leiris, Autobiography and Ethnographic Memory." *Cultural Anthropology* 5: 270–91.

Callaway, H. 1992. "Ethnography and Experience. Gender Implications in Fieldwork and Texts." In *Anthropology and Autobiography*, edited by J. Okely and H. Calloway, 30–49. London: Routledge.

Clifford, J. 1986. "On Ethnographic Allegory." In *The Predicament of Culture. Twentieth Century Ethnography, Literature, and Art*, edited by J. Clifford and G. Marcus, 98–121. Cambridge, MA: Harvard University Press.

_____. 1988. *The Predicament of Culture. Twentieth Century Ethnography, Literature, and Art*. Cambridge, MA: Harvard University Press.

Clifford, J. and Marcus, G. E. eds. 1986. *Writing Culture*. Berkeley, CA: University of California Press.

Crapanzano, V. 1985. *Tuhami: Portrait of a Moroccan*. Chicago, IL: University of Chicago Press.

Dumont, J. 1978. *The Headman and I*. Austin, TX: University of Texas Press.

Dwyer, K. 1999. *Moroccan Dialogues: Anthropology in Question*. Baltimore, MD: Johns Hopkins Press.

Ellis, C. 2004. *The Ethnographic I. A Methodological Novel about Autoethnography*. Walnut Creek, CA: Altamira Press.

Fischer, M. J. 1986. "Ethnicity and the Post-Modern Arts of Memory." In *The Poetics and Politics of Ethnography*, edited by J. Clifford and G. E. Marcus, 194–233. Berkeley, CA: University of California Press.

Geertz, C. 1973. *The Interpretation of Cultures*. New York: Basic Books.

_____. 1983. *Local Knowledge: Further Essays in Interpretive Anthropology*. New York: Basic Books.

_____. 1986. "Making Experiences, Authoring Selves." In *The Anthropology of Experience*, edited by Turner V. and Bruner E., 373–80. Urbana, IL: University of Illinois Press.

_____. 1988. *Works and Lives: The Anthropologist as Author*. Stanford, CA: Stanford University Press.

Iser, W. 1974. *The Implied Reader*. Baltimore, MD: Johns Hopkins University Press.

King, W. D. 2008. *Collections of Nothing*. Chicago, IL: University Of Chicago Press.

Leiris, M. 1934. *L'Afrique Fantôme*. Paris, Gallimard.

Madden, R. 2010. *Being Ethnographic*. Sage: London.

Malinowski, B. 1922. *Argonauts of the Western Pacific*. London: Routledge.

Motzafi-Haller, P. 1997. "Writing Birthright. On Native Anthropologists and the Politics of Representations." In *Autoethnography. Rewriting the Self and the Social*, edited by D. E. Reed-Danahay, 195–222. Oxford: Berg.

Myerhoff, B. 1978. *Number Our Days: A Triumph of Continuity and Culture among Jewish Old People in an Urban Ghetto*. New York: Simon and Schuster.

Myerhoff, B. and Ruby, J. 1982. "Introduction." In *A Crack in the Mirror: Reflexive Perspectives in Anthropology*, edited by J. Ruby. Philadelphia, PA: University of Pennsylvania Press.

Price, S. 2004. "Michel Leiris, French Anthropology, and a Side Trip to the Antilles." *Politics, Culture & Society* 22: 1.

Rabinow, P. 1977. *Reflections on Fieldwork in Morocco.* Berkeley, CA: University of California Press.

_____. 1986. "Representations Are Social Facts. Modernity and Post-Modernity in Anthropology." In *The Poetics and Politics of Ethnography*, edited by J. Clifford and G. E. Marcus, 234–61. Berkeley, CA: University of California Press.

Reed-Danahay, D. E. 1997. "Leaving Home: Schooling Stories and the Ethnography of Autoethnography in Rural France." In *Autoethnography. Rewriting the Self and the Social*, edited by D. E. Reed-Danahay, 123–43. Oxford: Berg.

Shostak, M. 1981. *Nisa: The Life and Words of a !Kung Woman.* Cambridge, MA: Harvard University Press.

Strathern, M. 1985. "Dislodging a World View: Challenge and Counter-Challenge in the Relationship between Feminism and Anthropology." *Australian Feminist Studies* 1, no. 1: 1–25.

Part VI
Conclusions

14

The Inferential Context of Self-Observation

Joshua W. Clegg

The chapters in this volume have suggested to me four basic arguments that might profitably frame future self-observation theory and practice: (1) the familiar dualisms of enlightenment thinking continue to muddle our thinking about self-interpretation and should be abandoned; (2) the immense complexities involved in self-observation research require a more sophisticated epistemological framework, one that allows us to situate self-interpretative activities within the dynamic and socio-culturally embedded relationships and practices where they are enacted; (3) the notion of self, psyche, or consciousness implied, even required, by such a reformulation of the self-observation context is one that is neither "inside" nor "outside" but is, rather, enacted, emplotted, dialogically construed and negotiated; and (4) though this reformulation of both self and self-observation helps make sense of psychological traditions of self-knowledge, it also shows their fundamental limits, not because they are based on "subjective" sources of knowledge, but because any genuine knowledge of another's consciousness is also knowledge of its excess, its transcendence, no matter the methods employed.

Dualism and Its Discontents

The story of introspection makes abundantly clear the political nature of the dualism that has long presided over psychology. The canonical history of our discipline has perpetuated a mythical "controversy" rooted in "the essentially private nature of introspection" (Brock 2012, 34) as opposed to the "publicly observable facts" (34) of behavioral science but a closer historical analysis suggests that "the ban on introspection is better seen as a social taboo rather than a rational response to a crisis" (37). We tell the story of introspection in a way that implies our evolution beyond the private, idiosyncratic, and unreliable methods of self-observation and that pointedly ignores the obvious facts that early self-observation research was not, in fact, unreliable nor idiosyncratic (e.g., there are probably no more enduring findings in the history of psychology than Ebbinghaus' memory research) and that we have not ceased to employ methods of self-observation (though many of these are decidedly less sophisticated than those of the early introspectionists).

As Costall (2012) argues, the principle consequence of this illusory history is a methodological dualism that radically de-privileges self-knowledge:

> The unthinking distrust of introspection within modern psychology goes hand in hand with the unchallenged prestige of methodological behaviorism. Neither are the result of critical disciplinary reflection, but stem from a dualism of the subjective and the objective that has insinuated itself into psychological thought through a potent historical myth. (Costall 2012, 77).

This hollow objectivism at the core of our discipline has persistently sabotaged any attempts to account for self-knowledge and it has done so through an insistence that the various forms of psychological knowledge be separated and ordered along a rigid hierarchy of the knowable.

Though the dualism of objectivism has served particular political ends (as Brock, Young, and Costall all show in this volume), this philosophical tradition is ultimately artificial and futile. Objectivism rests on the assumption that it is possible to observe objects as they are, independent of interpretation or perspective—in other words, that some kinds of observation do not involve self-observation. But this distinction does not withstand scrutiny. All observations come from somewhere; as Costall (2012) says, "It is only subjects who can be objective" (77). The meaning of all observations, including self-observations, is found not in the abstracted, independent content of "data" or "reports" but in the concrete, contextualized negotiations of meaning that constitute such observations. The fundamental observational datum, then, is essentially a complex, dynamic relationship whereby mutual inferences are negotiated, and this is as much true for observations of behavior as it is for the various forms of self-observation. Ultimately, then, the problems of self-observation are the problems of knowledge, and of all psychology, and we gain nothing from the segregationist pretense of objectivity.

The Inferential Context

If we take it as given that self-observation, like all forms of observation, is constituted fundamentally in a dynamic relational context, then interpreting self-observations will require an interpretation of the inferential relationship within which it is constituted. Much of the current volume has, in fact, focused on the specific qualities and requirements of the inferential contexts unique to self-observation and a review of some of the principle themes elaborated should suffice to characterize what I mean by inferential negotiations. These themes can be organized around two basic turns in the negotiation: (1) establishing trust and (2) examining and negotiating shared frames of reference.

Establishing Trust

One of the most basic negotiations involved in self-observation research concerns decisions about the trustworthiness of both researchers and self-observers. The researcher's mistrust of participants has been almost axiomatic in psychology. Boring (1953), for example, argued that this mistrust was at the core of the behaviorist objection to introspective methods: "the important thing is to see that Watson, in attacking introspection, was objecting, not to the use of words by the subject, but to trusting the subject to use the words only with those meanings that the experimenter wishes the words to have" (185). This fundamental empiricistic angst has led many psychologists to avoid, or at least re-brand, any methods that relied on self-observation, but as we have already seen, there is no avoiding self-observation if we are to do psychology at all.

The self-observation researcher, then, must exercise at least a modicum of trust to even begin the research process, but the self-observer must also make the choice to trust the researcher. In every self-observation context, the self-observer makes decisions about how much to tell and so there is never any guarantee that any given set of self-reports "consist of all the information the subjects have about their own cognitive processes" (Gaillard et al. 2006, 714). In any reliable self-observation, then, "the partners must rely on each other and trust is a critical component of the alliance" (Heavey 2012, 107).

The inevitable implication of this interpretive alliance is that the meaning of any self-observation report cannot be divorced from the substance of the negotiations that constitute it—to know what is "observed" requires that we know about the quality of the relationships between observers and interpreters and the implicit and explicit conversational turns that frame the inferential negotiations. Wagoner's (2012) recounting of Binet's attempts to replicate "two-point" threshold research is an elegant case in point. Binet found that posthoc qualitative reports revealed complex unreported meaning negotiations as participants interpreted researcher instructions in idiosyncratic ways, negotiations that radically transformed the meaning of the "reports" generated. Even in the most basic psychophysical research, then, the meaning and substance of the "observation" is inseparable from the interpretive relationship within which it is set.

Sharing Frames of Reference

The development of a reliable interpretive relationship is, of course, the practical core of self-observation research. The authors in this volume have discussed numerous principles central to this activity, most of which can be broadly organized around the task of sharing frames of reference, first, by interrogating and expressing individual frames of reference, positionality, and context and, second, by negotiating, or co-constructing, shared frames of mutual intelligibility.

The interrogation of one's own frame of reference is critical for both self-observers and for those who interpret those observations because the meaning of an experience, its literal nature, is constituted by the social, cultural, and psychological realities within which it is constituted. An indispensable turn in the self-interpretive conversation, then, is the interrogation of the lived worlds that frame experience: "self observation is just as much a matter of observing ourselves acting, living, and interacting, as it is a matter of inward introspection" (Brinkmann 2012, 200). Indeed, "we literally study ourselves when we begin to analyze the material objects that we possess, for example. These are often extensions of the self's capabilities (glasses, computers, notebooks, etc.) or social identity (clothes, car, house) and are in that sense co-constitutive of the person's attributes" (202).

This self-contextualization is also important for the researcher or interpreter, as his or her experiences and frames of reference co-determine the meaning of a self-observation—"the knowledge of the other progresses together with the knowledge of the self" (Fasulo 2012, 268). The interpretation of "data" is not simply a re-presentation of the "subject's" experience but is a curation, a re-narration, an interpretation through multiple levels of reflection:

> There are multiple layers of self-observation in narrative work: (a) the subject reflecting upon the ways that he/she observes himself/herself, and (b) the researcher reflecting upon himself/herself reflecting upon the subject's self-reflections. (McCarron 2012, 225)

Inattention to these complex circuits of interpretation and self-interpretation is, I would argue, precisely the reason for the poverty and unreliability of much self-observation research and so cultivating a more embedded and reflexive interpretive context is an indispensable starting-place for self-observation.

But the cultivation of reflexivity around our frames of reference is not simply a matter of paying special attention to culture or context; it requires training, something that the earliest traditions of self-observation recognized as fundamental to meaningful self-reports. In this volume, Heavey (2012) has argued that our patterns of reflection and description become more reliable and evocative with intentional training: "subjects must be taught to examine their inner experience carefully, to explore the nooks and crannies of their pristine inner experience to discover what might be present" (109). Gould (2012) also highlights the central role of practice in developing the capacities for self-observation. In fact, Gould argues persuasively for very different competencies being involved in different forms of self-observation—he argues, for example, that conscious reflection may actually interfere with the perception of experiences that are nonconceptual.

Though we no longer cultivate robust traditions of self-observation training, there is no doubt that learning to be reflexive about one's own frames of reference requires skill and experience. And this task is made even more complex by the fact that it is inseparable from the larger requirements of negotiating or co-constituting shared frames of reference. "Observations" become "reports" through the co-constitution of a world: "both the researcher and the research participant are informed by that shared world, its historical, cultural, moral, and physical contours, even as they themselves collaborate in the constructive interpretation of its reality and meanings" (Gantt and Thayne 2012, 165). The research process is always embedded in and enacts this co-constitution of a shared world of meanings. The choices we make about the subjects, means, and meanings of interpretive activity frame what we take to be our phenomena—"self-observation can be many different things depending on which aspects of the self that researchers intend to capture" (Brinkmann 2012, 203)—and the whole complex of intentions, conventions, and purposes that researcher and participant share predetermine how those phenomena are understood. The relational context of our interpretations, then, is inseparable from, and constitutive of, those interpretations and just as we must cultivate reflexivity in the process of observation, we must do the same in the discursive process of interpretation. Furthermore, without the documentation of, and reflection upon, these relational processes of interpretation, no self-observation report can be fully understood.

Some ways that such reflexive interpretive processes could be cultivated include the intentional use of ambiguity and metaphor, as Wagoner (2012) suggests, or perhaps some of the narrative methods described in the final section of this volume. Whatever methods are employed, the intelligibility of shared inferences cannot be simply assumed but "the subject and investigator have to work, sometimes painstakingly, to develop the skills and language to communicate about the (possibly) unique inner experience of the subject" (Heavey 2012, 109). This negotiational quality, inherent in all kinds of interpretation, implies that research findings should not be collapsed into simplistic statements of static fact, owned by the researcher. Self-observation findings, rather, should be conversations, negotiations, not foreclosed and colonized meanings, canonized to an uncomplicated universal knowledge base.

The Conversational Consciousness

Implicit in this way of conceptualizing self-observation is a kind of radical reconceptualization of the self that is being observed. A negotiated conceptualization of self-observation findings depends on a consciousness that is not an inaccessible homunculus, but one that is expressible in the lived, shared world of meaning. The model of consciousness that arises from this line of thinking is one that does not live either "inside" or "outside." As Downs (2012) argues: "All knowledge is not within the mind or in the external world, but is a meaningful intentional act" (176), an act that "when considered as an intention, extends beyond me into the world around me: into my context, my culture, its history, and my history" (178). Consciousness as enacted in this way, imparts a very different character to self-knowledge. Such knowledge is not the "catching oneself in the act and thereby encountering oneself as object" that, as Mark Freeman (2012) argues, "cannot help but deform and distort the very phenomenon it seeks to understand, precisely by its reliance on an objectified and objectifying form of seeing" (240). An enacted consciousness is one we narrate, an "emplottment, which involves composing ourselves as protagonists into a storyline" (McCarron 2012, 224).

To put the argument another way, a psychology of self-observation is meaningless and fundamentally distorting if its object is the Cartesian black box—there is no real knowledge of this mythical entity. But consciousness as enacted, as instantiated in conversation, as constituted in the appropriation, transformation, and embodiment of our shared historical and cultural texts, is a genuinely meaningful psychological phenomenon. The black box consciousness is not one we can have anything to say about, as it remains both unknowable and inexpressible, but the enacted, storied, embodied consciousness is a fitting site for self-observation research.

And Yet

Though we gain some intelligibility, some theoretical clarity, by recasting self-observation in terms of inferential negotiations around an enacted consciousness, we do not gain anything like certainty or transparency: "what is it that allows for self-observation rather than self-deception or self-obfuscation? Well, strictly speaking, nothing: there are no guarantees" (Freeman 2012, 255). But why are there no guarantees? We have long told ourselves that self-observation is unreliable and uncertain because it is "subjective"—that is, "inside," "biased," hopelessly idiosyncratic—but this really has nothing to do with the perilous nature of self-observation. There is no kind of knowledge that is not idiosyncratic, that is not given meaning in local, personal, perspectival contexts. What makes self-observation uncertain is the same thing that makes all knowledge uncertain— namely, that language always expresses excess, bears the face of the transcendent without collapsing it to the immanent. Language both reveals the consciousness of another and the rupturing excess of the other—both that we can, in some sense, know another but that, ultimately, she will never fully be known. There are no guarantees in self-observation, as there are none in any form of research, because both self and other have already flown, have already transcended what we very briefly understood, and so already demand a new gesture of understanding.

References

Boring, E. G. 1953. "A History of Introspection." Psychological Bulletin 50, no. 3: 169–86.

Brinkmann, S. 2012. "The Practice of Self-Observation in the Phenomenological Traditions." In *Self-Observation in the Social Sciences*, edited by J. W. Clegg, 195–219. New Brunswick, NJ: Transaction Publishers.

Brock, A. C. 2012. "The History of Introspection Revisited." In *Self-Observation in the Social Sciences*, edited by J. W. Clegg, 25–43. New Brunswick, NJ: Transaction Publishers.

Costall, A. 2012. "Introspection and the Myth of Methodological Behaviorism." In *Self-Observation in the Social Sciences*, edited by J. W. Clegg, 67–80. New Brunswick, NJ: Transaction Publishers.

Downs, S. D. 2012. "A Phenomenologically Informed Theory of Self-Observation: Intra-Spection as Hermeneutic Reduction on the Self." In *Self-Observation in the Social Sciences*, edited by J. W. Clegg, 173–194. New Brunswick, NJ: Transaction Publishers.

Fasulo, A. 2012. "Self-Observation in Ethnographic Writing." In *Self-Observation in the Social Sciences*, edited by J. W. Clegg, 259–274. New Brunswick, NJ: Transaction Publishers.

Freeman, M. 2012. "Self-Observation Theory in the Narrative Tradition: Rescuing the Possibility of Self-Understanding." In *Self-Observation in the Social Sciences*, edited by J. W. Clegg, 239–257. New Brunswick, NJ: Transaction Publishers.

Gaillard, V., Vandenberghe, M., Destrebecqz, A., and Cleeremans, A. 2006. "First- and Third-Person Approaches in Implicit Learning Research." *Consciousness and Cognition: An International Journal* 15, no. 4: 709–22.

Gantt, E. E. and Thayne, J. L. 2012. "A Conceptual History of Self-Observation in the Phenomenological Tradition: Brentano, Husserl, and Heidegger." In *Self-Observation in the Social Sciences*, edited by J. W. Clegg, 147–171. New Brunswick, NJ: Transaction Publishers.

Heavey, C. L. 2012. "Confronting the Challenges of Observing Inner Experience: The Descriptive Experience Sampling Method." In *Self-Observation in the Social Sciences*, edited by J. W. Clegg, 103–119. New Brunswick, NJ: Transaction Publishers.

McCarron, A. 2012. "A Practice of Self-Observation in Narrative Psychology." In *Self-Observation in the Social Sciences*, edited by J. W. Clegg, 223–238. New Brunswick, NJ: Transaction Publishers.

Wagoner, B. 2012. "Language in Self-Observation." In *Self-Observation in the Social Sciences*, edited by J. W. Clegg, 83–101. New Brunswick, NJ: Transaction Publishers.

List of Contributors

Svend Brinkmann is professor of psychology in the Department of Communication & Psychology at Aalborg University, Denmark, where he serves as the codirector of the Center for Qualitative Studies. He is interested in the philosophy, history, and methodology of psychology and other human sciences. His most recent book (2012) is Qualitative Inquiry in Everyday Life.

Adrian C. Brock is a lecturer in psychology at University College Dublin in Ireland. After taking an honours degree in Psychology in Manchester, England, he studied History and Philosophy of Science at the University of Cambridge. He then moved to York University in Toronto, Canada, to do his PhD with the eminent historian of psychology, Kurt Danziger. He is particularly interested in the history of psychology in developing countries and this was the main focus of his edited book, *Internationalizing the History of Psychology* (2006).

Joshua W. Clegg is assistant professor of psychology at John Jay College of Criminal Justice and The Graduate Center, City University of New York. His empirical research focuses on social alienation and the social psychology of environmental sustainability; his theoretical and historical work focuses on research methodology and philosophy of science. He is the editor of *The Observation of Human Systems*.

Alan Costall is professor of theoretical psychology and Deputy Director of the Centre for Situated Action and Communication at the University of Portsmouth. His theoretical and historical work examines the origins of dualistic thinking that pervades modern psychology. His research explores the implications of a broadly ecological approach to the human sciences. Recent publications include *Doing things with things* and *Against theory of mind*.

Samuel D. Downs will receive his doctorate in applied social psychology this year (2012) from Brigham Young University. His work focuses on the philosophical and empirical study of contextual influences. More specifically, he studies the contextual influences on ethical behavior, classroom outcomes, and choice. He is also interested in the philosophy of social science, particularly psychology.

Alessandra Fasulo's research focuses on communicative practices in naturalistic settings and on autobiographical narratives in both ordinary conversation and written memoirs. She has carried out ethnographic research on the everyday life of family and on workplace interactions. She is currently conducting research on communication with children with learning disabilities, and on object-related memories in older people.

Mark Freeman earned his PhD in the Committee on Human Development at the University of Chicago and is currently distinguished professor of ethics and society in the Department of Psychology at the College of the Holy Cross. He is the author of *Rewriting the Self: History, Memory, Narrative* (1993); *Finding the Muse: A Sociopsychological Inquiry into the Conditions of Artistic Creativity* (1994); *Hindsight: The Promise and Peril of Looking Backward* (2010); and numerous articles on memory, self, and autobiographical narrative. He also serves as editor for the Oxford University Press series "Explorations in Narrative Psychology."

Edwin E. Gantt is an associate professor in the Department of Psychology at Brigham Young University. He received his doctorate in clinical psychology from Duquesne University in Pittsburgh, Pennsylvania, where he studied existential, phenomenological, and hermeneutic approaches to psychological theory. Currently, his research focuses on issues in philosophy of social science, psychology of religion, and the implications of Levinasian phenomenology for psychological accounts of moral agency and altruism. He has authored numerous scholarly articles in these areas, as well as coediting (with Richard N. Williams) the book *Psychology-for-the-Other: Levinas, Ethics, and the Practice of Psychology.*

Stephen Gould is a professor of marketing in the Zicklin School of Business, Baruch College, The City University of New York. He has published numerous articles in such outlets as the *Journal of Consumer Research, Psychological Review, Journal of Business Ethics, Journal* *of International Business Studies, Marketing Theory, Consumption, Markets and Culture, Journal of Business Research,* and *American Journal of Preventive Medicine,* among others. In particular, his work is informed by his lifelong introspective and experiential quest in its personal and research dimensions. He has also emphasized the psychological dimensions of Asian thought and meditation in relation to Western thought and research.

Christopher L. Heavey is an associate professor of psychology. His research involves using descriptive experience sampling to explore inner experience. Descriptive experience sampling is a qualitative method that uses a random beeper to cue subjects to pay attention to their ongoing inner experience as they go about their normal daily activities. Particular interests include the inner experience of individuals suffering from mental illnesses such as depression and bipolar disorder as well as the experience of emotion.

Andrew McCarron is a poet and personality psychologist born and raised in the Hudson River Valley. He was educated at Bard College, Harvard University, and the Graduate Center of the City University of New York. He teaches at Bard College and Trinity School.

Jeffrey L. Thayne is a graduate student in the Department of Psychology at Brigham Young University where he is studying theoretical and philosophical psychology. His current research focuses on issues related to moral agency, ethical obligation, and constructivist psychology, particularly in regards to the work of the American psychologist George Kelly and the French philosopher Emmanuel Levinas.

Brady Wagoner completed his PhD in psychology at the University of Cambridge and is now associate professor at the Aalborg University (Denmark). He has received a number of prestigious academic awards, including the Sigmund Koch Award, Gates Cambridge Scholarship, and the Jefferson Prize. His books include *Symbolic Transformation: The Mind in Movement through Culture and Society* (2010), *Dialogicality in Focus: Challenges to Theory, Method and Application* (2011), *Development as a Social Process: Selected Writings of Gerard Duveen* (in press), and is currently writing Bartlett in Reconstruction: Where Culture and Mind Meet. Additionally, he is on the editorial board of several international Journals, including *Culture & Psychology* and is founding coeditor of the journal *Psychology & Society.*

Jacy L. Young is a doctoral student in the History and Theory of Psychology programme at York University in Toronto. She is currently working on a project on the methods psychologists and educators used to interrogate child life in the late nineteenth and early twentieth centuries.

Index